Ermolao Barbaro's
On Celibacy 1 and 2

BLOOMSBURY NEO-LATIN SERIES

Series editors: William M. Barton, Stephen Harrison, Gesine Manuwald and Bobby Xinyue

Early Modern Texts and Anthologies
Edited by Stephen Harrison and Gesine Manuwald

Volume 5

The 'Early Modern Texts and Anthologies' strand of the *Bloomsbury Neo-Latin Series* presents editions of texts with English translations, introductions and notes. Volumes include complete editions of longer single texts and themed anthologies bringing together texts from particular genres, periods or countries and the like.

These editions are primarily aimed at students and scholars and intended to be suitable for use in university teaching, with introductions that give authoritative but not exhaustive accounts of the relevant texts and authors, and commentaries that provide sufficient help for the modern reader in noting links with classical Latin texts and bringing out the cultural context of writing.

Alongside the series' 'Studies in Early Modern Latin Literature' strand, it is hoped that these editions will help to bring important and interesting Neo-Latin texts of the period from 1350 to 1800 to greater prominence in study and scholarship, and make them available for a wider range of academic disciplines as well as for the rapidly growing study of Neo-Latin itself.

Also available in this series:
An Anthology of British Neo-Latin Literature by Gesine Manuwald,
L. B. T. Houghton and Lucy R. Nicholas
An Anthology of European Neo-Latin Literature edited by
Gesine Manuwald, Daniel Hadas and Lucy R. Nicholas

An Anthology of Neo-Latin Literature in British Universities
edited by Gesine Manuwald and Lucy R. Nicholas
Ermolao Barbaro's On Celibacy 3 and 4 *and* On the Duty of the
Ambassador *edited by Gareth Williams*
Japan on the Jesuit Stage by Akihiko Watanabe
Roger Ascham's Themata Theologica by Lucy R. Nicholas

Ermolao Barbaro's
On Celibacy 1 and 2

Edited by Gareth Williams

BLOOMSBURY ACADEMIC
LONDON • NEW YORK • OXFORD • NEW DELHI • SYDNEY

BLOOMSBURY ACADEMIC
Bloomsbury Publishing Plc
50 Bedford Square, London, WC1B 3DP, UK
1385 Broadway, New York, NY 10018, USA
29 Earlsfort Terrace, Dublin 2, Ireland

BLOOMSBURY, BLOOMSBURY ACADEMIC and the Diana logo are trademarks of Bloomsbury Publishing Plc

First published in Great Britain 2024
Paperback edition published 2025

Copyright © Gareth Williams, 2024

Gareth Williams has asserted his right under the Copyright, Designs and Patents Act, 1988, to be identified as Author of this work.

Cover image: *Portrait of Hermolao Barbaro*, c. 1520–ante 1521, Raccolte d'arte della Pinacoteca Civica di Palazzo Volpi, here reproduced with the permission of the Musei Civici di Como

All rights reserved. No part of this publication may be reproduced or transmitted in any form or by any means, electronic or mechanical, including photocopying, recording, or any information storage or retrieval system, without prior permission in writing from the publishers.

Bloomsbury Publishing Plc does not have any control over, or responsibility for, any third-party websites referred to or in this book. All internet addresses given in this book were correct at the time of going to press. The author and publisher regret any inconvenience caused if addresses have changed or sites have ceased to exist, but can accept no responsibility for any such changes.

A catalogue record for this book is available from the British Library.

A catalog record for this book is available from the Library of Congress.

ISBN: HB: 978-1-3501-4943-4
      PB: 978-1-3501-4942-7
      ePDF: 978-1-3501-4945-8
      eBook: 978-1-3501-4944-1

Typeset by RefineCatch Limited, Bungay, Suffolk

To find out more about our authors and books visit www.bloomsbury.com and sign up for our newsletters.

Contents

List of Illustrations	viii
Preface	ix
List of Abbreviations	xiii
Introduction	1
I: The crisis	1
II: *De coelibatu*	4
Composition and textual history	4
The content of the four books	7
De coelibatu in the context of Venetian humanism	9
The originality of Francesco Barbaro's *De re uxoria*	12
De coelibatu and *De re uxoria* in dialogue	17
The authorial self in *De coelibatu*	21
III: Picturing Ermolao Barbaro	24
IV: Style and technique	29
Note on the Text and Translation	48
On Celibacy Preface: Text and Translation	50
On Celibacy Book 1: Text and Translation	52
On Celibacy Book 2: Text and Translation	100
Bibliography	165
Index of Passages	179
General Index	185
Index of Latin Words	192
Index of Greek Words	193

Illustrations

1 *De coelibatu* 1.1.7-1.2.1, here reproduced from MS Classe II 9, Biblioteca Comunale Ariostea, Ferrara, with the permission of the Servizio Biblioteche e Archivi del Comune di Ferrara — 6
2 *Portrait of Hermolao Barbaro*, c. 1520–*ante* 1521, Raccolte d'arte della Pinacoteca Civica di Palazzo Volpi, here reproduced with the permission of the Musei Civici di Como — 25
3 Vittore Carpaccio, *St. Ursula's Arrival in Rome*, part of his *Saint Ursula* cycle, 1488–95. Gallerie dell'Accademia, Venice — 28

Preface

The modest aim of this volume and its companion-piece in the *Bloomsbury Neo-Latin Series* is to do what they can to enhance the modern visibility, especially in Anglophone circles, of a truly remarkable figure in the history of Italian humanism: Ermolao Barbaro (1454–93). In his short life Barbaro played an important role in the evolution of Aristotelian studies in northern Italy and far beyond, and he was a pioneer in creating a 'scientific' basis for the textual study of such authors as Dioscorides and, most famously, the elder Pliny. Despite his life-long devotion to his literary studies, Barbaro also served the Venetian state with distinction on a number of diplomatic missions – only to fall into disgrace when, in 1491, he was appointed Patriarch of Aquileia without Venetian permission. Disowned by his home state, he lived his last years in Rome before he was claimed by the plague in July 1493.

Barbaro's record of scholarly achievement in his brief life is nothing short of extraordinary, in terms of both the breadth of his studies and the learning of his copious writings. The two works that are presented in the paired volumes of this edition belong to very different phases of his existence. On the one hand, his *De coelibatu* (*On celibacy*) was written in his late teens, and amounts to a highly idealized charter for the single life in devotion to contemplation – a far cry from the personal, familial, and career expectations incumbent on a Venetian of Barbaro's aristocratic station and pedigree. On the other hand, his *De officio legati* (*On the duty of the ambassador*), probably written in mid- to late-1489, offers a concise codification of how the ambassador should conduct himself in loyal duty to his state – an intriguing document for Barbaro to have penned, given that a year or so thereafter he caused outrage in Venice by his appointment to Aquileia. The present study centres on the tension between these two works: if the one is a youthful call to independence from the patrician Venetian way, the other is far more conformist in its call to civic duty, with the claims of the self always secondary to the demands of the state apparatus.

The tension between the two works was adroitly expressed through their juxtaposition in Vittore Branca's pioneering textual edition of 1969: this was the first printed edition of *De coelibatu*, and only the second (after Hrabar 1906) of *De officio legati*. The texts as presented in my paired volumes are based on my own examination of the sole extant manuscript of *De coelibatu* and, in the case of *De officio legati*, on Branca's edition, which itself relies on the ten manuscripts that were known to Branca. Quite apart from the practical difficulties posed by the Covid-19 pandemic in the preparation of this study, I make no claim to the editorial competence that *ab initio* construction of the text of *De officio legati* would now require.

The two volumes of this edition present what is, to my knowledge, the first complete translation into English (or any other language) of *De coelibatu*, and the first complete English version of *De officio legati* (cf. in Italian Rinaldi 2013–14). The current project is motivated by three further factors, the first of them predicated once more on Branca's 1969 edition. For all its striking originality in making accessible to a modern audience these two important but previously unheralded works, Branca supplied relatively little in the way of annotation that would reveal the richness of Barbaro's learned allusiveness and the complexity of his engagement with the literary and philosophical storehouse on which he draws so prolifically, especially in *De coelibatu*.[1] Hence the notes that accompany the present translations are designed to shed some useful light on the sheer breadth of learning that the young Barbaro already had at his disposal in *On celibacy* – and on his ability to apply that learning with an easy touch, an enviable fluency in a vast range of sources, and a keen eye for wit and sparkle.

Second, beyond the Ciceronian cast of Barbaro's Latinity in both *De coelibatu* and *De officio legati*, considerable attention is given in this edition to his highly creative adaptation of Cicero's *De officiis* in particular, especially in Barbaro's treatment of the familiar tension from antiquity onwards between the claims of the contemplative life on the one hand and its active alternative on the other. In my treatment of this Ciceronian component, a central objective is to explore how, in Barbaro's hands, classical reception is hardly a passive exercise in re-invoking a hallowed cultural past, but a dynamic mode of appropriation, re-interpretation, and improvisation: Barbaro applies his Cicero in a forward-looking way, articulating his response to the particular socio-political climate of his contemporary Venice through a Ciceronian lens whose focus has been carefully recalibrated to fit his late Quattrocento times. In this respect, 'classical reception' is an inadequate term for the capacities of literary response to the classical past that I claim for Barbaro in these pages.

---

[1] Cf. in review Scaglione 1972: 339: 'The only criticism one could offer to this otherwise admirable publication concerns the very limited scope of the exegetic apparatus. The text is usually plain enough, but not always; several passages demand explanation or interpretation, and literary or historical references are frequent.'

Third, much important light has been cast in recent scholarship on the originality of Barbaro's *De officio legati* in the history of Renaissance writing on diplomacy, not least because of his focus on the permanent or 'resident' ambassador as opposed to the envoy sent on short-term, ad hoc missions. *De officio legati* plays an important part in Barbaro's life story as recounted in my two volumes, especially in its uneasy relationship with his position on public service in *De coelibatu*. In my second volume, however, much effort is also made in the introduction and annotations to *De officio legati* to view that work on its own terms as a charter of sorts for a 'modern' diplomatic ethos and practice that were far removed from the world of medieval diplomacy.

The two volumes of this edition are designed to be stand-alone productions as much as possible: in both cases, the Abbreviations and Notes on the Text(s) and Translation(s) are pertinent only to the given volume, and the Bibliography and Indices in each are volume-specific. Much cross-reference is nevertheless made between the two volumes, especially in the annotations to the four books of *De coelibatu*: in such cases, simple reference is made in the annotations in the first volume to (e.g.) '3.5.10 and n. 73' in the second volume, and vice versa; outside the annotations, cross-referencing follows volume and page number (e.g., 'See Vol. 1 Intro. pp. 14–15'). In the introductions and in the annotations to *De coelibatu* and *De officio legati*, all translations are my own unless otherwise stated.

This study owes many debts. I am grateful for the insights received after presentations at Queen's University, Ontario, and at the University of Manchester in March 2022. Dr Mirna Bonazza of the Biblioteca Comunale Ariostea di Ferrara offered invaluable help in facilitating access to the sole extant manuscript of *De coelibatu*; and I am grateful to Mr Luca Gavagna for his expertise in preparing a digital reproduction of that manuscript. For advice on other fronts I am most grateful to Anthony D'Elia and especially to Tommaso Gazzarri, whose interventions at critical moments enabled me to make contact with various Italian institutions. But my greatest debt is to my friends Katharina Volk and James Zetzel, both of whom read through the entirety of my translations not just with their usual generosity and patience, but also with their typical acuity and eye for precision. I am also most grateful to Katharina for the many suggestions that informed and improved the annotations on multiple fronts, and to Jim for the wealth of practical guidance that he offered on many points along the way, not least in textual matters. I am further indebted to Joseph Solodow for his insights on several particularly thorny problems in the translation. I thank Alice Wright, Lily Mac Mahon, and Zoë Osman for skillfully steering the book through the production process at Bloomsbury Press, and the editors of the Bloomsbury *Early*

Modern Texts and Anthologies series for enthusiastically supporting this project from the outset; anonymous readers for the press also offered many points of help that have much improved the end product.

I am also most grateful to Merv Honeywood and his team at RefineCatch Limited for their expertise in formatting the completed manuscript for publication. Last, and most important of all: this book would not exist without the inspiration provided by Lucy R. Nicholas.

New York City
May 2023

Abbreviations

Apul.	Apuleius (b. *c.* 125 CE)
Apol.	*Apologia*/Apology
De dog. Plat.	*De dogmate Platonis*/On Plato and his doctrine
Met.	*Metamorphoses*
Arat.	Aratus (*c.* 315–240 BCE)
Phaen.	*Phaenomena*
Arist.	Aristotle (384–322 BCE)
De an.	*De anima*/On the soul
De nob.	*De nobilitate*/On noble birth
EN	*Ethica Nicomachea*/Nicomachean ethics
Hist. an.	*Historia animalium*/History of animals
Int.	*De interpretatione*/On interpretation
Metaph.	*Metaphysica*/Metaphysics
Part. an.	*De partibus animalium*/On the parts of animals
Pol.	*Politica*/Politics
[Arist.]	
Ath. Pol.	*Athēnaiōn politeia*/The Athenian constitution
August.	Augustine (354–430 CE)
De bon. coni.	*De bono coniugali*/On the good of marriage
Caes.	C. Iulius Caesar (*c.* 100–44 BCE)
Civ.	*Bellum civile*/Civil war
Cels.	A. Cornelius Celsus (*fl.* 1st century CE)
Med.	*De medicina*/On medicine
Cic.	M. Tullius Cicero (106–43 BCE)
Ac.	*Academica*
Am.	*De amicitia*/On friendship
Brut.	*Brutus*
Cael.	*Pro Caelio*/For Caelius
De or.	*De oratore*/On the orator
Div.	*De divinatione*/On divination
Fin.	*De finibus*/On ends
Inv.	*De inventione*/On invention
Leg.	*De legibus*/On the laws
Luc.	*Lucullus*
Man.	*Pro Lege Manilia*/On the Manilian law
Marcell.	*Pro Marcello*/For Marcellus

Mur.	Pro Murena/For Murena
Nat. D.	De natura deorum/On the nature of the gods
Off.	De officiis/On duties
Opt. gen.	De optimo genere oratorum/On the best kind of orator
Orat.	Orator
Parad.	Paradoxa Stoicorum/Stoic paradoxes
Red. pop.	Post reditum ad populum/The speech delivered before the people after his return from exile
Rep.	De republica/On the republic
Sen.	De senectute/On old age
Tusc.	Tusculanae disputationes/Tusculan disputations
Verr.	In Verrem/Against Verres
Dante	Dante Alighieri (c. 1265–1321 CE)
Inf.	Inferno
Diod. Sic.	Diodorus Siculus (fl. 1st century BCE), author of a universal history from mythical times down to 60 BCE
DK	H. Diels and W. Kranz, eds. Die Fragmente der Vorsokratiker. 6th edn. 3 vols. Berlin, 1952.
D. L.	Diogenes Laertius (fl. 3rd century CE), biographer of the ancient philosophers from Thales to Epicurus
Fest.	Sex. Pompeius Festus (late 2nd century CE), abridger of M. Verrius Flaccus' *De verborum significatu/On the meaning of words*
De verb. sign.	De verborum significatione/On the meaning of words
Gell.	Aulus Gellius (2nd century CE), Roman miscellanist and author of the 20-book *Noctes Atticae* (*Attic nights*)
Hdt.	Herodotus of Halicarnassus (b. c. 485 BCE)
Hipp.	Hippocrates (c. 460–375 BCE)/Hippocratic Corpus
Nat. hom.	De natura hominis/Nature of man
Hom.	Homer (c. 8th century BCE)
Il.	Iliad
Od.	Odyssey
Hor.	Horace (Q. Horatius Flaccus, 65–8 BCE)
Carm.	Carmina/Odes
Serm.	Sermones/Satires

Isid.	Isidorus Hispalensis (*c.* 560–636 CE), bishop of Seville
Etym.	*Etymologiae*/Etymologies
Jer.	Jerome (Eusebius Hieronymus, *c.* 345–420 CE)
Adv. Iovinian.	*Adversus Iovinianum*/Against Jovinian
Ep.	*Epistulae*/Letters
Liv.	Livy (Titus Livius, 59 BCE–17 CE)
LM	A. Laks and G. W. Most, eds. *Early Greek Philosophy*. 9 vols. Loeb Classical Library Volumes 524–532. Cambridge, MA, and London, 2016.
LSJ	H. G. Liddell and R. Scott, eds. *A Greek-English Lexicon*. 9th edn, rev. H. Stuart Jones. Oxford, 1925–40.
Man.	Marcus Manilius (early 1st century CE)
Astron.	*Astronomica*
Nep.	Cornelius Nepos (*c.* 110–24 BCE)
Arist.	*Life of Aristides*
OLD	P. G. W. Glare, ed. *Oxford Latin Dictionary*. Oxford, 1982.
Ov.	Ovid (P. Ovidius Naso, 43 BCE–17 CE)
Fast.	*Fasti*/On the Roman calendar
Paus.	Pausanias (*fl. c.* 150 CE), author of the 10-book *Description of Greece*
PL	J.-P. Migne, ed. *Patrologiae Cursus Completus, Series Latina*. Paris, 1844–55.
Pl.	Plato (*c.* 429–347 BCE)
Ap.	*Apologia*/Apology
Leg.	*Leges*/Laws
Phd.	*Phaedo*
Phdr.	*Phaedrus*
Prt.	*Protagoras*
Plin.	Pliny the elder (C. Plinius Secundus, *c.* 23–79 CE)
NH	*Naturalis historia*/Natural history
Plut.	Plutarch (L.[?] Mestrius Plutarchus, *c.* 46–after 120 CE)
Mor.	*Moralia*
Vitae	*Lives*
Aem.	*Aemilius Paulus*
Arist.	*Aristides*
Cat. mai.	*Cato maior*/Cato the elder

Lyc.	*Lycurgus*
Sol.	*Solon*
[Plut.]	
De lib. educ.	*De liberis educandis*/On the education of children
Quint.	Quintilian (M. Fabius Quintilianus, *c*. 35–after 96 CE)
Inst.	*Institutio oratoria*/The orator's education
Sall.	Sallust (C. Sallustius Crispus, 86–*c*. 34 BCE)
Iug.	*Iugurtha*/The war with Jugurtha
Sen.	Seneca the younger (L. Annaeus Seneca, *c*. 4 BCE–65 CE)
De matr.	*De matrimonio*/On marriage
Dial.	*Dialogi*/Dialogues
Ep.	*Epistulae*/Letters
Q. Nat.	*Quaestiones naturales*/Natural questions
Soph.	Sophocles (*c*. 496–406 BCE)
Aj.	*Ajax*
El.	*Electra*
Ter.	Terence (P. Terentius Afer, *c*. 195–159 BCE)
An.	*Andria*
Haut.	*H(e)autontimorumenos*
Theoc.	Theocritus (*c*. 300–after 260 BCE)
Id.	*Idylls*
V. Max.	Valerius Maximus (*fl*. early 1st century CE), author of the 9-book *Facta et dicta memorabilia*/Memorable doings and sayings
Vell. Pat.	C. Velleius Paterculus (*c*. 19 BCE–after 30 CE), Roman historical writer
Virg.	Virgil (P. Vergilius Maro, 70–19 BCE)
Aen.	*Aeneis*/Aeneid
Vitr.	Vitruvius Pollio (*fl*. 1st century BCE)
De arch.	*De architectura*/On architecture
Xen.	Xenophon (*c*. 430–350 BCE)
Cyr.	*Cyropaedia*/The education of Cyrus

Introduction

I: The crisis

Our story begins with a long letter, one of the last extant from a sadly truncated life, that bears the date January 7 1492 – a letter penned at Rome by Ermolao Barbaro (1454–93), the accomplished scion of one of Venice's most illustrious aristocratic families, and 'the *Wunderkind* of late Quattrocento Venetian humanism'.[1] Addressed to the humanist Jacopo Antiquario of Perugia (*c.* 1444–1512), Barbaro's missive recounts to his friend the extraordinary circumstances in which Ermolao's life was transformed on March 2 1491, when he was serving as Venice's ambassador to the Papal Curia in Rome.[2]

On that March day Marco Barbo, the Patriarch of Aquileia, passed away. Located near the Adriatic coast in what is now the Friuli-Venezia Giulia region of northeastern Italy, Aquileia was founded as a Roman colony in 181 BCE and grew into a thriving military and commercial hub down to at least the end of the fourth century CE. An episcopal see from the third century CE, it later became an ecclesiastical state of the Holy Roman Empire. The Patriarchate remained politically and territorially powerful through the Middle Ages, but its longstanding rivalry with Venice culminated in the hostilities that led to the Venetian conquest of Friuli in 1420. The Patriarchal State was incorporated into the Republic of Venice in 1445; thereafter, Venetians always held the Patriarchate until it was finally suppressed by Pope Benedict XIV in 1751.

Hence the crisis that engulfed Barbaro: on March 6 1491 he was nominated as Marco Barbo's successor by Pope Innocent VIII. Barbaro acquiesced in obedience to the Pope but without Venetian consultation or permission; although staunch in his Christian devotion, he had yet to take religious orders.[3] His nomination was viewed favourably elsewhere in the Italian peninsula,[4] but the Venetian Senate was quick to express its displeasure at what it perceived as an egregious act of disloyalty; on March 11 Barbaro was summarily removed from his ambassadorship in Rome.[5] His patrician friend and fellow humanist of the highest distinction, Girolamo Donato (*c.* 1456–1511), was dispatched there to order him back to Venice so that he could account for his actions, and his father, Zaccaria, was pressured to induce Ermolao to return; but all to no avail. Barbaro remained in Rome, resentful of the Republic's treatment of him and distressed at the disgrace brought upon the family name, but absorbed nonetheless in his beloved humanistic studies. Matters remained at an impasse until Barbaro died, probably of the plague, on July 24 or 25 1493,[6] at the age of only thirty-nine. On November 4 1493 Pope Alexander VI named Nicolò Donato, Venice's nominee, as the new Patriarch of Aquileia; and so ended the convoluted saga that had dragged on for almost three years.

Barbaro's letter to Antiquario records his own version of events. He remains strong and resolute, he insists, and steadfast in his endurance. For when the storm began to break, his conscience was clear:

> There was no resort to base conduct, or to entreaties. The Pope made his approach when I knew nothing of the matter and my thoughts were entirely elsewhere; he chided me when I was astonished and dumbfounded at the unexpected development; he turned to intimidation when, in my reluctance, I resorted to delaying tactics; and he brought force to bear when I sought to excuse myself and wrangled as much as I could in the circumstances.[7]

To whom did Barbaro owe his primary allegiance, the Pope or Venice? The decision was not hard, as 'I thought that the authority of the Supreme Pontiff, to whom I am subject after God, was to be placed above all things.'[8] His conscience was clear ('And still all is innocent, there is no transgression, no wrong done, and I have no reason for anguish');[9] yet there was no disguising the great wound (*magnum vulnus*)[10] caused by the Republic's anger towards him, by its refusal to sanction his nomination to the Patriarchate, and by its failure to take into account the sterling service that Ermolao and his forebears had long given the Republic. But there was a silver lining: his new-found freedom from his official duties on Venice's behalf brought a welcome release from all the anxiety, nuisance and risk that went with those duties.[11] Already in a previous letter of April 11 1491 Barbaro had written to Antiquario as follows:

> I live in good cheer, I live in freedom, I live for literary studies; the whole of me covets them after many years when not even half of me could pay them attention.[12]

However tragic the circumstances in which Barbaro became alienated from the Republic, he at last found a form of escape that he had long craved. 'A large part of my life, as you know, has always been devoted to literary studies,' he wrote on April 12 1491 to the Florentine humanist poet Ugolino Verino (1438–1516); 'now it will be the entirety of it.'[13]

Years before, Barbaro had yielded to the career expectations of one of his standing within the Venetian patriciate. So in a letter to Antonio Calvo of July 22 1491:

> I was born for literary studies, I was devoted to literary studies, I cannot be without literary studies, I can only be without the interferences that hinder, get in the way of, and keep me away from my studies. I have held many distinguished offices in the Republic, with what trust, reputation and esteem I wouldn't say. It is satisfying to have spent twelve years altogether, but eight of them continuously, in service to the Republic; yet that whole time was virtually lost to literary studies.[14]

The story of Barbaro's fall from grace at Venice and yet of his yearning for release from the burdens of office crucially conditions our approach to the two texts that are presented in the paired volumes of this edition. First, *De coelibatu* (*On celibacy*), written in Naples in 1472–3 when Barbaro was just eighteen; in Naples because he accompanied his father's retinue there during Zaccaria's term of service as Venetian ambassador to the Neapolitan court in 1471–3.[15] Some seventeen years later Barbaro composed the short tract *De officio legati* (*On the duty of the ambassador*) after his return to Venice from Milan, where he had served as Venetian ambassador to the Sforza court in 1488–9. Barbaro's motivation in penning this work has been variously interpreted in modern scholarship, and different dates of composition have been posited for it.[16] But the mainstream position taken here[17] is that *On the duty of the ambassador* surely falls within the time-window between April 1489, when he returned to Venice from Milan, and May 1490, when he departed for Rome to serve as ambassador to the Papal Curia.

Quite apart from the young Barbaro's precocious show of learning in drawing on an impressive array of classical and postclassical sources and influences in *De coelibatu*,[18] the intricate case against marriage that he articulates in that work amounts to a remarkable position for a Venetian aristocrat of Ermolao's generation to take. The work is a charter of sorts for an existence that rejects a central tenet of patrician civic ideology at Venice: individual fulfillment was to be found first in the family and ultimately in the state, with the patriarchal family structure functioning as an analogue of the state; the patrician family discharged its duty to the Republic by ensuring its own self-reproduction in terms of both bloodline and nobility of character, thereby forming in its image each next generation of Venice's ruling elite.[19] Hence the immediately arresting effect of *De coelibatu* as a tract that is in a sense fundamentally un-Venetian. But how then to understand *De officio legati*, a work in which diligent obedience to the state is all? This work was written only shortly before Barbaro caused outrage in Venice by his perceived act of betrayal: how to reconcile the public face that he shows in *De officio legati* with his private yearning for an existence unhampered by official service? And how to view his sermon on fidelity to the state in *De officio legati* in light of the message that he preaches in *De coelibatu* – that the celibate's self-fulfillment at a remove from the Venetian *cursus* is an eminently worthy and justifiable life-path that is endorsed by divine sanction?

Central to the storyline that dominates this study, then, is the life-long drama of Barbaro's divided loyalties to the self and to the state: on the one hand, there was the pressure of conformity to the traditional obligations, expectations, and career path of his patrician class at Venice, and, on the other, the gravitational pull to an existence devoted to his beloved literary studies. Much of his life consisted of an uneasy compromise between these different callings until matters came to a head when he made his decisive choice in early 1491. Such is the background to our treatment in this volume of *De coelibatu* Books 1 and 2, and then of *De coelibatu* Books 3 and 4 and *De officio legati* in the second volume.

II: *De coelibatu*

Composition and textual history

'You ask if I am married,' Barbaro writes on 1 February 1486 to the learned Carmelite scholar-monk of Ghent, Arnold of Bost (1445–99):

> I am not, nor do I even think of a wife. It is enough for me to be busily preoccupied with literary studies; moreover, quarrelsome they are not. Again, nothing is as inimical to literary studies as the yoke of marriage and caring for children. I don't condemn marriage; without it, not even literature would have existed. But I yearn to be a man of letters, an observer of God, of the stars, and of nature, free and released from this shackle.[20]

Arnold's query appears to have been prompted by a remark that Barbaro made in a previous letter of 1 June 1485 to his friend in Ghent. In reply to Arnold's request that he give an account of his studies, Barbaro writes as follows in that earlier missive:

Introduction 5

> In my eighteenth year I composed in boyish fashion two books *On celibacy*. In my nineteenth year I translated Themistius and published [that translation] at twenty-six, at twenty-five I rendered the rhetorical books of Aristotle, at twenty-eight Dioscorides, and at thirty the entirety of Aristotle's logic.[21]

This extraordinary record of productivity for one so young powerfully underscores the sheer depth and consistency of Barbaro's life-long devotion to scholarship. But his remarks on marriage in his 1486 letter to Arnold are also entirely consistent with the position that he took in *De coelibatu* some thirteen years earlier – proof positive that *De coelibatu* was hardly just an audacious literary experiment or jeu d'esprit when he was eighteen, but truly a declaration of personal intent.

Barbaro's autograph original of *De coelibatu* is lost, and the work survives in a single known copy that is now housed in the Biblioteca Comunale Ariostea in Ferrara.[22] Beyond Barbaro's own allusion to the treatise in his 1485 letter to Arnold, *De coelibatu* is mentioned in Johannes Trithemius' *De scriptoribus ecclesiasticis* (*On church writers*) of 1494, along with the mysterious attribution to Ermolao of an otherwise unknown *De re uxoria* (*On marriage*) in verse.[23] Ermolao's eminent grandfather, Francesco Barbaro (1390–1454), had in 1415 composed what quickly became a celebrated prose work entitled *De re uxoria*.[24] Whether or not Trithemius confused grandfather and grandson in misattributing a poetic *De re uxoria* to Ermolao, a different confusion meant that as late as 1897 *De coelibatu* was wrongly attributed to the grandfather.[25] These missteps were at last rectified by Vittore Branca: after an initial article in which he freshly announced Ermolao's *De coelibatu* to the world with a concise overview of the Ferrara manuscript and its thematic content, Branca published the sole modern edition of the work (together with *De officio legati*) half a century ago.[26] The text in the present edition is based on my own consultation of the Ferrara manuscript; all points of departure from Branca's 1969 edition and/or the manuscript are incorporated in my textual apparatus, and certain cases that warrant fuller explanation are treated in my Note on the Text and Translation.[27]

The elegant Ferrara manuscript – its elegance is sampled in Figure 1 – is the work of Antonio Sinibaldi (1443–*c*. 1502), but the circumstances in which he was commissioned to prepare his version are beyond recovery. Already active as a scribe in Florence by 1461, Sinibaldi moved to the Aragonese court in Naples in 1469. He returned to Florence in 1476 but was back in Naples by 1477; after reverting to Florence in 1480-1, he remained there for good, a preeminent scribe in Florence for the rest of the century.[28] At the end of his version of *De coelibatu* he signs off (in Latin) as follows: 'Antonius Sinibaldus the Florentine, the scribe of King Ferdinand [I of Naples, 1423–94], transcribed this work at Naples, May 31 A.D. 1473.'[29] Sinibaldi's copy was executed just a few months after Barbaro had completed his original; for Ermolao signs off by dating that original to *Kalendis Februarii MCCCCLXXII*, i.e., 1 February 1473 by the Julian calendar.[30] The manuscript's lack of final finish is reflected in the blank spaces that usually presuppose Greek words or phrases. In addition to these omissions, errors and infelicities in the transcription process suggest that Sinibaldi was not necessarily working from an original (or a copy of it) that was polished and approved by Barbaro himself, and that that source text was itself hard to decipher in places.[31] But Sinibaldi's version is also incomplete because of the acts of vandalism that were inflicted on it in later ages – an unfortunate measure of how richly it was illuminated. The first page evidently contained the start of the dedication to Ermolao's father, Zaccaria, presumably with the treatise's formal title before it; both are lost with that first page, as is the beginning of Book 1 on the third page, where the head letter must have been sumptuously decorated, as it is at the openings of Books 2, 3, and 4; and a single page in Book 3 (f. 84) has also been removed, possibly because it bore an illustration in miniature of Mt. Olympus.[32]

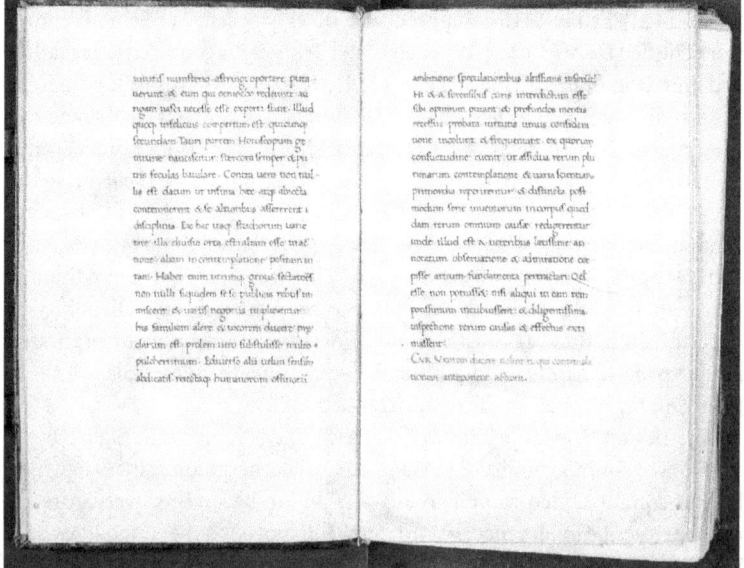

Figure 1 *De coelibatu* 1.1.7–1.2.1, here reproduced from MS Classe II 9, Biblioteca Comunale Ariostea, Ferrara, with the permission of the Servizio Biblioteche e Archivi del Comune di Ferrara.

The content of the four books

Directly after his prefatory dedication to Zaccaria, Ermolao itemizes the contents of the four books of *De coelibatu*, but the loss of the third page means that only the full entry for Book 1 and the start of that for Book 2 survive on the verso side of the second page. By celibacy Ermolao means not just abstaining from marriage, but also abstention from sexual relations of any kind (cf. 2.2.2); the state of physical purity that Barbaro urges is inseparable from his celibate's commitment to the contemplative as opposed to the active life. His chief aim in Book 1 is to establish not just why the contemplative celibate will reject marriage, but also why a celibate existence is both superior to and happier than the active life of civic engagement (1.2-6). A central strategy that Barbaro deploys here is to present the contemplative life as no less capable of contributing to the communal benefit than the active life, and therefore *itself* a form of 'active,' socially utilitarian service.[33]

After vindicating the life of contemplative celibacy in Book 1, Barbaro turns in Book 2 to the qualities that are to be looked for in the boy destined for that existence. Beyond the celibate-to-be's inherent capacities and physical robustness, his parents are to do all they can to support his progress, not least by ensuring that he receives a solid religious grounding at an early age, that he is educated privately at home by an elderly male tutor of unimpeachable character, and that he is sheltered in adolescence from household servants of the opposite sex (2.3-4). Yet the boy's natural aptitudes remain paramount, and so the last part of the book focuses above all on his good physical health and his stability of temperament (2.5-6). He shows every sign of developing into a philosophical sage such as the serene and virtuous contemplative configured in the ancient Stoic tradition.[34] From a Christian perspective, however, his specialness is also conveyed though his pious devotion and proximity to God – a point underscored early in Book 2 through the etymological relation that Barbaro draws between <u>caelebs</u>/<u>caelibatus</u> and <u>caelestis</u> ('heavenly').[35] But at no point in *De coelibatu* does Ermolao expand explicitly or in detail on faith per se as *itself* a form of encouragement to the chaste life. In order to present the contemplative celibate as a valuable, 'active,' and therefore praiseworthy contributor to the communal interest, Ermolao pushes to an extreme the idea that God favours such a person over all other mortals. But despite its strong Christian accent, the work is hardly a charter for monastic celibacy, and the celibate ideal that it aims for is one of self-discovery, not self-denial or self-sacrifice.[36]

After a brief summary of the topics covered in the first two books (3.2), and after concise coverage of what it is to live chastely both within and then outside marriage (3.3-4), Book 3 is dominated first by the forms of behaviour that are to be scrupulously avoided by the celibate-to-be: sensory pleasure, overindulgence in food and drink, consorting with the opposite sex, and an irregular pattern of sleep (3.5). Self-control is all, the Aristotelian golden mean its guiding principle.[37] But after first expatiating on the precautions to be taken by the celibate, Book 3 focuses secondly on the treatments to be applied so as to keep him safe from contamination: moderation of his appetites in accordance with his own needs and nature, an appropriate degree of detachment from social intercourse, and properly regulated sleep (3.6).

The first part of Book 4 is more abstract in feel, as if Barbaro's exploration there of the nature of contemplation (4.1) elevates the treatise, and the celibate himself, to a more ethereal plane.[38] After the social distancing that Ermolao recommends in Book 3, he enforces a different but complementary distance in 4.1 between lofty contemplation on the one hand and, on the other, the everyday values (e.g., desire for wealth, social position, material pleasure, etc.) that predominate in life at ground level, so to speak. This distance is again discernible in Barbaro's tailoring in 4.2 of the familiar humanistic curriculum to the rarified needs of the celibate-to-be: by turning his mind to geometry, music, arithmetic, and the visual arts/optics, the young man acquires a mathematical grasp that equips him for his higher studies, not least in the astronomical branch of natural science (cf. 4.2.4-5). The study of eloquence is hardly a priority (4.2.10-20), given the celibate's detachment from the civic arena where rhetorical skill comes into its own. In requiring the student to pay close attention to dialectic (4.2.26-30), Barbaro eschews the sophistic quibbling and sleight of hand that too often blight the discipline, at least as he finds it habitually practiced; the celibate's dialectical training instead sharpens the intellect for his high-minded immersion in moral philosophy and natural science (the latter including 'the investigation of matters pertaining to the gods and to mortals,' 4.2.31). Beyond this customized shaping of the humanist curriculum to serve the celibate, Barbaro also reverts to Cicero's *De officiis* (*On duties*) in an extended section (4.2.37-56) that importantly complements and rounds out his appropriation of that work in Book 1.[39]

As Book 4 hurries on to its conclusion, Barbaro neatly forestalls any impression that the celibate shaped in his pages must be a model of pinched severity and earnest self-containment; hence the appealing dash of colour with which Ermolao pictures him as vivacious and cheerful in outlook, affably enjoying the company of friends, vibrant in spirit as in body (4.2.72-87), and even 'a kind of likeness on earth, and an attestation, of the blessedness of God' (4.2.88). Just before the close, Barbaro goes out of his way to add a brief but important coda that is strikingly forward-looking for its time: he explicitly states that women are no less capable than men of achieving the end-goal of celibacy as set out in his four books (4.2.91-6) – a radical departure from the male-oriented asceticism and frequent misogyny of medieval writing on monastic celibacy.[40]

The promise that Barbaro requires in the celibate-to-be for growth into the mature adult celibate has important implications for the portrayal of childhood and adolescence in *De coelibatu*. No full attempt can be made here to assess the place of *De coelibatu* in the complex and much contested terrain of modern scholarly approaches to childhood in the Renaissance and beyond – not least the question of whether the concept of childhood as a separately (and often sentimentally) defined phase of human existence was an early modern construct.[41] Barbaro presents the pathway for the celibate-to-be as steady and predictable so long as he follows the protocols and educational program that Ermolao prescribes for him. In this respect, the early development of the celibate in *De coelibatu* is no discrete phase before he advances to his different, mature self, but a formative stage en route to, and inseparable from, that predestined future. And that continuity of experience is also critically manifested on a sexual front: the innocence of the child and adolescent anticipates the simple continence that Barbaro associates with the mature celibate – a childlike simplicity (*nēpiotēs*) in adulthood that was already valorized in the early Church.[42]

De coelibatu in the context of Venetian humanism

The hint of individuality conveyed by the celibate's characterful vivacity has important implications for the place of *De coelibatu* in the fifteenth-century evolution of Venetian humanism. As Venice expanded into the Terraferma from the late fourteenth century onwards, and as mainland cities such as Bassano, Vicenza, and especially Padua gradually came under Venetian control, the humanistic tendencies that had taken root in the mainland began to infiltrate the Republic and lent impetus to a movement that was already incipient there. Petrarch for one was an influential presence in Padua and also Venice, where he resided (thought not continuously) between 1362 and 1368, and where he championed the establishing of a public library based on his own collection; after that proposal ultimately came to nothing, Petrarch departed from Venice, but the humanistic seed had been sown.[43] In the subsequent decades the Republic's territorial expansion required a larger bureaucratic apparatus to deal with the volume of correspondence generated by that expansion;[44] more notaries and scribes were needed, and, in turn, there was an increasing demand for teachers of Latin who looked to the Classics for models of stylistic purity and elegance of form. Beyond this practical requirement, the study of material culture through such lenses as numismatics and epigraphy, and the rediscovery of lost works such as Cicero's letters, Quintilian's *Institutio oratoria*, and Lucretius' *De rerum natura*,[45] fostered a deeper engagement with the totality of ancient social, political and literary culture. This process was further advanced by the rise of the study of Greek in Italy in the early fifteenth century; and the diffusion of Greek was much accelerated by the arrival in the peninsula, and especially in Venice, of many émigré scholars after the fall of Constantinople in 1453.[46]

These humanistic developments were hardly exclusive to Venice in the Italian peninsula; but Venetian humanism was nevertheless highly distinctive because it was inseparable from, and largely deployed to affirm and celebrate, the myth of Venice as a society committed to *unanimitas*, or the subordination of individual interests and ambitions to the single, collective will.[47] 'The result,' as Craig Kallendorf well puts it, 'was a humanism of moral severity, pronounced piety, and committed republicanism – a humanism, in other words, that privileged certain traditional, fixed beliefs over disciplinary modes of enquiry.'[48] For all its rigidity of principle, however, Venetian humanism evolved over time, and three broad phases are identifiable according to the scheme influentially proposed by Margaret King.[49]

The first humanist generation delineated by King[50] was born in the last decades of the fourteenth century and witnessed Venice's early expansion into the mainland; this generation consisted mostly of nobles who sought to integrate humanist values and methodologies within the traditional *mores* of the ruling patrician class. Educated by professional humanists, many of them itinerant rather than permanent settlers in Venice, this generation could find respite from their civic responsibilities and their subordination to the imperative of *unanimitas* in their humanistic studies. Here the individual was able to challenge and assert himself more freely, thereby affirming his own intellectual and cultural identity;[51] but immersion in the classical tradition could also be directed to the patriotic end of finding in the ancient canon ample support for Venice's self-idealization as a unique Republic that was heir to the greatness of classical Rome.[52] This nostalgia for the Roman past makes its presence felt in *De coelibatu*, and not just through Barbaro's frequent recourse to anecdotes and moralizing *exempla* that feature eminent Romans;[53] at many moments the work appears situated not in the early 1470s but in ancient Rome itself, as when Ermolao anachronistically writes of the gladiatorial arena (cf. 1.6.3, 3.5.33) as if it were a familiar living institution in the flexible textual 'present.'

The second generation identified by King[54] came of age in the early decades of the fifteenth century, when Venice was engaged almost continuously in campaigns to extend and consolidate its mainland territories, and when its maritime empire and precious trade routes were coming under increasing threat from the Turks in the eastern Mediterranean. This was a phase in which humanistic skill was deployed by the Republic to argue its case and defend its interests before friend and foe alike. Venetian civic humanism reached maturity in these decades; but by arming the word in defense of Venetian ideology and strategic policy, this era tempered the 'enthusiastic classicism'[55] that characterized the first generation. By the emergence of King's third generation, born after 1430,[56] the humanistic cause was already well embedded in Venice, and it was further consolidated by the arrival of often transient foreigners, especially after 1453, and then by the rapid rise of print culture in the Republic.

But Venetian humanism also witnessed a growing malaise in this third generation. The myth of Venice was tested by external factors (especially the challenge posed to Venetian self-assurance by the Turkish threat in the east), but also by internal ones. The foreign scholar humanists who had served as cultured companions to patrician nobles and taught their sons gained a measure of independence through the alternative livelihoods provided by the printing presses.[57] The dissemination of Graeco-Roman texts from those presses encouraged a scientific approach to textual criticism, and the likes of Poliziano and Barbaro pioneered a new methodological rigour in the areas of manuscript collation, the reconciling of facts and assertions as differently reported by different sources, and the holistic study of Latin texts in relation to the Greek tradition. But this philological turn also gave rise to a certain desiccation of the word: as Anthony Grafton puts it, Poliziano 'belonged to a whole generation of humanists who turned – in Rome and Venice as well as Florence – from the oration to the emendation, from an audience of eager young citizens to a reading public of crabbed, jealous scholars.'[58] In Venice, many patricians settled for a relatively passive role as humanistic patrons rather than as active practitioners. Much humanistic engagement began to be characterized by an ornamental tendency, as opposed to being the force of self-expression and individual fulfillment that it had been in the first two generations.[59] The myth of *unanimitas* was also strained by widespread corruption among nobles in office, and frequently by a reluctance to serve in the first place; many tried to avoid office by quickly resigning from it, pleading cause for exemption, or trying not to be elected through such tactics as absenteeism abroad, finding fault with the election process, or nullifying their candidacy through breaches of the law.[60] Other patricians, whether disillusioned by the responsibilities traditionally incumbent on their class or alienated from the machine-like functionality of the Venetian bureaucracy, sought refuge and self-realization in the inner life through philosophical contemplation, monastic devotion, or immersion in humanistic scholarship.[61]

Against this background, Ermolao Barbaro's fall from grace in 1491 offers a spectacular example of this third-generation alienation, or escape, from the patrician *cursus*. But King's tripartite model also neatly differentiates three generations of the Barbaro family: born in 1422/3, Zaccaria, Ermolao's father, was a second-generation humanist, but our spotlight now falls on Francesco in the first generation.[62] Born in 1390, Francesco was 'the intellectual giant certainly of this generation, and (rivaled only by his own grandson and the son of his friend Leonardo Giustiniani) perhaps of the whole course of fifteenth-century humanism.'[63] One of Francesco's many contributions to the early development of Venetian humanism and its ideological mission was his 1415 *De re uxoria* (*On marriage*) – for King, 'the first major work of Venetian humanism' and the source of 'its legitimation.'[64] How, then, to understand Ermolao's *De coelibatu* in relation to his grandfather's *De re uxoria*, that cornerstone of Venetian humanistic discourse?

The originality of Francesco Barbaro's *De re uxoria*

In the first half of the fifteenth century, what Stanley Chojnacki characterizes as a 'new articulation of patrician culture' in Venice reinforced 'the formal dominance of the father in public and private life.'[65] Laws enacted in 1414 and 1430 established procedures for inspecting and recording the genealogical qualifications of those claiming noble status by birth; the names of mothers were also required as a way of curbing relationships between patrician men and lower-order women.[66] The patrician father's public status was replicated in the patriarchal structure of the domestic sphere; and yet, though subordinate to their husbands, married noblewomen acquired, as Chojnacki puts it, 'a new symbolic importance as part of their class's effort to achieve a castelike distinctiveness in the early Quattrocento.'[67] But one consequence of this stress on inherited nobility was that marital alliances became a central means by which patrician families guarded their survival and prestige. In turn, as fathers sought to arrange marriage settlements for their daughters with powerful and affluent families, dowry inflation meant that siblings of a new bride were frequently disadvantaged by the uneven distribution of the familial patrimony. Hence in 1420 the Venetian senate limited dowries to 1,600 ducats, an amount raised to 3,000 ducats in 1505 – an increase that reflected the scale of violations and the continuing pressure of dowry inflation after 1420.[68] Beyond the consequence that one daughter's marital prospects could be very negatively affected by her sister's high dowry, patrician sons were also hit hard. Their plight contributed to the growing cohort of unmarried nobles in fifteenth-century Venice, where Chojnacki estimates that almost half of adult male nobles remained bachelors.[69] As for voluntary bachelorhood, sexual factors doubtless played a part, whether because of homosexual leanings or the freedoms available to unmarried heterosexuals; so rife was prostitution in Venice that regulation of it in the later fourteenth century was intensified in the early fifteenth.[70] Some noble bachelors simply rejected the role of familial patriarch and its attendant pressures. But in the fifteenth century increasing numbers were drawn specifically to a life of celibate study or contemplation, monastic or otherwise;[71] hence the importance of *De coelibatu* as an informal Quattrocento mission statement of sorts for such an existence.

In their different responses to this sociocultural picture, Francesco's *De re uxoria* and Ermolao's *De coelibatu* are more complementary than contradictory; *De coelibatu* is even in a sense wedded to Francesco's tract through its many explicit points of contact with, adaptation of, and reaction to it.[72] *De re uxoria* amply reflects the humanist influences that Francesco had imbibed from his early teachers in Venice and Padua. Under Gasparino Barzizza (1360–1431) in Padua, he honed the stylistic manner and techniques of Ciceronian Latin that are fully on display in *De re uxoria*.[73] In Venice in July 1414 he began to study Greek under Guarino Guarini (1374–1460, also known as Guarino da Verona or Guarino Veronese), who was himself one of the pioneers of Greek studies in Renaissance Italy;[74] Francesco bears witness at the end of *De re uxoria* to his remarkable progress in Greek under Guarino's guidance in 1414–15.[75] Another formative influence on the young Francesco was Zaccaria Trevisan (*c.* 1370–1414), the carrier of the Petrarchan torch at Venice and hence 'the prototypical figure of Venetian humanism'.[76] A measure of his importance in Barbaro's cultural formation is that he is fondly commemorated in the dedicatory preface of *De re uxoria*;[77] but Trevisan's presence there also symbolically preannounces the deep humanist credentials of a work that is steeped in such newly propagated 'classics' as Xenophon and Plutarch on matters of domestic management and the rearing and educating of children. Guarino's influence is especially marked in this respect, as he played a key role in the diffusion of Xenophon and Plutarch in early Quattrocento Venice.[78] Through its innovative recourse to such sources, and in its larger indebtedness to the Graeco-Roman canon, *De re uxoria* is a state-of-the-art humanist production in its literary form and texture – and no less groundbreaking on a thematic front.

Francesco visited Florence in the summer of 1415, and during his stay he became acquainted with several of the leading Florentine humanists of the day.[79] He also established warm relations with the Medici family, especially Lorenzo de' Medici (1395–1440, known as 'the Elder' to differentiate him from Lorenzo the Magnificent, 1449–92). Lorenzo's engagement in 1415 to the highborn Ginevra Cavalcanti[80] prompted Francesco to compose *De re uxoria* as a wedding gift for his friend; it was probably completed over the winter of 1415–16, after Francesco had returned to Venice and before the marriage in early (mid-February?) 1416.[81] The work soon made its mark in Italian humanist circles: its popularity is attested by its survival in more than a hundred manuscripts, by the multiple print editions that followed its 1513 *princeps* in Paris, and by numerous translations into Italian, German, French, and English.[82] A dedicatory address to Lorenzo is followed by an introductory section on 'what marriage is' (*Quid matrimonium sit*) before the main body of the work proceeds in two movements (*not* two books), the first on the factors to be considered in choosing a wife, the second on the responsibilities incumbent upon her.[83] Francesco himself was twenty-five at the time of writing, and as yet unmarried,[84] and so in his prefatory letter he acknowledges all that he has learnt from the married Trevisan 'in conversations about this matter we had from time to time. In these he gravely expounded to me nearly the whole of the elegant science of marriage as taught by the ancients.'[85] Guarino too was surely influential, and not just because of his own experience of marriage;[86] a vocal opponent of the ancient and medieval anti-marriage tradition, Guarino revived the ancient form of the epithalamium in pioneering what became the thriving Renaissance tradition of the wedding oration.[87]

De re uxoria is as original in substance as it is state-of-the-art in its humanistic form: 'with his emphasis ... on the family as the basic unit of state and society, and on the duties of wives in this context, Barbaro created a new literary genre,' giving 'the conventional treatise on family life a new twist.'[88] In particular, by predicating noble succession on the wife's own nobility of birth and her rearing and educating of her offspring in the image of her own virtue, the work is unprecedented in the importance it attaches to the role of women in safeguarding the institution of the patrician family. In this respect Francesco is for King 'the first champion of maternal capacity in the domain of the family, and an advocate of the other voice'[89] who departs radically from the rabid misogyny that had characterized the anti-marriage tradition from antiquity onwards.[90] Ermolao himself predictably draws on that tradition in *De coelibatu*, notably through his allusions to one of its mainstays, Jerome's *Adversus Iovinianum* (*Against Jovinian*) of 393 CE.[91] Along with Jerome, Augustine played a key role in shaping the Western Church's doctrine on marriage. On the basis of the prelapsarian sacrament conjoining Adam and Eve in Genesis with the injunction to 'be fruitful and multiply and fill the earth and subdue it' (1.28), Augustine defended marriage in his *De bono coniugali* (*On the good of marriage*) of 401 CE. But for Augustine God's command to multiply sanctioned sexual intercourse only for the purpose of procreation; reproductive union was blessed before the Fall, but intercourse thereafter was contaminated with evil. Even though Augustine defends marriage and finds within it a means of remedying and regulating lust, it remains inferior to continence.[92]

The claims of holy abstinence and virginity as propagated by Jerome and Augustine were profoundly influential throughout the Middle Ages. At the dawn of humanism in Italy, Petrarch notably shows and shares the misogynistic traces of this tradition in extolling the contemplative life at a remove from the distractions of marriage, family, and civic engagement.[93] But by the late fourteenth century the social upheavals and depopulation precipitated by plagues, wars, and internal factionalism within city-states caused attitudes to marriage to shift; the anti-marriage tradition was hardly displaced, but it came under fresh challenge. Hence the important contribution of Coluccio Salutati (1331–1406), chancellor of Florence from 1375 to his death: he is hailed by Anthony D'Elia as 'the first humanist to reevaluate marriage in the light of these social and economic changes.'[94] Moving away from the anti-marriage stance that he had taken in championing the contemplative life of religious commitment over that of the active layman in his *De seculo et religione* (*On the world and religious life*) of 1381–2, Salutati reversed his position by 1393: the active life of civic engagement is equal in merit, even superior, to that of contemplative withdrawal.[95] He married in 1392, albeit with concerns that marriage was incompatible with his studies – only to find his fears groundless and to harden in opposition to the anti-marriage tradition and to contemplative celibacy at a remove from the civic arena.[96]

Salutati's shifting stance on marriage matters here because of his pivotal role in initiating at Florence, through his advocacy of humanistic education, the ideology of a civic humanism that was committed to the active life: humanistic study perfected the citizen, and his perfected virtue was expressed in civic participation.[97] It was in this climate that Francesco Barbaro visited Florence in 1415, almost a decade after Salutati's death; and Francesco's *De re uxoria* is inflected as much by this Florentine discourse as it is by Venetian introspection about the role of marriage in perpetuating the bloodline and values of the patrician family. The work looks both ways in this respect, setting the two Republics in dialogue with other;[98] and another contact-point between them was the problem of dowry inflation in both places.[99] Early in the dedicatory letter to Lorenzo, Francesco laments how 'today, men … burden themselves with debt so as to give rich gifts to those who are already rich';[100] this en route to explaining why he gives *De re uxoria* as a gift to his friend – a gift more valuable than any material offering that Francesco could possibly bestow on a man of Lorenzo's wealth, and all the more precious because it comes 'not from Francesco's fortune, but from your friend

Francesco.'[101] Behind the charm of this gesture lies a barely concealed allusion to the inflationary culture of the nuptial dowry, a feature of the work encoded in its very title. The Latin phrase *res uxoria* can refer simply to matrimony,[102] but it is also used of 'a wife's property' in Roman legal terminology – a connotation doubtless familiar to Francesco from his study of civil and canon law in Padua in 1408–12.[103] The title *De re uxoria* is thus, as King puts it, 'in fact a trick, a riddle, a clever pun'[104] whose ambiguity she preserves in rendering the title *De re uxoria* not as plain *On marriage* but as *On the wealth of wives*. But what sort of wealth does the title then imply?

Fundamental to *De re uxoria* is Francesco's rejection of the importance all too often attached to the financial dowry that the wife brings to the union: her greatest wealth lies above all in her virtue and good birth. This ordering of priorities is emphatically reflected in how he organizes his subject matter in the work's first movement, on choosing a wife. He follows ancient practice, he asserts, in evaluating a prospective wife according to five criteria, each of them treated in its own section in this first part of the treatise: 'her character, age, descent, beauty, and wealth.'[105] This order is for King nothing short of 'startling'[106] in countering the reader's expectations by relegating beauty and wealth so far down the list and immediately prioritizing virtue in III:

> Virtue, then, is the preeminent requirement, whose power and worth is so great that, even if other qualities are lacking, yet the marriage should be considered a good one . . . we consider virtue in a wife of such great importance that, if our fortune permits (*si fortunae nostrae patientur*), we should either pay no attention to the size of her dowry, or settle for a very small one, in order to obtain domestic honour and harmony.[107]

Elsewhere, Francesco hardly denies the value of material wealth (hence the rider in 'if our fortune permits' above), but the onus remains on virtue:

> Now, as planned, I shall speak about wealth (*divitiis*) . . . Since therefore we value all that promotes the worthiness and honour of marriage, and our own ease, abundance, possessions, and riches, we must husband such wealth for its dignity and utility, whose fruits are gratitude, liberality, and magnificence, virtues which shine indeed with a supreme splendor.[108]

So with beauty, Francesco 'would value it highly' only if conjoined with 'noble character and other admirable qualities';[109] what matters is not a beautiful physique per se, but one well equipped for 'the duty to procreate offspring.'[110] In the second movement, on the wife's responsibilities, the opening chapters on obedience and conjugal love give way to five sections that are 'decidedly repressive in intent':[111] not just the regulation of her behaviour, of her appetites in food and drink, and of her manner of dress, etc., but even '[the suppression of] normal energies and emotions in order to meet the marital ideal.'[112] For all his movement away from the misogyny of the anti-marriage tradition, Francesco underscores through these chapters on regulation and self-control the wife's subordination to her husband through the limits and constraints imposed by marriage. Yet the crowning section on the rearing of children (XVIII) offsets this subordinating tendency by stressing the wife's vital role both as the physical nurturer of her children (via gestation, birthing, and breastfeeding) and subsequently as the inculcator of religious and moral instruction in them. For all her subordination to her husband, and beyond material circumstance, the truest wealth within the union lies with his wife herself: *De re uxoria* is the telling of that untold wealth.

De coelibatu and *De re uxoria* in dialogue

Experience of Francesco's originality of approach in *De re uxoria* encourages us to look for a similar enterprise – even a no less startling effect – in Ermolao's *De coelibatu*. Far from contradicting or countermanding his grandfather's treatise, *De coelibatu* is better viewed as a diptych-like complement to it,[113] and not just because Ermolao hardly launches a systematic attack on the institution of marriage per se or denies the benefits and pleasures it can bring (cf. 1.5.8-15, 1.6.2: 'I maintain that intimate companionship with a wife of the greatest respectability ... is a pleasant thing'). Much more important for now is Cicero's role in connecting *De coelibatu* and *De re uxoria*, and not just at the level of the Ciceronian style and diction that pervade both works.[114] Poggio Bracciolini (1380–1459) for one nicely articulates the particular Ciceronian feature that concerns us in *De re uxoria*. In a letter to Guarino of 31 December 1416, Poggio thanks him for sending on a copy of *De re uxoria*; he writes with nice irony that before he read the work he had little intention of marrying, but that he had still less intention afterwards, now that he knew what marriage really involved.[115] But he admired the novel subject matter, the orderliness of the presentation, the attractive style, and the dignified expression, all of which culminates in this:

> Francesco Barbaro seems to me to have written a second book *On duties*, but on wifely duties – so perfectly does he reproduce Cicero in his expression.[116]

The paradigmatic influence of Cicero's *De officiis* is duly highlighted by Francesco's latest editor, Claudio Griggio, for whom the Ciceronian tract is remade in *De re uxoria* with a topical relevance to the socio-political realities of marriage and family in Quattrocento Venice.[117]

It is this remaking of Cicero that Ermolao emulates in *De coelibatu*, but in ways that importantly modify his grandfather's approach in *De re uxoria*. Three features of Ermolao's emulative technique stand out for now, the first his extended engagement in Book 1 of *De coelibatu* with *De officiis* 1 and the provocation of Cicero's stance there that the glory of virtue lies wholly in action (1.19); Ermolao strives to answer the time-honoured objection that the contemplative celibate's existence is inferior to the *vita activa* of public service. In 1.4 he embarks on a complex and, in places, a somewhat tendentious[118] refutation of Cicero's portrayal of the active life as superior. Ermolao's strategy here is partly defensive; but he also shows a more aggressive side in re-channelling and turning in his favour various features of Cicero's own argument in *De officiis* 1. At several points Ermolao casts the celibate as vigorous and 'active' in his contemplative pursuits – endeavours by which he makes a valuable contribution to society at large.[119] The implication is that through this shared commitment to action in different spheres, Cicero's man of action and Ermolao's 'active' contemplative celibate are reconcilable as variations of a shared typology. In this way Ermolao adjusts the Ciceronian blueprint in *De officiis* 1 in his favour. But Barbaro offers no acknowledgement that, after enthusiastically endorsing the active life early in *De officiis* 1, Cicero himself takes a more nuanced approach to the *vita contemplativa* later in the book. So at 1.71:

> Men of outstanding ability who have devoted themselves to learning rather than choose public life, or those who have retired from public life hampered by ill health or some quite serious cause, should therefore perhaps be excused when they yield to others the power and the praise of governing.[120]

Then at 1.155:

> But note that those who have devoted their entire life to learning things have, after all, managed to contribute to the benefits and advantages of mankind. They have educated many to be better citizens and more beneficial to their countries.[121]

In effect, in configuring his 'active' celibate, Barbaro turns to his advantage what was *already* a concession made by Cicero in the mid- to later stages of *De officiis* 1. To put the point differently, Barbaro exploits what he saw to be the shifting ground of Cicero's own argument: on offer in *De coelibatu* 1 is not so much a response to *De officiis* 1 as a remaking of it, with Barbaro building on a premise (the contemplative's 'active' potential) that surfaces only secondarily in his Ciceronian source-text.

Second, in his treatment in Book 4 of moral philosophy as part of the humanist education of the celibate-to-be, Ermolao engages once more with *De officiis* 1; this return to Cicero helps to unify *De coelibatu* through a form of ring-compositional coordination between the first and last books. Following the Stoic Panaetius of Rhodes (*c.* 185–109 BCE), Cicero identifies the four parts of the Panaetian *honestum* ('the honourable') as follows in *Off.* 1.15:

> Everything that is honourable arises from one of four parts: it is involved either [i] with the perception of truth and with ingenuity; or [ii] with preserving fellowship among men, with assigning to each his own, and with faithfulness to agreements one has made; or [iii] with the greatness and strength of a lofty and unconquered spirit; or [iv] with order and limit in everything that is said and done (modesty and restraint are included here).[122]

The rest of *De officiis* 1 is dominated by Cicero's discussion of each of these four parts in turn: wisdom (1.18-19); social virtue, including justice (1.20-41) and liberality (1.42-60); greatness of spirit (1.61-92); and decorum and its related virtues (1.93-151). Ermolao takes up his own discussion of these virtues in *De coelibatu* 4, in circumstances that importantly supplement his defense of the contemplative life in his first book. If he is seen to prevail there over Cicero's championing of the active life in *De officiis* 1, a further challenge remains: if the celibate's *vita contemplativa* is fully vindicated as, in its own way, no less 'active' and valuable to the community than the *vita activa*, how are the four parts of the Panaetian *honestum* as distinguished in *De officiis* 1 to be reconciled with and mapped on to the celibate life? Ermolao rises to this challenge in 4.2.37-61, first treating justice (§§39–47) and liberality (§§48–9) and then turning to greatness of spirit (§§50–4) and decorum (§§55–6) before reverting in §§57–9 to wisdom, the virtue that led off the Ciceronian sequence. Throughout this section Ermolao's direct dialogical engagement with Cicero is evident in his many explicit evocations of *De officiis* 1.[123] His standard technique in this section is to begin with the Ciceronian definition of the given virtue before going his own way, configuring out of each of the four virtues a double valence of equal pertinence to both the active life and the *vita contemplativa*.[124] By this means Ermolao again conspicuously reworks a major feature of *De officiis* 1, as if amending or updating the Ciceronian charter so as to accommodate the celibate. Through this remaking of *De officiis*, he in effect does for the celibate what Francesco did for the noble wife in *De re uxoria*.

Third, Ermolao not only emulates Francesco's own creativity of response to Cicero's *De officiis*, but also aligns the celibate with the noble wife as shaped in *De re uxoria*. Before arguing in *De coelibatu* 1 that a celibate existence is more pleasurable than married life, Ermolao first defines what marriage is; his definition in 1.5.1 directly echoes Francesco's in *De re uxoria*,[125] and he then goes on to offer a de facto summary of the structure and content of his grandfather's treatise.[126] Through this early précis of Francesco's work and of the qualities to be looked for in the noble wife, Ermolao gently invites a comparison that surely becomes more compelling as the celibate's necessary attributes and education are delineated in ever more detail as the work progresses: for all their obvious differences, his celibate emerges as a virtuous counterpart of sorts to the noble wife. Take, for example, Francesco's strictures on food and drink in the second part of *De re uxoria*:

> Now we shall consider food ... Who doubts that those delicacies that the multitude believes afford us the good life instead tear at and shatter the sinews of virtue? Who is so abstemious that he is not swiftly corrupted by them? Who has been so lost to these pleasures, that sobriety, vigilance, caution, cannot recall him to the joy and honour of a moderate existence?[127]

This paragraph would hardly be out of place in *De coelibatu*, where, in the matter of the sensory pleasures of food and drink, abstention and control of the appetites are enjoined on the celibate (3.5.9-21) as they are on Francesco's noble wife. In the second movement of *De re uxoria* moderation is not only granted its own subsection (XII) as a quality that informs all aspects of the noble wife's conduct; by implication, it also permeates her habits of speech and silence (XIII), her manner of dress (XIV), and her physical appetites (XV, XVI),[128] just as moderation and the golden mean are enshrined as guiding principles for the celibate.[129] Certainly, both Francesco's noble wife and Ermolao's celibate are shaped within a familiar matrix of philosophical and humanistic ideals and sources that profoundly influence both *De re uxoria* and *De coelibatu*.[130] But beyond the familial linkage of the two works at an authorial level, and beyond their shared responses to or re-makings of Cicero's *De officiis*, the noble wife and the celibate are themselves closely related, as if different versions of the same virtuous typology – even perhaps a textual mother and son, as it were, like-minded and mutually affirming.

For Chojnacki, Francesco's stress on the mother's role in preserving the purity of patrician lineage at Venice, and his disapproval of the importance too often attached to the material dowry, 'prefigured the legislation of the 1420s.'[131] When, some sixty years later, his grandson penned *De coelibatu* in Naples, Ermolao's physical detachment from Venice offers a suggestive analogy for the 'external' perspective that his treatise brings to bear on patrician marriage in the Republic: experience of the Neapolitan court and its distinctive strain of 'royal humanism' offered something different from the particular constraints of the Venetian humanistic model.[132] We saw earlier how the myth of the Serenissima was tested in Margaret King's third generation of Venetian humanism, not least through disillusion with the demands of the Venetian civic *cursus*.[133] For King, *De coelibatu* fits this larger pattern of frustration: it constitutes 'the quiet but potent manifesto of Venetian humanism's most genuine rebel,'[134] and Ermolao's defense of celibacy is 'a plea for individual self-determination in a social context where family and state limited the possibilities for self-determination.'[135] But elsewhere King describes *De coelibatu* in words that are especially telling:

> Barbaro must forge a new vision of the ideal life that would be met with public applause, not condemnation: such a life would be nonpolitical on the one hand and nonmonastic on the other.[136]

The stress that Ermolao places on the contemplative life as itself 'active' and capable of benefiting society at large now becomes all-important. However rebellious *De coelibatu* is in articulating an existence away from the public *cursus*, Ermolao remains committed to the *vita activa* in this special sense. The point is implicit in King's words above, but to spell it out more starkly: Barbaro relies on this 'active' interpretation of contemplative celibacy to cast his new vision of the ideal life as worthy of public applause, not condemnation. On this approach, his rebellious streak in *De coelibatu* only extends so far: he tries to work within the familiar paradigm of Venetian service to the state by making the case for 'active' contemplation. Here was a strategy by which the young man could theorize his way out of what became a far more intractable problem when he eventually collided with the realities of state service: fine theoretical distinctions counted for less at that point, and there was no easy exit from his official commitments.

The authorial self in *De coelibatu*

One of the most appealing aspects of *De coelibatu* is the sheer vibrancy of the writing: beyond the largely Ciceronian stamp of his Latinity,[137] Ermolao's textual personality shows dash and panache; he keeps varying the pace and tone of his authorial voice as he progresses through the changeful movements of theme and content across the four books; and in his liveliness of self-presentation he fully, and surely self-consciously, resembles the genial, quick-witted, and energetic celibate he pictures late in Book 4.[138] The text abounds with colourful *exempla* and anecdotes featuring famous names from the Graeco-Roman past;[139] there are many flashes of wit, fully in keeping with the Ermolao who reveals himself in his letters;[140] in the manner of a moralizing Seneca, he rises to peaks of outrage and takes on imagined opponents in the rough-and-tumble of diatribe-like debate;[141] he deploys extended sequences of complex and occasionally convoluted argument;[142] he engages deeply with certain influential source texts,[143] but elsewhere touches on complex philosophical technicalities with a more allusive, seemingly professorial brevity;[144] his lengthy discourse on the humanistic curriculum in 4.2 is inflected by the tradition of such pedagogical treatises as Pier Paolo Vergerio's *De ingenuis moribus et liberalibus adulescentiae studiis*, as was Francesco Barbaro's *De re uxoria*;[145] and in his frequent recourse to Aristotle and the Greek medical theorists,[146] he already shows at eighteen his profound engagement with the texts and interests that would define his scholarship for years to come.

For present purposes, it is important to view *De coelibatu* in the context of Ermolao's writings on Aristotle in particular for two reasons. First, the youthful sense of mission and appetite for provocation that he shows in *De coelibatu* are fully reflected, and much magnified, in his subsequent work on Aristotle. Already before twenty, we recall,[147] he had embarked on his Latin translation of the corpus of Themistius, the fourth-century CE author of explanatory paraphrases of numerous Aristotelian works.[148] After returning from Naples in 1473, Ermolao lectured on Aristotle in Padua in 1474–9,[149] drafting a summary of the *Nicomachean ethics* that was published only decades later.[150] The first edition of his translation of Themistius was published in 1481, but already by then he had made a start on his ambitious plan to translate the whole of the Aristotelian corpus. Ermolao's preoccupation with Aristotle was inseparable from the latter's larger imprint on Venetian humanism: as universal systems of order that structured reality within a hierarchical model of authority, both Aristotelian philosophy and Christianity offered important holistic paradigms for Venice's ideological mission and governmental stability at home (in its myth of one-state *unanimitas*) and abroad (in its seaborne empire).[151] Ermolao was hardly alone in promoting the fusion of the Aristotelian and the humanist traditions in the Republic,[152] but he was outspoken in his denunciations of the current climate of Aristotelian studies, especially as practiced in Padua.[153] What he objected to were the accretions of misinterpretation that he and like-minded thinkers attributed to such factors as the use of unreliable translations, the biases of the Latin scholastics, and the influence of the Arabic commentator Averroes (1126–98). For Ermolao, only by returning to the original Greek texts and their ancient commentators such as Themistius could Aristotle be properly read and his authentic views recovered. In his own renditions of the Greek Ermolao applied a philosophy of translation ('not just turning, but turning well')[154] that avoided a bare literalism and aimed for 'a kind of middle elegance'[155] – a 'philosophy' of style that set him at odds with Giovanni Pico della Mirandola (1463–94) in their famous debate on the role of eloquence in philosophical exposition.[156]

What Ermolao sought to achieve was nothing less than a radical reform of Aristotelianism that would reverse this tide of error. In the dedicatory letter that he addressed to Pope Sixtus IV (1414–84) in his 1481 edition of Themistius, he writes as follows:

> I have expended very great effort in this exposition, not so much because I could not be helped at all by those authors who have previously commented abominably and ignorantly (*barbare*) on Aristotle as because [I could not be helped] by those, too, who lay claim to eloquence in Latin in our own times and have rendered the Greek commentaries on that philosopher. Most of these, while attacking the ignorance of others, have betrayed their own ignorance.[157]

Ermolao's waspish barbs here are offset by the witty play on his name in *barbare* (a recurring play in and beyond this letter[158]): a Barbarus valiantly battles barbarian ignorance. He launches similar broadsides elsewhere,[159] but what matters for now is the habit of mind that connects *De coelibatu* with what came afterwards. The independent spirit on show in that youthful treatise is symptomatic of the boldness of initiative – the reformist zeal – with which Ermolao set about helping to forge a new humanist/anti-scholastic Aristotelianism.

Secondly, Ermolao's own stated motivation for sanitizing Aristotle in this way is revealing. After publishing his Themistius in 1481, he embarked on a translation of the first-century CE physician and botanical pharmacologist Pedanius Dioscorides' Greek *On medical material*. It is likely that he completed this translation in 1481–2; he went on to supplement it some years later, plausibly in or around 1489, with the appendix encased in his so-called *Corollarium in Dioscoridem* (*Supplement to Dioscorides*).[160] The *Corollarium* and his translation were published only posthumously, in the 1516 edition curated in Venice by Giovanni Battista Egnazio.[161] In that edition a preface to the opening book of the *Corollarium* is written in the first person[162] – for John Riddle, *Egnazio*'s preface in imitation of Ermolao's first-person voice;[163] but for Giovanni Pozzi the content and tone of the preface are too finely calibrated about the man and his works, too personally revealing, to be the work of anyone but Barbaro.[164] If the preface was indeed penned by Ermolao himself, it appears to have been written no earlier than very late 1492, given that he refers in that preface to the publication of his *Castigationes Plinianae primae* (*First corrections of Pliny*) on Pliny's *Natural History*; a second set of Plinian *Castigationes* was to follow in early 1493. His prefatory dedication of the first set to Pope Alexander VI is dated 25 August 1492, and Barbaro signs off at the end of his *First corrections* on 24 November 1492;[165] hence the later date of the *Corollarium* preface.

In surveying Ermolao's past scholarly endeavours, this preface is strikingly reminiscent of his letter to Arnold of Bost of June 1 1485 that we touched on earlier.[166] In contrast to that letter, however, the preface begins by stressing Barbaro's commitment to the utilitarian benefit of his scholarship. Whether their topic is historical or lodged in a different branch of study, he writes, authors generally have no greater concern than to 'have regard for the life and benefit of mortals' (*ut vitae usuique mortalium consulant*). He had admired this turn of mind from boyhood, he says, and so he had devoted to his studies all the time that he could secure away from his private and public responsibilities. He had long striven to be helpful to the lives of humankind through his painstaking efforts (*ut studio, cura industriaque mea vitae hominum prodessem*), and to win esteem for those strivings. Let others be the judge of whether he has earned that esteem; but he can testify on his own behalf that he 'had exerted himself with the intention of directing to the profit and advantage of humankind (*ad mortalitatis fructum et utilitatem*) all that he was capable of achieving in thought and writing.' Even if this preface is ascribed (with Riddle) to Egnazio, not Ermolao, Egnazio well captures the essence of the man in this late phase of his short life: Ermolao himself uses the same language of utilitarian benefit (*utilis, utilitas, prodesse*) in his dedicatory letter to Pope Alexander VI at the start of his *Castigationes Plinianae primae*.[167]

This stress on Ermolao's utilitarian motivation in his scholarship has important implications for the 'active' dimension of the *vita contemplativa* in *De coelibatu*. Viewed in isolation, his argument to that 'active' effect in *De coelibatu* may appear opportunistic and more contrived than compelling, even though it has strong ancient precedents.[168] In retrospect, however, the utilitarian intent of his 'active' service in rendering Themistius, say, or in repairing the text of Pliny, can now be seen to continue a commitment to the *commune bonum* that Barbaro had already asserted in *De coelibatu* all those years before.

III: Picturing Ermolao Barbaro

Ermolao's impassioned commitment to the single life in *De coelibatu* will now importantly inform our effort to put a face on the verbal picture of him that has been sketched so far. His image is known today partly from an unattributed oil portrait on wood that resides in the Pinacoteca Civica di Palazzo Volpi in Como, Lombardy (Figure 2). This portrait belonged to Paolo Giovio (1483–1552), the distinguished Italian physician, historian and prelate who assembled the renowned art collection known today as the

Figure 2 *Portrait of Hermolao Barbaro*, c. 1520–*ante* 1521, Raccolte d'arte della Pinacoteca Civica di Palazzo Volpi, here reproduced with the permission of the Musei Civici di Como.

Giovio Series.[169] That collection of portraits of famous men was originally housed in a museum constructed specially for it on the shore of Lake Como. The Como version of Barbaro was in turn copied by Cristofano dell'Altissimo (c. 1525–1605) as part of a commission received from Cosimo I de' Medici: from 1552 down to 1589, Cristofano copied at least 280 of the portraits in the Como collection. The collection of copies deriving from the Giovio Series has been housed in the Uffizi Gallery since 1587, six years after the Uffizi's foundation in 1581; hence the portrait of Barbaro that today hangs in Florence.[170]

The Como portrait is known to have come into Giovio's possession no later than the summer of 1521;[171] apart from the Uffizi version, it was also the source of the engraving executed by Tobias Stimmer (1539–84) for the 1577 Basel edition of Giovio's *Elogia virorum literis illustrium* (*Praises of men distinguished in letters*).[172] But what was Giovio's original based on? If not a portrait of Barbaro from life, from what source did it derive? Giovio's representatives are known sometimes to have acquired copies of figures drawn from large-scale group-compositions. One Venetian painting on this scale included, in the cast of eminences that it pictured, Barbaro as well as Angelo Poliziano and Girolamo Donato (that hallowed trinity of humanists); this was one of the canvases that hung in the Sala del Maggior Consiglio in the Palazzo Ducale and were destroyed in the great fire that swept through the Doge's Palace in December 1577.[173] But another Venetian painting survives that shows an image of Barbaro – an identification made in a poem on the picture written probably around 1504 by the humanist Pierio Valeriano (1477–1558).[174]

The picture in question is one of the cycle of nine canvases by Vittore Carpaccio (c. 1460–1525/6) that depict the life, martyrdom, and apotheosis of St. Ursula.[175] Her legend has numerous variants, but Carpaccio appears to have followed the version recounted in the famous *Legenda Aurea* (*Golden Legend*) of Jacopo da Varagine (c. 1230–98), an Italian translation of which was published in Venice in 1475. According to this version, Ursula, the mythic fourth-century daughter of the Christian king Notus (or Maurus) of Brittany, was betrothed to the pagan prince Etherius; the betrothal was effectively coerced, as Etherius' father threatened to destroy Notus' kingdom if the match was refused. But the betrothal came with a condition: that Etherius convert to Christianity and allow Ursula to make a pilgrimage to Rome. The pilgrimage happened, and Etherius joined her on it, together with her ten ladies-in-waiting, each of them attended by a thousand virgin escorts. At Rome Ursula and Etherius received the blessing of Pope Cyriacus, but thereafter (at least according to the narrative sequence of the *Legenda Aurea*[176]), in her sleep, Ursula had a premonition of her own martyrdom. That vision was fulfilled when, on her return from her Roman pilgrimage, she reached Cologne and was there slain by the Hun army; given the Ottoman threat to Venetian interests in the eastern Mediterranean in the late fifteenth century, the Huns are tellingly depicted in the guise of the Turks in Carpaccio's rendition. With Ursula's Christian martyrdom now complete, the final canvas shows her in the presence of God, elevated in her ascension above her virgin companions. Carpaccio's cycle is generally dated to between 1490 and 1500. It was produced for the Scuola di Sant'Orsola in Venice; after the Scuola's suppression under Napoleon in 1806, it was moved in 1810 to the Gallerie dell'Accademia in Venice, and there it resides today.[177]

The canvas that concerns us for now features Ursula's arrival at Rome (Figure 3): as she kneels beside Etherius to receive Pope Cyriacus' blessing, the figure who stands prominently behind Cyriacus and holds his train is shown turning his gaze away from the betrothed couple. This figure bears a striking resemblance in both his physiognomy and the direction of his look to the Barbaro captured in the Como portrait: the implication is that Giovio's original of Ermolao, the one later copied by Cristofano dell'Altissimo, was modeled on Carpaccio's version. It remains conceivable that Giovio's original was modeled specifically on the version that hung in the Sala del Maggior Consiglio and perished in the 1577 fire; but since that version was itself painted in the first years of the sixteenth century, a decade or so after Ermolao's death, it too presupposes a model – and the trail of clues leads back once more to Carpaccio, or to the model on which Carpaccio himself relied.[178] After all, Carpaccio's *St. Ursula's Arrival in Rome* was probably painted after 1490, the year in which Barbaro departed for Rome, where he would ultimately remain in exile from Venice down to his death in 1493; Carpaccio must have painted him not from life, but from a pre-existing model. Moreover, Barbaro's death presumably explains why, despite his public disgrace in Venice, he could yet be shown on Carpaccio's canvas: the Aquileia controversy did not efface the fact that Barbaro was 'undoubtedly the greatest scholar of Latin and Greek literature the city had produced to that point.'[179]

But if we accept that Ermolao Barbaro is shown in this eye-catching pose and position in Carpaccio's canvas, why his averted gaze? An important clue is offered by the long shadow cast over the St. Ursula cycle by the politics of aristocratic marriage at Venice. As we have seen,[180] the institution of marriage played a vital role in the safeguarding of patrician self-identity and hereditary succession in the Republic. The stability of that structure was increasingly tested by the rise of new wealth and by the social ambition that it fueled; marrying 'up' into the impoverished nobility led to dowry inflation, and the purity of the closed patriciate's identity was challenged by marriage between different social orders. The St. Ursula cycle is heavily implicated in this

Figure 3 Vittore Carpaccio, *St. Ursula's Arrival in Rome*, part of his *Saint Ursula* cycle, 1488–95. Gallerie dell'Accademia, Venice.

discourse by 'speak[ing] firmly of aristocratic marriage appropriately sanctioned and properly managed.'[181] In light of his *De coelibatu*, does Barbaro look away disapprovingly from the couple as they kneel before Pope Cyriacus? Or can we detect a sympathetic union of sorts between Ermolao and Ursula? After all, her martyrdom in a sense begins when she succumbs to the arranged match with Etherius, and it is completed when she succumbs to the infidel Huns in Cologne. Hence the possibility that Barbaro and Ursula are to be viewed as kindred spirits in their breaking away from the traditional protocols of aristocratic marriage, she through spiritual devotion, he through devotion to the life of the mind. In effect, as Elizabeth Rodini observes, 'perhaps the two figures are paired here as contrasting models of behaviour, or perhaps as two sides of the same coin.'[182]

As he turns away from Ursula and Etherius, this Barbaro is also far detached from Venice in Carpaccio's spatial setting of Rome. If Carpaccio deliberately fused these literal and figurative modes of alienation, he offers an insightful reading of the life in coordinating Ermolao's physical distance from Venice with his rejection of core Venetian marital values. But whether pictured as an idealist condoned or as a misfit who stands aloof, Barbaro is unmistakably a striking presence here, and one that 'surely drew attention, invited speculation, and gave prominence, in one form or another, to matters of patrician obligation and civic duty':[183] a multi-faceted, enigmatic and ambiguous figure to the last.

IV: Style and technique

Martin McLaughlin well captures Barbaro's stylistic versatility by setting certain sub-tendencies (e.g., in some letters, the 'urge to lower the tone of the Latin with common or technical words') against his more 'official' manner:

> Yet outside his letters and the technical *Castigationes Plinianae* (1492), Barbaro displays a more conformist, almost Ciceronian Latin. In his official dedications and epistles, such as those to Sixtus IV and Alexander VI, in his political orations, and in his two treatises *De Coelibatu* and *De Officio Legati*, Barbaro writes a Ciceronian language that eschews the archaisms and preciosities of his letters to close friends.[184]

No attempt can be made in the brief space below to offer anything like a full analysis of this Ciceronian accent in our two featured works. The aim is rather to offer a broad-brush sketch of how *On celibacy* as well as *On the duty of the ambassador* relate to Barbaro's larger 'philosophy' of style; and then to illustrate some of his more conspicuous tendencies in *De coelibatu* in particular – an approach that will throw into relief the smoother, less variable register of *De officio legati*.

Two conjoined factors importantly condition our approach to Ermolao's Latin style. The first concerns his famous correspondence with Giovanni Pico della Mirandola (1463-94) on the compatibility of rhetoric and philosophy.[185] In a letter of April 5 1485 to his young friend in Florence,[186] Ermolao is coruscating in his condemnation of the crude Latin of scholastic philosophy – part of his broader campaign to launch a humanist reformation of Aristotelianism by resisting what he sees as the coarseness of scholastic approaches to the discipline, and by insisting that the Greek texts should be read and interpreted in the original language, and rendered in an accessible and elegant Latin.[187] Pico's reply of 3 June[188] took Barbaro by surprise in its defense of the scholastic cause: however crude their Latinity, what matters for the scholastics is the unadorned substance of argument. Asserting a rigid dichotomy between rhetoric and philosophy, Pico associates eloquence with the charms of persuasion, whereas logic cuts through superficial appearances to the truth beneath; rhetoric deals in seduction, philosophy in reduction to fact. Yet layers of humour and irony greatly complicate the serio-ludic tone of Pico's letter.[189] The elegant Latin of his defense, the breadth of his humanist learning as evidenced in his allusions to multiple sources, his ample use of rhetorical devices, and above all the paradoxical way in which he eloquently defends the scholastic approach in the voice of a scholastic spokesperson ('one of the slightly more eloquent ones' whose remit it is 'to champion his barbarism as little like a barbarian as possible'):[190] all of these features and more make it hard to gauge Pico's full or true intent. In a further twist late in the letter, he suddenly qualifies his defense of the scholastics ('I do not fully agree with their opinions') and then asserts that he has argued as he has so that he might 'test his abilities' in the disputational arena:[191] just how sincere or committed has his defense been all along?

Beyond the surface ironies and the serio-ludic complexion of his letter, however, Pico suggestively offers a synthesis of the scholastic and humanist approaches: his letter is humanistic in style, scholastic in substance – as Jill Kraye puts it, a combination of 'discordant movements' by which Pico deploys 'scholastic philosophy to discover the truth and humanist rhetoric to make others see the light.'[192] Pico's last words in the letter impute a similar versatility to Barbaro himself as one who is 'among philosophers ... the most eloquent, among the eloquent the most philosophical.'[193] In his first, brief response to Pico's letter, Barbaro immediately identifies a fundamental irony in Pico's defense: 'Yet what a ridiculous thing it is: a barbarous man [i.e., Barbaro himself] defends eloquence, while you, an eloquent man, defend its want.'[194] Barbaro's second, far longer response[195] powerfully exploits that irony by pointing out the contradiction in Pico's use of eloquence to defend the scholastics' lack of eloquence: was his friend's letter not meant as a learned joke, Barbaro suggests, with Pico's scholastic spokesperson showing a humanistic eloquence and learning that automatically undermined his own defense of scholasticism?[196]

This amiable exchange of views, this battle of wits, has too often been reduced to a polarizing vision of Pico and Barbaro as opposites: Pico the champion of philosophy, Barbaro of eloquence.[197] It cannot be stressed enough that Barbaro favours not the cultivation of elegant artifice just for its own sake, but a middle way: the fusion of philosophical clarity and verbal finesse. So in his dedicatory letter to Pope Sixtus IV of his 1481 translation of Themistius, Barbaro sets out in manifesto-like terms how he has avoided rendering the Greek word-for-word but freely used metaphors and figures of speech, and also conceits that are 'in keeping with the Roman way'; he uses the language of play to describe his discretionary licenses (*lusimus arbitratu nostro*), but he has kept Themistius' thought intact; his aim has been not so much to render him as to compete with him.[198] The goal is thus a Latin version that is precise but polished, true to the thought of the original but attractively accessible and refined in its expression. In a separate letter in late 1483 to the apparently like-minded Nicoletto Vernia (*c.* 1427–99), professor of natural philosophy in Padua,[199] Barbaro laments not just the absence of eloquence in philosophy, but also the disease that has penetrated into the philosophical core of the exercise: 'I would certainly wish for refinement and elegance, but I do not require it; I require ideas. The evil has not settled just on the skin but has worked its way into the vital organs.'[200] The idea is primary, its eloquent expression desirable but ancillary.

The second factor that conditions our approach to Barbaro's style is the inseparability of 'word' and 'essence,' *verbum* and *res*,[201] that Vittore Branca identifies with Ermolao's conviction that '*humanitas* is not a matter simply of externals, of ornament; it is a spiritual entity which produces in man the true man, the citizen, man in his totality'; such *humanitas* 'reveals itself most fully in the word which, in turn, can never be detached from its root, the thought.'[202] This correspondence between inside and out, thought and its expression, gives an important ethical valence to the rhetorical task. The dignity of the idea is matched by its worthy articulation, and a disregard for eloquence amounts to a philosophical failure: 'Whoever seeks to separate philosophical thinking from the perfect means of expression can be no more than a common little philosopher, a philosopher of wood, in fact.'[203] Hence also the importance attaching to the word because it expresses the most dignifying aspect of humankind: it allows 'the highest exercise of his spirit, the communication of his thoughts.'[204] At this level of human operation we can begin to consort with and even resemble God, an idea that Barbaro already expresses in *De coelibatu*: through engagement in contemplation at a far remove from public life, the celibate is set 'to acquire understanding, to be as close as possible to God the maker, and, in short, to fulfill the promise to which [he] will be deemed to have been born' (4.1.16). Further, as an extension of the correspondence between inside and out, *res* and *verbum*, the study of truth in the world about us presupposes in us an existence of complete honesty without moral blemish. So in 1484, when he began lecturing on Aristotle in Venice, Barbaro impresses on his students the need not just for the hard work that true engagement with the Stagirite requires, but also for 'what I have found to be of the greatest weight and importance for philosophical studies,' the avoidance of indulgent pleasures (*voluptatum fuga*); he then specifies the pleasures of the stomach, sleep and sex.[205] Already in *De coelibatu* this *fuga voluptatum* is a fundamental first principle that Barbaro enunciates in similar terms ('a remarkable result of refraining from and avoiding desires [*ex abstinentia fugaque cupiditatum*] is that the work of the mind is briskly accomplished, and reflection on the loftiest matters leads to an upright life of decency,' 4.2.71); this after he has discoursed at length on the dangers of the stomach, sleep, and consorting with the opposite sex in Book 3 (esp. 3.5.7-51, 69-82). Already in *De coelibatu*, the correlation of thought and word, inner essence and outward expression, is paralleled by the correspondence between the celibate's inner purity and his external deportment.

For Branca, it was in the early to mid-1480s, in the years when Barbaro was turning his attention first to Dioscorides and then to the elder Pliny, that he began to modify his more youthful penchant for literary elegance;[206] this tendency is reflected in the stress that he places on the primary requirement of the idea, with eloquence desirable but less urgently so, in his 1483 letter to Vernia.[207] His laconic approach in the *Castigationes Plinianae* in particular epitomizes this prioritization of the bare substance (*res*); yet his technique of terse annotation in correcting the text of the *Naturalis historia* is itself consciously stylized in its lean, Pliny-like economy of words.[208] But this shift of emphasis to the clarity of the expressed idea sheds useful light on the *De coelibatu* in comparison with *De officio legati*. Certainly, in the latter case, Barbaro's treatment of diplomacy and the behaviour expected of the ambassador encourages an orthodoxy of style and diction that are markedly Ciceronian in colour, but by no means exclusively so;[209] in neither work can Barbaro be counted as a Ciceronian in the hard sense that he confines himself only to Cicero's own patterns of usage, and his technique is in this respect far more eclectic than one-directional.[210] But in contrast to the more orthodox classicism of *De officio legati*, Barbaro's style in *De coelibatu* shows all the signs of a young man's effervescent talent that has yet to cool into a settled maturity of form.

Three features of his style in *De coelibatu* warrant special emphasis for now. First, Cicero: given the deep Ciceronian coloration at the levels of both diction and style in Francesco Barbaro's *De re uxoria*,[211] Ermolao's close engagement with his grandfather's work predisposes us to expect a similar Ciceronian imprint in *De coelibatu*. His many close adaptations and almost verbatim reproductions of sections of *De officiis* in particular truly embed Cicero in Barbaro's text[212] – a technique naturalized within the larger span of the treatise by Ermolao's far wider cultivation of Ciceronian diction and mannerism, but with an eclectic outreach to other influences as well.[213]

Second, the quality of eloquence to be expected in the celibate. In his review in Book 4 of the disciplines that will shape the celibate's humanistic education, Barbaro plays down the importance of eloquence: why any pressing need for rhetorical skill if the celibate will not engage in public life (4.2.10-15)? What befits him instead is an unaffected, natural manner of speech (4.2.16):

> His speech should be plain, not highly adorned, not forced, and not variable, but weighty and consistent – in short, that one form of speech that was conferred on him by nature's will; it will not be inelegant, rough-and-ready, or furnished with no artfulness, but well-ordered through nature's kind indulgence.

The balanced approach envisaged here is in keeping with the celibate's more general adhesion to the Aristotelian 'middle way' in accordance with his own nature (cf. 3.6.15-17); but it also resembles the balance that Barbaro sought to achieve in translating Aristotle and his Greek commentators into a Latin that was neither inelegant nor overwrought, and was also unaffectedly direct in capturing the thought of the original.[214] Yet in light of how he characterizes the celibate's unforced ease of expression, plain and not highly adorned, to what extent does Barbaro's own style in *De coelibatu* posit or project a similar correlation between his 'natural' self and his quality of expression? His lively persona has already been likened to that of the genial and vibrant celibate late in Book 4.[215] Despite his evident mastery of complex sentence construction and rhetorical flourishes in the Ciceronian manner, it would be paradoxical for Barbaro to forge a highly contrived and artificial style that contravened the naturalness he looks for in the celibate; he surely requires a certain ease of stylistic flow so as to underscore his implicit identification with his subject.

Third, and to build on this last point, Branca elegantly captures the 'natural' verve of Barbaro's writing in this, his first extended literary undertaking:[216] the style appears bristling and showy, with many flashes of virtuosity and boldness, flamboyant syntactical structures and verbal combinations, eye-catching wordplay and colourful, sometimes bizarre *exempla* that are often drawn from obscure parts of the Graeco-Roman canon – an extraordinary demonstration of learning in one so young. The result is a text that exudes personality and youthful dynamism, but also the uneven hand of the apprentice.[217] There are inconsistencies of usage, grammatical quirks, abrupt shifts of tone from one passage of argument to the next, leaps of logic, and other idiosyncratic features that cumulatively contribute to the impression of an unvarnished authenticity of pen. Variant spellings abound in the sole extant MS (so, e.g., *nanque* 1.3.2, 1.4.2, 1.6.6, etc., but *namque* at 1.3.3; *coelebs/coelibatus* at 1.2.6, 3.4.1, 3.5.9, 44, 47, 61, etc., but *cael-* at 1.2.6, 8, 1.5.3, 5, 2.2.1-4, 3.5.82, etc.; *felix/felicitas* at 1.6.2, 4, 5, 6, 2.3.2, 3, 3.1.3, etc., but *foel-*

at 1.3.6, 3.5.46, 3.6.1, 4.1.17, 22, etc.).[218] Barbaro notably uses archaic *quor* (2.4.4, 15, 2.5.15, 3.5.56, 60, etc.), with *cur* found only once, in the title to 1.2; so too he deploys the archaic form of the relative pronoun (e.g., *quoius* at 1.4.5, 3.6.6, 4.2.73, 74, 79, etc.; *quoi* at 2.4.17, 3.5.81), but also *cuius/cui* at 2.4.16, 3.6.4, 11, 4.1.8, 4.2.39, etc.). Then there are grammatical and syntactical oddities:[219] when, in the correlative formation *quemadmodum . . . ita*, the *ita* clause consists of an accusative and infinitive construction, Barbaro sometimes constructs the correlative clause in that same way, and not with a finite verb (so 2.2.13, 3.6.28; cf. 3.5.45); he frequently uses the indicative, not the more normative subjunctive, in subordinate clauses in indirect discourse; and certain grammatical aberrations (possibly caused by scribal slips?) surely stand to be corrected (e.g., in 1.6.3 *aperturos* for *aperituros* and *amorem* for *amor*[220]). In contrast to these vagaries of usage, his habits in *De officio legati* are far more consistent and orthodox, not least in his use of standard word-forms: so, e.g., he never uses the archaizing relative in the latter work; he never deploys variant forms of the same word such as are found in the MS of *De coelibatu*, but he uses (e.g.) *iudicium* (§§14, 49; cf. *iudit-* at *De coelibatu* pref. 2, 2.3.23, 2.6.17, 18, 3.5.48), *societas* (§§3, 4; cf. *soci-* at *De coelibatu* 1.4.7, 8, but *soti-* at 1.2.4, 7, 1.4.21, 2.6.4, 3.6.40, etc.), and *officium* (§§2, 16; cf. *offic-* at *De coelibatu* 1.3.9, 3.6.35, 52, 4.2.2, 32, but *offit-* at 1.1.6, 10, 1.4.9, 14, 2.3.2, 2.5.1, etc.); and he tends to write in shorter units than in *De coelibatu*, avoiding periodic sentences with multiple subordinate clauses, and thereby achieving a more direct effect, as if the mature Barbaro aims more for lucidity than to impress.

As for Barbaro's stylistic preferences in point of detail, only a brief overview can be attempted here. In constantly striving to re-engage his reader in *De coelibatu*, he uses different registers of mood and tone according to the thematic movements that progress with season-like changefulness across the four books.[221] This medley of sequences enlivens Barbaro's overall arc of argument; but at the level of the individual sentence or groupings of sentences, wordplay and verbal effect are designed constantly to catch the eye, please the ear, and appeal to the imagination. The paratactic balancing of clauses, sentences, or phrases is often coordinated in two or three units that begin with the same or a similar word (e.g., 1.4.16 *insectabimur . . . illos qui. . . incusabimus . . . quia. . . vituperabimus . . . quia*; 2.2.24 *quid . . . quae . . . quis . . . quae*); correlative constructions are also very frequent (e.g., *quemadmodum/ut . . . ita* at 1.4.14, 1.5.5, 2.5.7, 9, 2.6.9, 14, 3.5.55, 62, etc.). Through their common recurrence, these balancing devices lend a continuity of feel and form to Barbaro's prose as he moves through his thematic permutations. Other features to watch or listen for include sonorous repetition (e.g., 1.4.7 *tum . . . tum . . . tum . . . tum*; 2.2.22 *si . . . si . . . si . . .*

quantum ... quantum); parallelism with chiasmus (ABBA, e.g., 1.4.5 *vitio mentis ... et animi perturbatione*; 1.4.19 *esse actionem aut actionem esse*), sometimes with neat variation (so, e.g., 1.4.24 *ab activo ... contemplativus ... activus a contemplativo*, where the chiastic arrangement of abl. and nom. case-endings is accompanied by the ABAB distribution of *activus* and *contemplativus*); the piling of like terms, often with asyndeton (e.g., 1.6.3 *miserantur, queruntur, obsecrant, clamant*); repetition of the same noun or adjective in different cases (polyptoton, e.g., 2.3.18 *urbe ... urbem*; 3.5.56 *mulierum ... mulieres ... mulierum ... mulieribus*), or of the same verb in different forms (e.g., 2.4.10 *viventibus viventes*; 3.5.51 *peccat ... peccandi*); striking paradox (e.g., 1.4.18 *sine legibus atque cum legibus vivat*); touches of sarcasm (esp. *nisi forte* at, e.g., 1.2.4, 2.3.3, 3.5.19, 3.6.26); sharp interjectory questions (e.g., 1.3.4 *Quo quid crudelius?*; 3.5.43 *Quo quid vanius?*); invented viva voce quotations (e.g., Diogenes the Cynic speaking at 2.5.15; imaginary interlocutors at, e.g., 3.5.40, 52); and carefully placed diminutives that evoke sensuous arousal (e.g., *dulciolae* at 3.5.36, *minutulas* and *motiunculas* in 3.6.26).

Many more features of this enlivening kind could be cited, all of them already encased in the classical Latin tradition and part of the humanistic repertoire. But while these techniques are conventional enough in the hereditary sense, Barbaro's deployment of them is relentless, inventive, and always striving for effect, so that *De coelibatu* is more than a carefully argued treatise. In its verbal theatrics it is in many ways a highly dramatized event – a 'natural' mirroring of the vibrant young man, we might say, just as the measured stylistic complexion of *De officio legati* reflects the steady manner of the seasoned envoy.

Notes

1 Ogilvie 2006: 122. For orientation on Barbaro's life and career, Stickney 1903; Ferriguto 1922; Paschini 1957: 11–42; Bigi 1964; Branca 1973: 238–9 n. 6, 1980: 128–31 n. 8, and 1998: 65–9 n. 10; King 1986: 197–205, 322–3; Céard 1997; Figliuolo 1999; Biow 2002: 104–20; Robuschi 2013–14: 258–69.
2 For the letter, Branca 1943: 2.72-7 *Ep.* CLIV with Paschini 1957: 30–2 and Figliuolo 1999: 138 n. 146.
3 On this point, Figiuolo 1999: 133 and n. 134, and cf. Vol. 2 p. 176.
4 Not least in Lorenzo the Magnificent's Florence: see Poliziano in Butler 2006: 42–5 (*Ep.* 1.13).
5 Further on what follows, Banfi 1950; Paschini 1957: 18–42; Branca 1970 = 1998: 174–9; King 1976: 42–3 = 2005: V 42–3 and 1986: 202–5; Queller 1986: 121–2, 188–9; Figliuolo 1999: 133–42; Robuschi 2013–14: 267–9.

6   For the date, July 24 the likelier day, Figliuolo 1999: 142 and n. 161.
7   Branca 1943: 2.73 *Ep.* CLIV.
8   Branca 1943: 2.74 *Ep.* CLIV.
9   Branca 1943: 2.74 *Ep.* CLIV.
10 Branca 1943: 2.74 *Ep.* CLIV.
11 Branca 1943: 2.77 *Ep.* CLIV.
12 Branca 1943: 2.65 *Ep.* CXLVI.
13 Branca 1943: 2.66 *Ep.* CXLVII.
14 Branca 1943: 2.70 *Ep.* CLII; on the problem of *which* Antonio Calvo is the recipient, King 1986: 345–6.
15 For Zaccaria's extensive diplomatic career and appointment to Naples, Branca 1969: 7 n. 3 with King 1986: 325–6.
16 See Vol. 2 pp. 174–9.
17 See further Vol. 2, pp. 175–6.
18 Beyond the riches of the library passed down by Ermolao's humanist grandfather Francesco (for whom pp. 12–17; on the library, Diller 1963 with Zorzi 1996, esp. 369–83 and Raines 2015: 102, and now Vendruscolo 2020), his time in Naples presumably gave ample access to learned circles (cf. p. 42 n. 146) and resources, esp. the royal Aragonese library (on its holdings before a sizable part of them was sold by Isabella del Balzo, Queen of Naples, in 1523 see López-Ríos 2002, with further bibliography on p. 201 nn. 2, 4, and 5).
19 See esp. King 1976 = 2005 V and 1986 ch. 2 on 'Themes: *Unanimitas*,' esp. 92–150, 192–205.
20 Branca 1943: 1.96 *Ep.* LXXVI; Garin 1952: 840–3.
21 Branca 1943: 1.92 *Ep.* LXXII. For Barbaro's work on Themistius see pp. 22, 23, 30–1; on Dioscorides, pp. 23–4; on Aristotle, pp. 22–3, 31, 33 with Kristeller 1948: 167 n. 2 for an overview of his Aristotelian translations (only that of the *Rhetoric* was printed, at Venice in 1544: see Marcon and Moretti 2015: 120–2 Cat. 6, and cf. pp. 42–3 n. 150 below). Barbaro's allusion to *two* books of *De coelibatu*, not four, is puzzling. The simplest explanation (cf. Branca 1969: 3 n. 1) is a scribal error in the sole MS containing this letter to Arnold, or in an antigraph of it. It is harder to believe (i) that *libros duos* could here connote different redactions of *De coelibatu*; (ii) that Barbaro seeks to re-conceptualize the work in two books to align it with the two movements of his grandfather Francesco's 1415 *De re uxoria* (but see p. 39 n. 83 below); or (iii) that since at the start of *De coelibatu* 3 he announces a major transition point as he moves to the 'considerably greater and more imposing task' (3.1.1) that awaits in Books 3 and 4, in his letter to Arnold he means a work in 'two movements.'
22 Classe II.9; for description of the MS, Branca 1952: 84–5 and 1969: 8–11 with Bonazza 2008 and 2017: 7.
23 Trithemius 1494: f. 127*r* and *v*. Further, Branca 1952: 84 and n. 1 and 1969: 6 n. 2 with 1998: 159 and n. 41 and Kravina 2021: 73 n. 305.
24 See pp. 12–17.

25 See Mazzatinti 1897: LXX and 176 no. 600; cf. Fava 1925: 26 for *De re uxoria* attributed to Ermolao.
26 Branca 1952 and 1969.
27 Pp. 48–9 below.
28 Further on Sinibaldi, Ullman 1960: 118–23 with Regnicoli 2018.
29 Branca 1952: 84 and 1969: 9.
30 February 1 1472 by Venetian fashion, the Venetian calendar year traditionally beginning on 1 March.
31 Further, Branca 1969: 11–12.
32 On this vandalism, Branca 1952: 85 and 1969: 10–11; Barbaro alludes to Mt. Olympus at 3.6.18.
33 See on this key point pp. 18–19, 21, 23–4.
34 See 1.4.2 and n. 54; 3.5.48 and n. 135; 4.1.13 and nn. 38, 43; 4.2.38.
35 See 2.2.2–3 and nn. 9–11, and cf. 2.6.18 and n. 174.
36 On this point, King 1976: 40 = 2005: V 40 and 1986: 200.
37 See 3.6.15 and n. 224.
38 See esp. the climactic accent in 4.1.22 ('For to the contemplative both happiness and God will be the same end, such that he doesn't engage in contemplation because of any external factor').
39 See on this Ciceronian dimension p. 19 and 4.2.39 n. 137.
40 See further pp. 14–15 and Vol. 2 Intro. p. 3.
41 See for concise overview of the modern scholarly debate King 2007.
42 See P. Brown 1988: 70–1, 127–8.
43 For Petrarch's influence, Branca 1973: 225–6, 231, 1996: 9–15, and 1998: 51–8 with Lazzarini 1963.
44 King 1986: 214 with n. 26 for bibliography.
45 See Reynolds and Wilson 1974, esp. 113–24, with Clark 1921; Weiss 1988, esp. 145–66 (epigraphy) and 167–79 (numismatics); Fantazzi 2014a.
46 See Wilson 2017 with Geanakoplos 1962, esp. 13–70.
47 See amid the copious bibliography King 1986, esp. 92–205 on *unanimitas*; Branca 1973: 218–20, 1996: 12–18, and 1998: 59–65; Kallendorf 1999: 20–4.
48 Kallendorf 1999: 23.
49 King 1986: 219–36 and 1988: 213–19 = 2005: II 213–19; cf. already the four-part schema in Branca 1963: 193.
50 King 1986: 219–25 and 1988: 213–14 = 2005: II 213–14.
51 On this point, Zorzi 1996: 369–70.
52 On this invented idealization, Brown 1996, esp. 8–9, 11–29, 103–5, 168–9, 277–8; Pincus 1992.
53 See, e.g., 2.5.2 and n. 106 (Ap. Claudius Caecus); 2.6.7 and n. 155 (L. Iunius Brutus); 3.5.58 and n. 145 (Cato the younger); 4.2.95 and n. 248 (Cornelia, mother of Tiberius and Gaius Gracchus), etc.
54 King 1986: 225–31 and 1988: 214–16 = 2005: II 214–16.
55 King 1986: 229.
56 King 1986: 231–6 and 1988: 216–19 = 2005: II 216–19.
57 King 1986: 232 and 1988: 217 = 2005: II 217.

58 Grafton 1983-93: 1.41; cf. Branca 1963: 196 ('una situazione stagnante e senza uscite').
59 King 1986: 233-4 and 1988: 219-20 = 2005: II 219-20.
60 On such abuses, Queller 1969 and esp. 1986 with King 1986: 192-5.
61 See King 1986: 195-6 with Chojnacki 2000: 249, 254.
62 On Francesco's life and career, Gothein 1932; Carotti 1937; Gualdo 1964; King 1986: 323-5; Griggio 2009; now Kravina 2021: 1 n. 1 for further bibliography.
63 King 1986: 223. Leonardo's son was Bernardo Giustiniani, that devoted servant of the state who 'had excelled in humanist studies and devoted his eloquent pen to the will of Venice' (King 38). See Labalme 1996 on Ermolao's own touching commemoration of the deceased Bernardo in a letter of consolation of March 15 1489 to Marco Dandolo (1458-1535), Bernardo's grandson (Branca 1943: 2.48-9 *Ep.* CXXXI).
64 King 1986: 223-4.
65 Chojnacki 2000: 246.
66 Chojnacki 2000: 247; cf. 30-1.
67 2000: 247.
68 Chojnacki 2000: 56-63, 67.
69 Chojnacki 2000: 249.
70 Chojnacki 2000: 36-7.
71 Cf. p. 11 above.
72 Note also that Francesco's *De re uxoria* is among several works that are known to have been copied by Antonio Sinibaldi, albeit the copies are now lost (see Ullman 1960: 121-2). His version of *De re uxoria* was executed for the Aragonese King, Ferdinand I, in 1473, as was his *De coelibatu* (see pp. 5-6 above): possibly a coordinated project?
73 For his association with Barzizza, Mercer 1979, esp. 28, 104-5, 115-16, 128, with Kravina 2021: 11 and nn. 38-9. For the Ciceronian accent cf. Gnesotto 1915-16: 14: 'Quanto Cicerone anche nel *De re uxoria*, dalla prima all'ultima parola!' (with illustration on p. 14 n. 2). But the Ciceronian imprint goes far beyond the stylistic: see Kravina 16 n. 53 on Cicero's importance as 'vero e proprio archetipo dell'etica di Francesco,' and cf. my pp. 17-18 for the impact on *De re uxoria* of Cicero's *De officiis* in particular.
74 See Wilson 2017: 49-54 with Geanakoplos 1962: 28-30 and King 2015: 3-5 and n. 11; for Guarino's life, Sabbadini 1891 with (concisely) Pistilli 2003.
75 XVIII.13 Griggio 2021: 290 (Gnesotto 1915-16: 99.25-100.6); tr. King 2015: 125.
76 King 2015: 2. Further on Trevisan, Gothein 1942 with King 1986: 436-7; Ferracin 2019; Kravina 2021: 11 and n. 36; Griggio 2021: 297-8 n. 9.
77 I.4, 10 Griggio 2021: 178, 180 (Gnesotto 1915-16: 24.12-18, 27.3-6); tr. King 2015: 66, 67. Trevisan is also hailed at the end, XVIII.13 Griggio 290 (Gnesotto 99.23-4); tr. King 124.
78 See Kravina 2021: 45-53. Of notable importance was [Plut.] *De liberis educandis*/*On the education of children*, a source of citations throughout *De*

re uxoria but esp. influential in the last section, XVIII; this text was translated into Latin by Guarino between 1411 and 1413 (see Kravina 51–3, and cf. p. 41 n. 130 below).
79 On this visit, Kravina 2021: 2–3 with King 2015: 6 and Sabbadini 1910.
80 For whom Kravina 2021: 2 and n. 5.
81 On the date of the work, Kravina 2021: 2–3 and n. 6; on the date of the wedding, Kravina 2 n. 4 and Griggio 2021: 295 n. 4 and 297 n. 8.
82 Kravina 2018: 418–22 and 2021: 146–9 lists 129 MSS; for the 1513 *princeps* and for a listing of translations, Griggio 2021: 157–62 with King 2015: 45–6.
83 In the edition of Gnesotto 1915–16 these two movements are entitled *Pars prior de delectu uxoris* and *Pars altera de uxoris officio* respectively. These titles, and those of the further subdivisions within each of the two parts, reflect not Francesco Barbaro's demonstrated authorial will but the editorial influence of the French jurist André Tiraqueau, who oversaw the 1513 Paris *princeps*. The basis for that edition was a version apparently copied late in 1428 in Guarino's own house from an original that was early in the tradition; but the subdivisions, absent elsewhere in the tradition, need not be Barbaro's own (further, Kravina 2021: 14, 101–2 with Griggio 2021: 157–8 and n. 10, 293 n. 1). King 2015 follows Gnesotto's division of the work (i.e., Dedicatory letter; Prologue: What marriage is; First part: On the choice of a wife, chs 1–7; Second part: On the duties of a wife, chs 1–9); but all references to *De re uxoria* in the present work follow Griggio 2021 in offering a single sequence, I to XVIII, from the *Prooemium* (the dedicatory letter) onwards. See also Griggio 293 n. 1 for correction of Remigio Sabbadini's miscasting of the work as in two books, for which Sabbadini 1915–19: 1.116 (*Ep.* 55.36–7: *accepimus librum illum de re uxoria: restat alter in manibus librarii* ['I have received that book *On marriage*: the other remains in the hands of the copyist']): *pace* Sabbadini 3.55, *alter* signals not the second of two books of *De re uxoria*, but *a second copy* of that work, or a copy of *a second work* other than *De re uxoria*.
84 He married Maria Loredan in 1419, and fathered four daughters and one son, Zaccaria (b. 1422/3), who was so named partly to commemorate Francesco's elder brother, partly Zaccaria Trevisan (King 2015: 1 n. 1, 8).
85 I.4 Griggio 2021: 178 (Gnesotto 1915–16: 24.16-18); tr. King 2015: 66. Trevisan had married in 1395 (King 3).
86 See Sabbadini 1891: 58 §136: thirteen children by 1441, all of them alive – quite an achievement for one who married at forty-five. For the number of children cf. Ludovico Carbone (1430–85) in his 1460 funeral oration (Garin 1952: 404: seven boys, six girls); Pistilli 2003: 359 refers to fifteen children in all (mentioning on p. 363 a daughter who died soon after birth in 1441, and a last daughter born in 1449).
87 See D'Elia 2004: 33–4, 40–4, 50, with a catalogue of Guarino's extant orations on pp. 163–7.
88 Kohl and Witt 1978: 186, cited by Kravina 2021: 2.
89 King 2015: 2; cf. on Francesco's originality also King 2014: 77–80.

90 For overview, D'Elia 2004: 11–34.
91 See 1.2.1 n. 24, 1.2.2 n. 26, and 2.2.19 n. 42 with D'Elia 2004: 15–16, 19–23.
92 Further on Jerome and Augustine D'Elia 2004: 16–18 with Walsh 2001: xii–xvii and P. Brown 1988, esp. 67–8 and 149–50 on post-marital continence; Jerome's *Adv. Iovinian.* is also characterized by Brown (p. 377) as 'a disaster ... a memorable statement of the ascetic viewpoint at its most unpleasant and impracticable.'
93 D'Elia 2004: 21–3, duly observing (p. 21) that, though Petrarch never married, he had a concubine and children. For the influential effect of the anti-marriage views of Boccaccio as well as Petrarch see Vecchio 1998, esp. 60–4. For a good example of the sheer rabidity to be found in the medieval tradition of anti-feminist/celibate misogamy, see Wilson 1985 on the anonymous thirteenth-century poetic satire *De coniuge non ducenda/On not taking a wife*, that 'heir to the prototype of this branch of misogamous satire, Juvenal 6' (p. 214).
94 D'Elia 2004: 24.
95 See D'Elia 2004: 24–5; for Salutati's *De seculo et religione*, Marshall 2014.
96 D'Elia 2004: 26–7.
97 See succinctly Nauert 2006: 30–1 on Hans Baron's concept of Florentine 'civic humanism.'
98 Cf. Kravina 2021: 5 ('un autentico dialogo tra le due Repubbliche').
99 See Kravina 2021: 7 and n. 21.
100 I.1 Griggio 2021: 176 (Gnesotto 1915–16: 23.5-6); tr. King 2015: 65.
101 I.3 Griggio 2021: 176 (Gnesotto 1915–16: 24.7-8); tr. King 2015: 65.
102 So, e.g., Ter. *An.* 829, Gell. 1.6.3.
103 See Kravina 2021: 9–10, 36 with Griggio 2021: 293 n. 1 (citing for *res uxoria* as 'dowry' Cic. *Off.* 3.61, Quint. *Inst.* 7.4.11, Gell. 4.3.1, 2) and King 2015: 4, 15–17.
104 King 2015: 17.
105 III.1 Griggio 2021: 188 (Gnesotto 1915–16: 32.15); tr. King 2015: 71. Francesco's terms are reproduced by Ermolao at 1.5.1, but there with 'beauty' and 'descent' reversed in order.
106 2015: 33.
107 III.1, 8 Griggio 2021: 188, 192 (Gnesotto 1915–16: 32.20-1, 36.9-12); tr. King 2015: 71, 74.
108 VII.1 Griggio 2021: 212 (Gnesotto 1915–16: 48.13-19); tr. King 2015: 84.
109 VI.6 Griggio 2021: 210 (Gnesotto 1915–16: 47.5-6); tr. King 2015: 83.
110 VI.1 Griggio 2021: 206 (Gnesotto 1915–16: 45.4); tr. King 2015: 81.
111 King 2015: 34.
112 King 2015: 35.
113 See Branca 1952: 85–6 and 1969: 5.
114 For this Ciceronian accent in *De re uxoria* see p. 13 and n. 73; in *De coelibatu*, pp. 18–19, 21, 29, 32 and 46 n. 213.
115 For the letter, Griggio 1999: 51–2 *Ep.* 9. Yet in 1436, at the age of fifty-six, Poggio married the eighteen-year-old Vaggia de' Buondelmonti, with whom

he went on to have six children; he justified his late choice to marry in his *Dialogus an seni sit uxor ducenda/Dialogue on whether an old man should marry* of 1437, dedicated to Cosimo de' Medici (see Kravina 2021: 59–60 and n. 233 with D'Elia 2004: 124–5 and Petrucci 1971: 643; for the work itself, Shepherd 1807 with Bruez 1998).
116 Griggio 1999: 51–2 *Ep.* 9.16-18; also quoted by Kravina 2021: 59.
117 Griggio 2021: 294 n. 1. Cf. Kravina 2021: 16 and n. 53, 104, and 139, and also the astute insight in Gnesotto 1915–16: 11: 'Zaccaria Trevisan seniore entra nella composizione del *De re uxoria* press' a poco come Panezio in quella del *De officiis* di Cicerone.'
118 See 1.4.1 n. 52; 1.4.4 n. 57.
119 See 1.4.4; 1.4.13-14 and n. 74; 1.4.24-6. Cf. 2.5.17 and n. 143; 3.6.7 and n. 209; 4.2.59-60 and nn. 188–9.
120 Tr. Griffin and Atkins 1991: 29. But after making this concession, Cicero continues in 1.71 by stressing that avoidance of civic duty 'without a reason' should not be 'counted as praiseworthy – indeed no, but rather as a vice.'
121 Tr. Griffin and Atkins 1991: 60. Cicero elaborates on the point in 1.156, in a context nonetheless arguing for the superiority of sociability (*communitas*) over pure learning (*cognitio*), i.e., a life devoted solely to contemplation at a remove from society and the communal interest is intolerable (further, Dyck 1996: 340-3 on *Off.* 1.153).
122 Tr. Griffin and Atkins 1991: 7. But see Dyck 1996: 83 on 1.11-17 and 98 on 1.15-17 for the possibility that this systematic elaboration of the four 'parts' in 1.15 is Cicero's own, and not Panaetian, and meant 'to insure that the main points, which are at the same time the major topics to be treated in *Off.* 1, have emerged clearly [from earlier in Book 1].'
123 See 4.2.39 and nn. 136–7, 139–40; 4.2.41 and n. 143; 4.2.48 and n. 156; 4.2.50-1 and nn. 160–2; 4.2.54 and n. 173; 4.2.55 and nn. 175–6; 4.2.58 and nn. 182–3.
124 For this doubling effect spelt out see esp. 4.2.59-60.
125 See 1.5.1 n. 95 with Griggio 2021: 302 n. 23.
126 See 1.5.2 and nn. 96–8.
127 XV.1 Griggio 2021: 262 (Gnesotto 1915–16: 80.5, 7–11); tr. King 2015: 109.
128 Cf. XII.1 Griggio 2021: 248 (Gnesotto 1915–16: 72.10-11); tr. King 2015: 103: '[The quality of moderation] is evident principally in a wife's expression, gestures, speech, dress, eating, and lovemaking.'
129 See esp. 3.6.15-17.
130 See for *De re uxoria* Kravina 2021: 36–57, and esp. 52 for the classic trilogy of humanistic pedagogy (Griggio 1991: 291 with Kravina 2016) formed by (i) [Plut.] *De liberis educandis/On the education of children* (via Guarino Guarini's Latin translation of between 1411 and 1413), (ii) *De ingenuis moribus et liberalibus adulescentiae studiis/The character and studies befitting a free-born youth* of Pier Paolo Vergerio (1370–1444; for this tract of *c.* 1402-3, Kallendorf 2002: 2–91), and (iii) Francesco Barbaro's *De re uxoria*. This tradition in turn informs *De coelibatu*, esp. in Ermolao's treatment of the rearing of the celibate-to-be in Book 2 and his humanistic

education in Book 4. For the influential Vergerio in particular see 4.2 n. 57; 4.2.32 n. 122; 4.2.37 n. 133; 4.2.82-3 nn. 226-7.
131 Chojnacki 2000: 59; see already p. 12 above.
132 See on this 'royal humanism' Stacey 2011 with Roick 2012; on the liberating effects of Ermolao's distance from Venice, Robuschi 2013-14: 262.
133 See p. 11 above.
134 1986: 197.
135 1976: 41 = 2005 V 41; 1986: 201.
136 1976: 38 = 2005 V 38; 1986: 198.
137 See pp. 29 and 32 below with 46 n. 213.
138 See esp. 4.2.72-80.
139 Cf. p. 10 and n. 53.
140 See, e.g., 1.1.8 and n. 18; 3.5.47 and n. 133; 4.2.73 and n. 207.
141 See, e.g., 2.3.10-16 (Barbaro rails against sexual impurity), 3.5.7-39 (on the vulnerabilities of the senses). For feigned debate, e.g., 1.3-4, 3.5.40-1, 52-3; 'diatribe-like' only in a loose sense, as no formal ancient genre of 'diatribe' now tends to be recognized (see Roller 2015: 63 with Williams 2015: 139-40).
142 See, e.g., 1.4 and nn. 57, 61; 3.6.18-48 and n. 230.
143 Beyond his engagement with Cicero's *De officiis* in Books 1 and 4 (for which pp. 18-19 above), see, e.g., his interplay with Aristotle's *Metaphysics* in 4.1 (esp. nn. 6, 11, 15, 18).
144 See, e.g., 1.6.4 and n. 122 on Potamo of Alexandria; 2.2.3-4 and n. 11 on 'naturalist' and 'conventionalist' approaches to naming; 3.6.13 and n. 220 on fixed and relative interpretations of the Aristotelian mean; 3.6.28-9 and n. 251 on mental impairment as susceptible (on the analogy of physical impairment) to therapeutic rehabilitation.
145 See p. 41 n. 130.
146 For the medical aspect, e.g., 3.5.75 and n. 173; 3.6.28-30 and n. 251; 3.6.49-53 and nn. 279, 281. Aristotle's recurring presence in my annotations on *De coelibatu* well exemplifies Barbaro's life-long absorption in the Stagirite. This preoccupation may have been importantly influenced by his interaction in Naples in 1471-3 with Giovanni Pontano (1426-1503) and the humanist academy (the Accademia Pontaniana) that the latter led there from 1471: see Rinaldi 2013: 345 and n. 10 with Falco 1987.
147 See p. 5 above.
148 On Ermolao's undertaking, Todd 2003: 64-6, 72, 74-7, 79, 91-2, 96-100.
149 For this time-range, Branca 1973: 238 n. 6 with 1998: 67 n. 10.
150 This *Compendium ethicorum librorum* (in fact 'a competent summary' of *EN* 1-6: Lines 2013: 181) was published in 1544 in Venice by Daniele Barbaro (1514-70), Ermolao's great-nephew. In 1484 (Bigi 1964: 97) Ermolao also drafted a *Compendium scientiae naturalis ex Aristotele*, which Daniele published in Venice in 1545. On both works and the dates of their many subsequent reprintings, Kristeller 1948: 167-8 n. 5 with Kraye 2008: 14-15 and n. 8. In addition, Barbaro's translation of Aristotle's *Rhetoric*

(executed in 1479, when he was twenty-five: see p. 5 above with Kristeller 167 n. 2) with a commentary by Daniele was published in Venice in 1544. Two letters of 1488 also refer to Ermolao's recently completed work on the *Posterior Analytics* (see Branca 1943: 2.33 *Ep.* CXV and 2.38 *Ep.* CXXI with Lohr 1968: 237).
151 See concisely King 1986: 182–6 with Branca 1996: 12–13 and 1998: 54–5.
152 See King 1986: 182 on Girolamo Donato, Niccolò Leonico Tomeo, and Giorgio Valla (with further names in her n. 266).
153 Further on what follows, Kristeller 1948, esp. 164–8; Branca 1973: 225–7, 1996: 26–8, and 1998: 70–3; Kraye 1996: 144–5 and 2008: 15–16; Mahoney 2004: 2–10; Bianchi 2007, esp. 51–3; Robuschi 2013–14: 262–4; Garrod 2014. But see also Bianchi 2003: 143–7 and 2007: 59–62 for the effects of the rise of print culture in the fifteenth century – a phenomenon that facilitated the simultaneous circulation of diverse materials on Aristotle (Hellenistic, Byzantine, Arabic, scholastic, humanistic), thereby creating an effect less of substitution than of juxtaposition; on this approach Bianchi adds important nuance to how the humanistic relationship to scholastic Aristotelianism is to be understood.
154 'I know how great a thing it is *non vertere, sed bene vertere*': Branca 1943: 1.14 *Ep.* XI = Todd 2003: 98–9 (to Francesco Tron, in Barbaro's dedicatory preface to his 1481 version of Themistius' paraphrase of *On memory and recollection*). See further pp. 30–1.
155 McLaughlin 1995: 240.
156 See pp. 29–31.
157 Branca 1943: 1.8 *Ep.* VIII = Todd 2003: 75.
158 See, e.g., Branca 1943: 1.13 *Ep.* X, 1.14, 15 *Ep.* XI, 1.20 *Ep.* XIV, 2.20 *Ep.* XCVIII, etc., with Kraye 2008: 19 ('the usual insider joke').
159 See, e.g., Branca 1943: 1.10–12 *Ep.* IX (to Antonio de Ferrariis, 1480), 1.12–14 *Ep.* X (to Giorgio Merula, 1480), 1.16–17 *Ep.* XII (to Girolamo Donato, 1480), 2.107–9 *Orat.* III (his inaugural lecture on Aristotle in Venice, November 22 1484; cf. on his new 'school' 1.78–9 *Ep.* LXI, to Merula, December 13 1484).
160 Further on the *Corollarium*, Egerton 1983: 561–8 with Reeds 1976: 524–5; Touwaide 2012; and Ramminger 2005 (the *Corollarium* as a philologically oriented supplement to, not strictly a commentary on, Dioscorides). For Barbaro working intensively on the *Corollarium* in 1488–9, see Pozzi 1974: 626, Riddle 1980: 27–8 and Vendruscolo 2017: 586–7; but for his further activity on it even down to his death in July 1493, Vendruscolo 591–5.
161 For details of this edition, Riddle 1980: 16.
162 Reproduced by Pozzi 1974: 622–3.
163 Riddle 1980: 46, 47. In the 1516 edition the preface is announced as *Ioannis Baptistae Egnatii Veneti in primum Corollarii librum Hermolai Barbari patritii Veneti et Aquileiensis patriarchae praefatio* ('Preface of the Venetian Johannes Baptista Egnatius to the first book of the *Corollarium* of Hermolaus Barbarus, Venetian patrician and patriarch of Aquileia'), but in

the 1530 edition (*Hermolai Barbari ... in Dioscoridem Corollariorum libri quinque*, Cologne, Johannes Soter) it is attributed directly to Barbaro himself (*Ermolai Barbari patritii Veneti et Aquileiensis patriarchae in primum Corollarii librum praefatio*).

164 Pozzi 1974: 622, pointing to 'una così lucida autocritica, una così netta presa di posizione morale.'
165 On the dates, Pozzi 1973-9: 1.xxxvii, 3 with Nauert 1980: 338.
166 See pp. 4-5; further on this link with the letter to Arnold, Pozzi 1974: 623.
167 Branca 1943: 2.78-80 *Ep*. CLVI = Pozzi 1973-9: 1.2 lines 7, 14-16, 30-1; further on this 'active' and utilitarian dimension to Barbaro's scholarship, Manetti 1971: 310.
168 Apart from Cicero in *De officiis* (pp. 18-19 above), see notably Sen. *Dial.* 8.3.4-5, 4.1-2, 5.8, 6.4-5.
169 For Giovio see Price Zimmermann 1995, esp. 159-62 and 206-8 on his collection.
170 For Cristofano, Meloni Trkulja 1985, and see on his Barbaro portrait and the circumstances of its production Branca and Weiss 1963: 35. It was executed no later than 1556, given Cristofano's inclusion of it in a list of completed portraits accompanying a letter of October 23 1556 (see Gualandi 1844-56: 1.371-4 no. 148 with Müntz 1901: 267 n. 1).
171 See Branca and Weiss 1963: 35, referring to a letter of August 28 1521 that mentions the Barbaro portrait (for the letter, Ferrero 1956: 92).
172 See Müntz 1901: 270-1 and 271 n. 1 for Stimmer; for the engraving, Giovio 1577: 69.
173 On this canvas, Branca and Weiss 1963: 38.
174 See Branca and Weiss 1963: 38.
175 On the legend and Carpaccio's selectivity of emphasis within it, Rodini 2013; concisely on the cycle, Matino and Brown 2020: 104-30.
176 See on this point Matino and Brown 2020: 119 (the placement of the canvas depicting Ursula's dream is different in the Carpaccio cycle, *preceding* that depicting her arrival in Rome).
177 On this history, P. F. Brown 1988: 279 with Matino and Brown 2020: 104-5.
178 On these points, Branca and Weiss 1963: 38.
179 So Pietro Bembo in his *Historia Veneta* (1.53 Ulery 2007: 62-3), the Latin version of which (duly censored by the Venetian authorities) was first published in 1551, the Italian version in 1552.
180 See pp. 12-13, 16-17.
181 Rodini 2013: 110.
182 Rodini 2013: 115.
183 Rodini 2013: 115. Cf. Labalme 1996: 342 for Carpaccio's Barbaro 'stand[ing] forever in the senatorial robes from which he was forever banned, almost completely detached from the religious events being enacted behind him, his face averted toward some private vision of his own, perhaps a perfect resolution of those conflicting allegiances whose incompatibility had sundered his life ...'

184 McLaughlin 1995: 244-5.
185 Cf. p. 23 above. For Barbaro's three letters, Branca 1943: 1.84-7 *Ep.* LXVIII, 1.100-1 *Ep.* LXXX, and 1.101-16 *Ep.* LXXXI = Garin 1952: 844-63 (with Italian translation). For Pico's famous letter of June 3 1485, Garin 805-23 (with Italian translation). For the assembled correspondence, Bausi 1998; with English translation, Breen 1952. The bibliography on these exchanges is voluminous, but see esp. Breen 384-91; McLaughlin 1995: 228-48; Margolin 1996; Panizza 1996, 1999, and 2000; Kray 1996: 145-6 and 2008 (with p. 13 n. 2 for further bibliography); Fantazzi 2014b: 146-7; Giglioni 2015: 252-3.
186 *Ep.* LXVIII in n. 185 above.
187 See pp. 22-3 above.
188 As cited in n. 185 above.
189 On this line, esp. Panizza 1999 and 2000 with Vickers 1988: 184-96.
190 Tr. Breen 1952: 395.
191 Tr. Breen 1952: 402.
192 Kraye 2008: 36.
193 Tr. Breen 1952: 402. Pico's characterization of Barbaro here itself elegantly adapts Cicero's similar conceit in reference to L. Licinius Crassus and Q. Mucius Scaevola Pontifex at *Brut.* 145 (cf. also 150).
194 Branca 1943: 1.100 *Ep.* LXXX; tr. Breen 1952: 402. For the play on Barbaro's name, cf. p. 23 and n. 158.
195 *Ep.* LXXXI in n. 185 above.
196 See Kraye 2008: 34.
197 On this point, Panizza 2000: 152-3 and 170 n. 2, citing the 'oppositional' view asserted by Kristeller 1964: 58.
198 Branca 1943: 1.9 *Ep.* VIII, where Barbaro's 'philosophy' of translation is itself strikingly Ciceronian in character (see esp. *Opt. gen.* 14). Cf. already on these points pp. 22-3 above.
199 For Vernia, Forlivesi 2020 with Branca 1973: 226 and 241 n. 16 (in Italian in 1998: 70-1 and n. 12); Grendler 2002: 287.
200 Branca 1943: 1.46 *Ep.* XXXI.
201 Already a Ciceronian preoccupation, as at *De or.* 3.19, 125, *Orat.* 72.
202 Branca 1973: 228; in Italian, 1996: 29 and 1998: 74, and cf. also Giannetto 1985: 183 and n. 241. Further on this 'ethicized rhetoric' as 'particularly deeply rooted within Venetian humanistic culture,' Cox 2003: 654.
203 Branca 1943: 1.17 *Ep.* XII; tr. Branca 1973: 228.
204 Branca 1973: 229; in Italian, 1996: 31 and 1998: 75-6.
205 Branca 1943: 2.109 *Orat.* III; further on this passage, Branca 1996: 31 and 1998: 76.
206 Branca 1996: 21-2.
207 See p. 31 above.
208 See Pozzi 1973-9: 1.clxi with McLaughlin 1995: 245.
209 Examples of non-Ciceronian diction: *internuntiare* in §3 (Cic. uses substantival *internuntius/-ia*, but not the verb); *repolire* §9; *superventus* §12;

vellicatim §20; *satagere* §22; *scrupulatim* §22; *aestuatio* §24; *dexteritas* §25; *sciscitatio* §44; *retaxare* §44; *praesumptio* §49.

210 On this point, McLaughlin 1995: 240, 241, 244–5, 246–8, 260-1.
211 See pp. 13 and n. 73, 17–18.
212 See, e.g., 1.3.9 and n. 47; 1.4.3-4 and nn. 55, 57; 1.4.7 and n. 62; 3.5.50 and n. 137, etc.
213 A single example for now can only be suggestive at best about the larger Ciceronian presence in the treatise, but consider a sample passage from the middle of the work (3.2), in a subsection summarizing the ground covered in Books 1 and 2. The following lexical items and/or verbal combinations are either first found in Cicero or notably frequent in him: 3.2.1 *rationis ... particeps*: cf. Cic. *Leg.* 1.22, *Luc.* 21, *Tusc.* 2.47; 3.2.2 *in actione*: *Off.* 1.19; *communem utilitatem*: *Fin.* 3.64, *Off.* 1.22, 1.31; 3.2.3 *valitudo, opes, ingenium*: in combination elsewhere only at *De or.* 2.46; 3.2.4 *muneribus ornatus*: *De or.* 1.115, *Leg.* 1.35; *honestatis ... appetentissimus*: *Tusc.* 2.58; *studiosissimus*: superl. first in Cic. (with gen., *Fin.* 4.61, *Tusc.* 2.58); *consilio et ... institutis*: in combination, *Marcell.* 29; 3.2.5 *dignitatem ostendit*: *Inv.* 2.107; *magnitudine non multitudine*: in combination in Caesar (e.g., *Civ.* 2.2.5), but more frequent in Cic. (*Inv.* 1.39, 2.168, *Man.* 14, *Red. pop.* 5); 3.2.6 *ut enim ... ita*: first attested, and frequent, in Cic. (e.g., *De or.* 1.120, *Leg.* 1.49, *Verr.* 2.3.39); *caelator*: first attested in *Verr.* 2.4.54, 63.
214 See pp. 22–3, 29–31 above.
215 See p. 21 above.
216 Branca 1969: 13–14.
217 Cf. Branca 1969: 13 ('un autore ancora nel pieno del suo tirocinio di scrittore').
218 See on these variations, and on Branca's resistance to imposing editorial standardization on them, Branca 1969: 13 with Manetti 1971: 310.
219 Some of them mentioned by Branca 1969: 13.
220 See on the latter case pp. 48–9 below.
221 See pp. 21–2 above.

Note on the Text and Translation

In keeping with the different life-stages at which Barbaro wrote *De coelibatu* and *De officio legati*, and given his very different thematic and literary agendas in the two works, the translations are cast in different registers in the paired volumes of this edition. The stylistic panache and versatility of *De coelibatu* demand in a translation at least the attempt at a matching liveliness of tone, a brisk pace that is in step with Barbaro's own accelerations, and adjustments of mood according to the shifting contours of his narrative. In particular, I have incorporated features of spoken English, especially contractions, in my version of *De coelibatu*, but not in that of *De officio legati*, where a more formal tone seems appropriate, and also a plainer uniformity of voice. The section divisions as marked in the Latin texts and their respective translations (1.1.1, 2, 3, etc.) follow those deployed by Branca in his 1969 edition. In the case of *De coelibatu*, I have also incorporated references to the page sequence in the sole extant manuscript of the work, i.e., 2r[ecto], 2v[erso], 3r, 3v, etc.

Unless otherwise noted, the text of *De coelibatu* 1 and 2 as given in this volume reproduces Branca's. His departures from the MS are listed below my text, as are my own departures from Branca's printed readings, including the correction of MS misreadings in his text. Spaces left blank in the MS (usually presupposing the insertion of one or more Greek words) are duly noted; and my apparatus also registers those places where my text departs from Branca's in matters of orthography and punctuation. For clarity, more notable departures from Branca and/or the MS are reasoned as follows:

Book One

1.4.12	*ut quam* [sc. *viam*] *sibi quisque munierit*: *quas* MS, *qua* Br., but for *munio -ire* standardly with acc. *viam* cf., e.g., Cic. *Cael.* 34, *De or.* 2.202, *Mur.* 48, *Tusc.* 1.32, etc.
1.4.23	*Nam activi hominis virtus in appetitu, qui cum ratione est, ... proculdubio consistat est necesse*: *cum ratione est* after Br. 67 n. 4; MS *non est* printed by Br., but see my n. 88 ad loc.
1.5.10	*parentum* MS, Wi.; *-ium* Br., but Barbaro elsewhere standardly uses *-um* as printed by Br. (cf. 1.6.2, 3, 2.3.1, 2, 3, 23, 25, 26, etc.).
1.6.3	*Atque ita fit ut omne studium et amorem praecipue parentum in filios magnum habere momentum nemo ire inficias audeat*: *amor*

	MS, Br., but the indirect statement introduced by *nemo . . . audeat* requires *studium et amorem* as acc. subj. of *habere*.
1.6.6	*difficillimum* after Br. 73 n. 2; MS *-ime* surely entered the text under the influence of *facillime* just above.

Book Two

2.2.2	*ab omni coniugii et congressus genere*: *omnis* MS, Br., but for *omni genere* + gen. cf. 1.5.5, 2.4.13.
2.2.7	*non nullos*: *nonnullos* Br. Br. prints MS *non null-* at 1.1.7, 8, 9, 1.4.6, 4.2.27, 72, but (*contra* MS) *nonnull-* here and at 2.6.4, 3.3.3, 3.5.67, 74, 3.6.12, 29, 35, 4.2.32, 52, 65; *nonnull-* with MS at 3.5.13.
2.2.11	*de iis qui se ipsis minora pertractant*: *ipsos* MS, Br., but an abl. of comparison is required in *se ipsis*.
2.2.19	*dum non Xantippem alteram fuisse non ignorassem*: *dum non* MS, but *non . . . non* is convoluted in sense (lit. '. . . not been unaware that not . . .'), whence *modo* is conjectured by Br. 79 n. 2 for the first *non*, to the effect of *dummodo* 'provided that'. But the second *non* is then hard to construe – unless the (excessively forced?) meaning of 'as long as I'd known that Xanthippe was one of the two' is that double wedlock here compensates for the shortcomings of a first wife.
2.5.6	*necesse est uti naturae incommodis atque iis legibus subiacere*: *subiacere* MS, *-eret* Br., but the imperf. subjunctive disrupts the prevailing primary sequence; hence *necesse est* with two infinitives in *uti . . . atque . . . subiacere*.
2.5.14	*a vehementi illa cogitationis intentione*: *vehementi* after Br. 92 n. 4; MS *-tis* is printed by Br., but the adj. better underscores the force of effort in *intentione*. For *vehemens/-enter* in proximity to *intentio* and cognates cf., e.g., Cic. *De or.* 2.211, Cels. *Med.* 3.21.1, Sen. *Ep.* 66.6, Q. *Nat.* 2.8.1, Apul. *Met.* 2.16.5.
2.6.16	*Hunc seducens a contemplando tantum se sciat pater sceleris admissurum . . .*: *seducens* after Br. 96 n. 3; *-ere* MS, but the inf. is grammatically incompatible with *se sciat pater . . . admissurum* [sc. *esse*].
2.6.16	*si factum ex filio turpe mancipium saevissimae genti venundaret*: *saevissime* MS, Br., but *-ae genti* neatly balances *turpe mancipium*, and *genti* in any case lacks force without a defining adj.

De Coelibatu

1 [....][1] [**2r**] pietate in re praesertim honesta imperabis. Illud mihi saltem solatio erit, qui, quae melior esset ac brevior ad bene vivendum via, si vel in mea ista adolescentia gloriari parumper licet, non penitus ignoraverim. Sed haec coram uberius atque apertius, si libuerit, disserentur. Satis etiam ea causa est tibi declarata quae animum potissimum meum induxit ut de coelibatu scriberem totumque id, qualecunque esset, tibi dedicarem. **2** Interim librum lege, mi pater, a filio proficiscentem observantissimo obletareque siquid erit iuditio tuo laudandum: nam dicere rogareve ut corrigas supervacuum est, cum quia in assentationem iam ea processit humanitas, tum vero maxime quia offitium tuum erit emendare et tu id mihi praestare debebis vel si nullum ea de re verbum fecissem. **3** In [**2v**] his autem voluminibus nihil erit quod prodesse possit tibi. Non enim instituuntur ii qui aut uxorem ducturi sunt aut qui iam, ut tu, duxerunt; nam in ea re paterni commentarii te adiuvare potuerunt; verum haec mihi fortasse proficient si id a te impetravero quod, ut honestum est, ita me spero a te praesertim facile consequuturum.

4 Ordo autem iste est.

Primus liber quatuor continebit:

Primum quor varia studia esse hominum coeperint, ut hic quidem ad res gerendas, ille vero ad contemplandum conferret sese.
Secundum quor uxorem ducere nolunt ii qui contemplationem anteponent.
Tertium quae[2] vita praestantior sit activine hominis an contemplativi.
Quartum quae[3] vita optabilior iocundiorve uxoriane an coelebs sit.

Secundus vero de iis tractabit quae in eo pu[...]

---

[1] F. 1 is missing, as is f. 3: see Intro. p. 6.
[2] quor MS.
[3] quor MS.

On Celibacy

[**Preface**]
1 [....] you[4] will exercise your authority with dutiful affection in a matter that is particularly honourable.[5] There will at least be comfort for me in the fact that (if even at this tender age of mine I'm allowed to boast for a moment) I have not been altogether unaware of what would be the better and quicker path to the good life. But these matters will be discussed more fully and more frankly face to face, if you want. You have also been sufficiently apprised of the motive that most led me to write on celibacy and to dedicate it all to you, such as it would be. **2** For the moment, father, please read the book that emanates from your most attentive son, and take pleasure in anything you find worth praising. For it's superfluous to tell or ask you to offer corrections – not just because that natural kindness of yours has already disposed you to say yes, but principally because it will be your duty to make corrections, and you will owe me that service even if I'd made no mention of the matter. **3** But there will be nothing in these books that could benefit you: there is no instruction for those who are set on marrying or who, as yourself, have already done so. In that area your father's treatise[6] could have helped you. But this undertaking will perhaps be to my advantage if I obtain from you a dispensation[7] that, honourable as it is, I hope accordingly to secure from you very straightforwardly.

4 This is the arrangement.
The first book will contain four parts:
First, why the pursuits of humankind began to be variegated, to the effect that one sort of person applied himself to a life of action, another to contemplation.
Second, why those who will prefer contemplation are unwilling to marry.
Third, which life is worthier, that of the active man or of the contemplative.
Fourth, which life is more desirable or agreeable, the married or the celibate.
The second book will deal with those matters that in that ...

---

[4] Zaccaria, Ermolao's father.
[5] Presumably Ermolao's preference for the celibate life.
[6] Francesco Barbaro's 1415 *De re uxoria*, on which see Intro. pp. 12–17.
[7] Not to have to marry.

[Primus liber]

1.1 ... **[4r]** quae sensibus atque oculis subiacent coniectari facillimum est. Qua propter et inanima quaedam sunt facta, quaedam animantia adiunctis [organis[8]] procreantur. Animantium quoque diversa sunt genera differentiis multiplicibus variata. **2** Nam, ut de reliquis taceam, alia quidem sensu dumtaxat ut bruta, alia vero ratione vivunt et sensu ut homines. Quare quemadmodum praesentia atque in oculis posita sensus agnoscit, ita et ea quae sensu solo moventur, praetermissa futurorum praeteritorumque cogitatione, ad ea se tantum accommodant quae sese sensibus percipienda offerre nunc possunt. **3** Iis vero quibus inest ratio atque animus remotiora deprehendendi latius vis animalis extenditur: nam et[9] praeteritorum habere memoriam possunt et futurorum certam prope definitamque senten[**4v**]tiam explicare. Solum autem hoc animal quosdam sibi fines et terminos in quos tendat statutos esse intelligit; caeterae vero animantes, utpote rationis expertes, aut parvam aut nullam omnino finium coniecturam colligere potuerunt.

 4 At nobis, quibus ut caeteris etiam rebus unum vivendi principium et finis est Deus, concessum esse caelitus arbitramur ut soli finem cognosceremus eumque, veluti quandam Platonis ideam, cogitatione assequi et contemplando liceret. **5** Ad id autem ut pervenire quandoque possent varium iter et

---

[8] Proposed by Br. 57 n. 1 to fill the blank in the MS.
[9] *et* Br. 57 n. 2 for MS *ut* to balance complementary *et* below.

[Book One]

1.1 [...][10] it is very easy for inferences to be drawn about things that submit to the senses and eyes. Hence also certain entities are inanimate in formation, while others are brought to life as animate beings through the addition of [sense-organs]. There are diverse kinds of animate beings, too, variegated by multiple points of difference: **2** to say nothing of all the other differences, some creatures live merely by sense perception, as brutish animals do; but others live by reason and sense perception, as humans do.[11] For that reason, just as sense perception registers things that are present and visible to the eyes, so also those creatures that are roused by the senses alone forego all reflection on the future or the past and adapt themselves only to those phenomena that can offer themselves for perception by the senses in the immediate present. **3** But in those beings that have reason and will, the natural capacity to encompass a more distant temporal range extends more widely: for they can both hold the memory of past events and articulate an almost sure and precise idea of events to come. Moreover, only this being understands that certain ends and limits have been established for it to strive towards; all other creatures, however, since they lack reason, can gather only a small inference, or none whatsoever, of those ends.

4 But we, for whom (as also for all other things) God is the sole beginning and end of existence[12] – we think that we have been granted the heaven-sent privilege of being the only ones to get to know that end, and of being allowed to grasp it through thought and contemplation, as if some Platonic idea.[13] **5** But to be able to reach that goal at some point, humans have devised for

---

[10] See on the mutilation of the beginning of Book 1 Intro. p. 6, and cf. 3.2.1 for a summary of the missing content.

[11] Participation in reason crucially distinguishes human from animal in the familiar Aristotelian/Stoic tradition echoed here (see, e.g., Cic. *Fin.* 2.45, 5.34, 38, *Leg.* 1.22 with Sorabji 1993: 7–29). But the broader influence of Cicero's *Off.* 1 in *De coelibatu* 1 (see Intro. pp. 18–19) suggests that Barbaro's specific source here is *Off.* 1.11.

[12] For the familiar phraseology cf. in the Latin Vulgate Revelation 1:8 ("'I am the Alpha and the Omega, the beginning and the end [*principium et finis*],' says the Lord God, who is, and who was, and who is to come, the Almighty'), 22.13.

[13] In accordance with the Platonic theory of Forms, for which 1.4.21 and n. 87.

multiplex sibi homines excogitaverunt. Quom enim, ut in una quaque re evenit, diversae atque impares hominum qualitates compararentur, necessarium visum est alias vias, eodem tamen ducentes, aperiendas esse, ut ii qui rectam fastidirent repetito ac circumducto parumper [5r] flexu in finem alacrius properarent.

6 Quare varia ac prope pugnantia offitia sibi homines vendicarunt, a quibus tamen si nunquam recesserint, non aeque finis refragetur sed idem sit prorsus aut quam simillimus. Iccirco autem variarum artium et dissimilium sectatores efficiuntur, quoniam et varia est et dissimilis cuiusque compositura: nam et astrorum vis, in quo quisque aut cadente cingitur aut oriente, non parvam affert nascentibus necessitatem. **7** Sed et locorum et patriae plurimus vigor et distincta varietas naturarum multiplicia hominum ingenia et appetitiones fecit et concitavit: nam et ad illiberalium artium studia tametsi cogi paupertate non nulli videantur, plurimi tamen natura ipsa feruntur, quemadmodum de iis Astronomi sentiunt quos, si Navi oriente nascantur, perpetuo naviculariae ser[5v]vitutis ministerio astringi oportere putaverunt, et eum qui Oeniocho redeunte aurigam nasci necesse esse experti sunt. **8** Illud quoque infelicius compertum est, quicunque secundam Tauri partem horoscopum geniturae nanciscitur stercora semper et putris feculas baiulare; contra vero non nullis est datum ut infima haec atque abiecta contemnerent et se altioribus assererent disciplinis.

themselves a route that has many varied options. Since (as happens in any and all situations) different and inconsistent properties of person were pitted against each other, it seemed necessary for diverse paths to be opened up, all of them nevertheless leading to the same goal, so that those who showed an aversion to the straight path would yet hurry to their end quite briskly despite, for a time, repeatedly making circuitous turnings.

6 Hence people in general have assumed for themselves a variety of almost conflicting duties;[14] nevertheless, if they've never walked away from them, the end-goal wouldn't thwart them to an equal degree, but it would remain precisely the same goal, or as like as possible.[15] For that reason devotees of a variety of different branches of knowledge emerge, since the configuration of each person shows both variety and difference; for the zodiacal influence that encompasses each of us by either its setting or rising bestows a considerable force of destiny on newborns. **7** But the very considerable influence both of our life-situations and of our place of origin, and the wide-ranging diversity of natures, have given rise to and stimulated a great variety of human aptitudes and aspirations: though a good number of people seem forced by poverty to apply themselves to ignoble pursuits, most are nevertheless carried along by their intrinsic nature – just as astronomers feel about those who, if they're born when the Argo constellation is rising, are thought to be necessarily bound for permanent deployment in service aboard ship;[16] or about the type who, in the astronomers' experience, was inevitably born a charioteer when the Rein-holder reappears.[17] **8** Likewise, a more unfortunate discovery was this – that anyone who got as his birth-sign the back end of the Bull would always be a shit-shifter ferrying fecal fetidness.[18] On the other hand, however, it's been granted to some people to keep well away from these bottom-end indignities, and to dedicate themselves to higher branches of study.

---

[14] Distributive in force: A's duties 'almost conflict' with those of B.
[15] I.e., different people take on different roles/duties in life; but their progress towards the shared end-goal (in 1.1.4, knowing God) is not consistent or equal in all cases.
[16] Barbaro means Argo Navis, the large southern constellation that was associated in the Greek tradition with the myth of Jason and the Argonauts (so, e.g., Arat. *Phaen.* 342-52). For the newborn under Argo as destined for a future at sea cf. Man. *Astron.* 5.32-56.
[17] The northern constellation of Heniochus, also known by its Latin name Auriga ('driver'). For those born under this sign cf. Man. *Astron.* 5.67-101.
[18] The constellation of Taurus: after the high-mindedness of, e.g., Manilius' portrayal of those born under Taurus (*Astron.* 5.140-51) – plain, industrious types who patiently work the land as if human oxen (cf. 4.150-1), or solid patriots such as Cincinnatus (*c.* 519–430 BCE), who by legend temporarily left the plow to lead Rome against her enemies (cf. 4.149) – Barbaro wittily descends into the mire. But perhaps more: given that only the forequarters of Taurus were visible (cf. Arat. *Phaen.* 322; Ov. *Fast.* 4.717-18; Vitr. *De arch.* 9.3.1 with Soubiran 1969: 132–3 ad loc.), Barbaro's back end of the Bull is itself a mere figment (my thanks to Katharina Volk for this point).

9 Ex hac itaque studiorum varietate illa divisio orta est, aliam esse in actione aliam in contemplatione positam vitam. Habet enim utrunque genus sectatores. Non nulli siquidem sese publicis rebus immiscent et variis negotiis implicantur: his familiam alere et uxorem ducere praeclarum est, prolem vero substulisse multo pulcherrimum. **10** E diverso alii, veluti sensibus abdicatis reiectaque humanorum offitiorum [**6r**] ambitione, speculationibus altissimis inseruntur. Hi et a forensibus curis interdictum esse sibi optimum putant et profundos mentis recessus probata virtutis unius consideratione incolunt et frequentant: ex quorum consuetudine evenit ut assidua rerum plurimarum contemplatione et varia scientiarum primordia reperirentur et distincta postmodum serie inventorum in corpus quoddam rerum omnium causae redigerentur. **11** Unde illud est a veteribus latissime annotatum: observatione et admiratione coepisse artium fundamenta pertractari; quod esse non potuisset nisi aliqui in eam rem potissimum incubuissent et diligentissima inspectione rerum causas et effectus extimassent.

[2] Cur uxorem ducere nolint ii qui contemplationem anteponent actioni.

2.1 [**6v**] Vacare autem illorum animos omni molestia et tumultu pernecessarium videbatur quibus ab actione et negotio sequestranda mens esset. Iccirco, ut Theophrastus scripsit, statutas fuisse philosophari volentibus apud aegyptios mansiones quibus non solum a cura rei familiaris sed etiam a publicis muneribus vacandum fuisset accepimus, ea scilicet ratione ne

9 From this diversity of pursuits, then, the following separation of categories has come about: one mode of existence is located in action, another in contemplation. Each of the two kinds has its followers.[19] On the one hand, a good many get involved in public affairs and engage in various sorts of business; for them, real respectability lies in supporting a household and marrying, but to have raised children is by far the most glorious aspect. **10** Others, by contrast, as if casting aside the senses and renouncing all desire for advancement in the service side of life, involve themselves in the loftiest forms of contemplation. They think that the best path for them is to be debarred from public responsibilities, and, esteeming as they do the contemplation of virtue alone, they dwell in the remote recesses of mind to which they constantly resort. From their habitual practice it came about that, through their unremitting consideration of a great many things, the diverse beginnings of scientific knowledge were discerned and, through a precise sequence of later discoveries, the causal origins of all things were assembled into a certain framework.[20] **11** Hence the following was very widely remarked upon by past ages – that through close observation and a sense of wonder the foundations of skilled knowledge began to be carefully investigated. This development could not have happened unless a few people had devoted themselves to that project above all, and appraised the causes and effects of things through the most painstaking examination.

[2] Why those who will prefer contemplation to action would not want to marry.

2.1 To the sort whose disposition was to be kept at a remove from action and business, it seemed very necessary for their minds to be free of all vexation and disturbance. For that reason, as Theophrastus wrote, we're told that in Egypt dwellings were established for aspiring philosophers who felt the need to be

---

[19] See on this time-honoured debate Intro. pp. 18–19, 21.
[20] Barbaro fuses traditional protreptic characterization of the contemplative life as nurturing our innate love of learning towards the acquisition of virtue (e.g., Cic. *Fin.* 5.48-60) with the idea that contemplation is itself 'active,' progressive, and productive in the knowledge it unveils (so, e.g., Sen. *Dial.* 8.5.3-8; cf. 1.4.14 and n. 74).

multarum rerum et dissimilium exercitatione abduceretur a contemplando animus et pulcherrimas desereret cogitationes. **2** Remedium itaque maximum atque utilissimum sibi ipsis sapientissimi illi Gymnosophistae excogitarunt, primumque ante omnia in animum induxerunt non esse sibi ducendas uxores si vacare magna molestia voluissent. Et Ciceronem ipsum accepimus, quom Publiae nuptias celebraret, interrogatum num ede[**7r**]ret[21] aliquid aut scriptitaret, non minus salse quam vere respondisse philosophiam simul et uxorem colere non licere. **3** Vix enim dici potest quantum haec cura distrahat a speculationibus mentem quantumque in minimis quibusque et abiectis moretur.[22] Adde quod ea est coniugiorum lex atque conditio, ut si curam suscipias inutilis, si deseras impius videare.

4 Nisi forte putandum est, quemadmodum in belli rebus plerunque contingit ut secum duces in castra uxores agant, profuturas etiam in contemplando aliquid si veluti sotias nobiscum advehamus. Nam et Cleopatra M. Antonium est in bellum prosequuta,[23] et Darii Persarum regis coniunx castra metata est; Semiramis quoque Assyriae regno per bellum potita dicitur, in quo quid differat vel si sotio marito duxisset in hostem exercitum non

---

[21] *aed-* MS.
[22] *-eretur* MS.
[23] *-uuta* MS; *-uunta* Br.

free not just of domestic responsibility but also of public duties;[24] the rationale, of course, was for the mind not to be drawn away from contemplation by being busied with many different things, and not to abandon its very beautiful meditations. **2** Accordingly, those famous sages of very great wisdom, the Gymnosophists,[25] devised a most effective and beneficial remedy for themselves, and their first determination before all else was that they should not take wives if they wanted to be free of great disturbance. And we hear that Cicero himself, when he was talking about his marriage to Publi[li]a, was asked whether he was publishing anything or in the habit of writing; and that, no less wittily than truthfully, he replied that it wasn't possible to tend to philosophy and a wife at the same time.[26] **3** Yes, because it can scarcely be said just how much this responsibility distracts the mind from its explorations, and the extent to which it wastes time on all the tiniest and most insignificant trivia. Moreover, such is the law of marriages, such the terms, that if you take on the responsibility you seem unfit for it, wicked if you abandon it.

4 Unless, perhaps, we're to suppose that, just as in matters of war it often happens that leaders take their wives with them into camp, wives would also be of some benefit in contemplation if we brought them along with us as if our comrades. For Cleopatra accompanied Marc Antony into war, and the wife of Darius, king of Persia, pitched military camp.[27] Semiramis, too, is said to have

---

[24] Theophrastus (c. 372–287 BCE) was Aristotle's successor as head of the Peripatetic school at Athens (for which n. 30 below). Barbaro draws on Jerome's *Adv. Iovinian.* of 393 CE: in asserting that marriage and celibacy were equally meritorious before God, Jovinian, the late fourth-century CE opponent of Christian asceticism, departed radically from the view, shared by Jerome, that celibacy was superior to marriage (cf. *Adv. Iovinian.* 1.16 [*PL* 23.246 §266]: 'Marriage replenishes the earth, virginity Paradise'). But in alluding to *Adv. Iovinian.* 2.13 (*PL* 23.316 §342), Barbaro misattributes to Theophrastus what Jerome there ascribes to the first-century CE Stoic philosopher and Egyptian priest Chaeremon of Alexandria. Theophrastus is mentioned just before Chaeremon in that same passage of Jerome; alternatively, or in addition, the misattribution may have arisen from confusion with (or cunning exploitation of?) Jerome's allusion to Theophrastus' 'book on marriage' (*liber de nuptiis*) in 1.47 (*PL* 23.288-9 §313 = Text 486 Fortenbaugh 2011: 410–15).

[25] Lit. 'naked philosophers,' the holy men of India, famed among the ancients for their asceticism (see Plin. *NH* 7.22 with Beagon 2005: 151).

[26] After divorcing his first wife of more than thirty years, Cicero married his young ward Publilia in late 46 BCE, but the union was short-lived (further on the episode, Treggiari 2007: 118–42 with Claassen 1996, and cf. 3.3.2 and n. 36). The anecdote is told (not of Publilia but of Cicero's refusal to marry his friend Aulus Hirtius' sister earlier in 46) by Jerome after Seneca: *Adv. Iovinian.* 1.48 (*PL* 23.291 §316 = Sen. *De matr.* fr. 30 Vottero 1998: 142–3).

[27] Cleopatra accompanied Antony at the fateful Battle of Actium (31 BCE), where Octavian crushed his rival (see, e.g., Virg. *Aen.* 8.671-713). If Darius I of Persia is meant, his wife, Atossa, allegedly emboldened him to invade Greece in 492 BCE (cf. Hdt. 3.134), only for that campaign to founder with the Athenian victory at Marathon in 490. These negative implications reinforce the irony already encased in 1.2.4 *Nisi forte putandum est* (cf. *OLD forte* 3b, 'esp. used to introduce an unlikely or absurd suggestion').

plane perspi[7v]cio. **5** Sed aperte concessum sit foeminarum ingenia praeclara et admirabilia esse et, ne suam sexui praestantiam invideamus, nostris non tardiora; non tamen in eum usum comparata esse dicendum est, ut regere sapienter et providere constanter possint. Nam et infirmitas, quae ex humetto atque impuro corporis statu proficiscitur, ad consilia altiora non sinit aspirare; et levitas, quae ex illa imbecillitate producitur, sententiae minuit firmitatem.

6 Nobis itaque, quibus de coelibum vita et moribus scribendum est, illud primum admonendum fuit ne ille, qui a nobis instituitur, animum inducat ad nuptias: hoc autem iccirco in initio positum esse voluimus ut, quemadmodum Peripatetici solent, veluti quaedam eius rei quae tractatur diffinitio protinus ac veluti titulus in fronte [**8r**] illucescat. Caelebs enim is vulgo ab omnibus dicitur qui caret uxore eamque sibi deligit vitam quae a rei cura familiaris sit quam remotissima. **7** Procedentibus vero libris ordine cuncta notabimus quae pertinere ad finem huius vitae adipiscendum cognoscemus. Quam rem antequam tractare incipiamus, ea videtur quaestio explicanda quae sit vita praestantior, an ea quae in sotietate et consuetudine hominum posita est, an quae in solitudine et tenebris iacere existimatur, idest an vita quae in actione consistit excellat eam quae est in contemplatione collocata.

acquired sovereignty over Assyria through war; I don't quite see what difference it makes even if in this case *she* had led an army against the enemy with her husband *her* comrade.[28] **5** But let it be openly acknowledged that the intellect of women is outstanding and worthy of admiration and – so as not to begrudge the female sex its own qualities of excellence – no less quick-witted than ours. Still, it has to be said that that intellect wasn't formed to give them the ability to rule prudently and to exercise consistent foresight; for the lack of robustness that originates from the impure moistness of their bodily condition doesn't allow them to aspire to a higher plane of reason, and the inconsistency resulting from that weakness reduces their firmness of intention.[29]

6 Accordingly, the first recommendation that was to be given by me in having to write about the life and ways of celibates was this: that the student trained by me should not turn his thoughts to marriage. The reason I wanted this point to be stated at the outset was so that, in the customary manner of the Peripatetics,[30] a certain defining of the matter at hand – a title-heading, as it were – should be made clear right at the start.[31] That's to say, he who doesn't have a wife and chooses for himself an existence that is as far removed as possible from domestic responsibility is commonly called by everyone a celibate. **7** Certainly, as my books progress in sequence, I shall draw attention to all the factors that I shall find relevant to attaining the end-goal of this existence. Before I begin to deal with this subject, the problem that has to be resolved first, it seems, is which existence is superior: that located in the societal conventions of humankind, or that which has the reputation of being a state of idleness in lonely obscurity; i.e., whether the life that resides in action surpasses that devoted to contemplation.

---

[28] Sammu-ramat, Greek Semiramis, queen of Assyria (*fl.* ninth century BCE). According to the tradition preserved in Diod. Sic. 2.6, she joined her first husband while he was on a campaign under Ninus, King of Babylon, and she distinguished herself by leading an attack on the city of Bactra; the infatuated Ninus sought to marry her, causing her husband (cf. Barbaro's *sotio marito*) to commit suicide. But Barbaro may also obliquely cast Semiramis as a negation of the celibate ideal, given her post-antique reputation for extreme sexual license, including incest and legitimizing marriage between parents and children: see Archibald 2001: 37–47, and cf. Dante *Inf.* 5.52–60 (Semiramis in the second circle of hell alongside – among other carnal sinners – Cleopatra).

[29] For all his stress on the female intellect as 'no less quick-witted than ours,' the effects of menstruation here reflect the Hippocratic/Aristotelian orthodoxy on male superiority that remained influential down to the sixteenth century and beyond: see Hufnagel 2012: 15–31 with Dean-Jones 1994, esp. 37–40, 41–5, 150–1, 178–9.

[30] The philosophical school founded by Aristotle, so called because of the walkways (Gk. *peripatoi*) of the Athenian Lyceum, where from *c.* 335 BCE he and his followers met.

[31] For this familiar stress on the importance of definitions see already Pl. *Phdr.* 237b-d with, e.g., Cic. *De or.* 1.209-13, *Rep.* 1.38.1-2; Barbaro here means Peripatetic propositional rigour of the kind that Cicero contrasts with Socratic non-assertion at *Ac.* 1.17.

8 Solutis siquidem iis, facile apparebit quid sit potissimum iis qui in coelibatu degunt in vita sequendum. Tetigerunt hanc et alii per transitum quaestionem: nos vero, quia praesentis operis propria videtur esse, libris nostris putavimus in[**8v**]serendam, eoque libentius faciendum id fuit quo intelligi apertius possit num vitae uxoriae praeferenda sit caelebs. **9** Id enim inprimis[32] hic agimus, ut quantum sit inferior illorum voluptas, qui uxorio muneri alligantur, appareat. Sed primum rationes illorum exponemus qui contra senserunt; deinceps dissolutis iis ad reliqua pergendi tempus erit. Breviter ergo hunc in modum dicamus.

[3] Quaestio quae vita praestantior sit, activine hominis an contemplativi.

3.1 Qui se a communi utilitate semper abducit ab hominum cadere ingenio existimandus est, quoniam natura ad operandum convivendumque hominem procreavit: item homini proprium ope consiliis auctoritate miseros et egentis sublevare. Eius qui se oculis hominum surripit et cuniculos semper colit et tenebras nullus [**9r**] esse in quanvis partem usus potest, non secus sane atque earum rerum quae mari naufrago absorbentur. **2** Praeterea si bonum est curis vacare omnibus, melius utique fiet si plures quam si unus eam deligant vitam, praestantius nanque quo latius bonum est. Optimum ergo videbitur si iter id omnes ingrediantur; quod manifeste non solum est falsum sed etiam periculosum.

---

[32] *inprimis* MS; *in primis* Br.

8 If these matters indeed get resolved, the direction that is most to be pursued in life by those leading a celibate existence will easily become apparent. Others, too, have touched on this problem[33] in passing. But because the problem is seen to have a special relevance to the present work, I thought it had to be included in my books; and that was to be done all the more gladly so that it could be more clearly understood whether a celibate existence is to be preferred to married life. **9** For my agenda here is above all this: to clarify just how much less is the enjoyment of those who are bound to marital duty. But I shall first set out the reasoning of those who have felt the opposite; then, after that reasoning has been refuted, it will be time to proceed to the remaining matters. Let's briefly talk, then, as follows.

[3] The problem of which existence is superior, that of the active person or of the contemplative.

3.1 One who always distances himself from the communal advantage has to be thought of as lapsing from human inclination, since nature created humankind to live an active life of shared fellowship;[34] likewise, it is a defining human characteristic to support the wretched and needy through help, advice, and leadership. One who withdraws from human sight and always stays in obscure rabbit-holes cannot be of any value to any extent whatsoever – no different, indeed, from the value of the possessions swallowed up by the sea in a shipwreck. **2** Moreover, if it's a good thing to be free of all responsibilities, it will surely become better still if more people choose that existence than if just one does; the wider its reach, the more impressive the good. It will therefore seem the best course if everyone embarks on it – a prospect that is clearly not just deluded but also fraught with danger.

---

[33] Which existence is superior, the active or the contemplative.
[34] Ciceronian phraseology, Stoic in tenor: on natural *communis utilitas* cf. *Fin.* 3.64, *Off.* 1.22, 31, 52; 3.28, 30.

3 Cito namque genus humanum interiret si nulla procreandae sobolis ratio haberetur: cito etiam tot praeclarae urbes, tot aedificia, tot fana, tot artes, tot immerentium artificum monumenta, tot virorum illustrium memoriae funditus delerentur. **4** Quo quid crudelius? Addendum etiam illud quod neque sperare amplius claros imperatores liceret, neque eos homines, quorum virtutem etiam mortuorum non solum laudamus sed etiam [**9v**] colimus et admiramur. Quid quod ab immanissimis baeluis pygmaeorum more quottidie[35] vexaremur, si nullus armorum usus, nulla rei militaris disciplina, nullum robur, nulla calliditas marcescentibus animis et studio alieno fractis extaret? **5** Frustra nobis oculi atque sensus illaque ipsa vis animorum essent concessa, nisi liceret uti concessis. Frustra pedes et crura reliquo corpori natura commisisset, nisi et incedere et currere pro temporis necessitate possemus. Frustra etiam ipsae instrumentorum omnium artifices manus validis lacertorum toris substentatae circumquaque agiles mobilesque et ad opus promptae velut extrinsecus fuissent adiunctae, nisi ad plurimos casus opis suae ministerium adhibere debuissent.

---

[35] *quot-* Br., but cf. 3.5.24 (MS *quott-* retained by Br.).

3 Why? The human race would quickly die out if no consideration were given to producing offspring; quickly, too, would so many distinguished cities, so many buildings, so many shrines be completely destroyed, so many crafts, so many monuments of undeserving craftsmen,[36] so many memorials of distinguished men.[37] **4** What could be crueler than this? The further point to be made is that it would no longer be possible to hope for famous leaders, or for the sort of people whose virtuous qualities we not only praise but also revere and admire even when they are dead. What of the fact that we would be harassed like pygmies[38] on a daily basis by the most savage beasts, if no practical experience of arms were to be found, no military training, no force of strength, and no shrewdness of initiative, while minds were enfeebled and broken by focusing on a pursuit that doesn't belong to us? **5** To no purpose would our eyes and senses and that very force of mind have been granted to us, if it were not possible to employ what we've been granted. To no purpose would nature have connected our feet and legs to the rest of our body, if we weren't able to walk and run according to the needs of the moment. To no purpose, too, would our hands have been added on as if from the outside, had they not had to apply to so many eventualities the service of their assistance – our hands, themselves the skilled makers of every kind of tool, undergirded by the strong musculature of the upper arms, and nimble and pliant in all directions, and quick to meet a task.[39]

---

[36] I.e., not deserving oblivion.
[37] In reviewing the case against celibacy, Barbaro revisits a line of argument – societies depend on marriage and procreation for continuity and prosperity (cf. n. 24 above) – that extends back at least to Plato and Aristotle, but which gained renewed urgency because of the socio-economic upheavals of the fourteenth and fifteenth centuries; hence the pivotal significance of Coluccio Salutati in humanist reevaluation of the claims of marriage (see Intro. p. 15). This revisionist stance is starkly reflected by the Vestal Virgin who speaks against chastity in Lorenzo Valla's 1431 *De voluptate/On pleasure* (1.45.1-11). Along the way the Vestal deploys the survivalist argument voiced here by Barbaro (cf. 1.45.5: 'Do you not see, O wisest of men, what a disaster humankind would suffer if all were as we [sc. the Vestals] are? Truly the race would be finished'; tr. Hieatt and Lorch 1977: 125). Further on Valla's work and its modified title over three bouts of revision, 3.6.16 n. 226.
[38] A dwarf-like people in conflict with the cranes, a legend extending back to Homer: cf. *Il.* 3.2-6 with Beagon 2005: 157 on Plin. *NH* 7.26 and Dasen 1993: 175–8.
[39] For the familiar argument of the hands, senses, etc., as granted by divine beneficence for human utility see Cic. *Nat. D.* 2.140-6 (senses) and 150-1 (hands; cf. also *Off.* 2.12) with Pease 1955–8: 2.916, 939.

6 Quid tam multa? Contemplativi hominis finem quid aliud prae [**10r**] se ferre arbitramur quam inertiam quandam et ignobilitatem? Activi contra diligentiam atque praestantiam? Ille enim, ut verum sciat et sibi ipsi dumtaxat prosit, conventus coetusque hominum reformidat; hic, ne solus sit quispiam foelix, forensibus et publicis rebus se reddit instructum, adesseque, in hominum oculis versari vult ut et domi et foris praesto sit omnibus. **7** Nonne et Aristoteli placet hunc esse qui non solum ea quae ad actionem pertinent componat et instruat, verumetiam[40] qui, quom leges omnibus statuat, praesit etiam iis quae ad contemplationem attineant? Nam et curat ut studiosi sint in re publica homines et disciplinis omnibus modum quendam et metam praescribit. **8** Nam et apud Romanos filii senatorum decreto publico in Aetruriam ad per[**10v**]discendas augurum disciplinas mittebantur, et Persarum instituto adolescentes omnes sese ad studia conferebant, quorum utrunque is qui erat in actione et rei publicae administratione imperabat. Quare, quoniam activus moderator[41] et rector est contemplandi, praestantior proculdubio habeatur necesse est. **9** Qua in re optime sensisse Cicero videri potest. Is, quom omnem animi motum cogitationemque aut in consiliis capiendis de rebus honestis et pertinentibus ad bene beateque vivendum aut in studiis scientiarum cognitionisque posuisset, utrunque ad actionem ordinavit: quamvis[42] enim perdiscendas esse homini has artes dicat, quae in veri investigatione versantur, harum tamen studio a rebus gerendis abduci contra officium esse arbitratur. Quare virtutis, inquit, laus omnis in actione consistit.

---

[40] *verumetiam* MS; *verum etiam* Br.
[41] Perhaps MS *-atur* (so Br. 62 n. 1)?
[42] Br. inconsistently prints the abbreviated form in the MS sometimes as *quamvis* (cf. 1.4.21, 1.6.5, 2.4.1, 2.5.7, 3.6.11, 4.2.93), sometimes *quanvis* (cf. 3.4.5, 3.5.4, 38, 51, 3.6.39).

6 Why such a litany? What do we think the contemplative's end-goal displays other than a certain indolence and a lack of distinction? What, by contrast, the active man's, if not attentiveness and preeminence? For the contemplative, in his quest for truth and to benefit only himself, shies away from social intercourse and gatherings; the active man, so that no one prospers just on his own, makes himself ready and available for public and state affairs, and he wants to be helpfully at hand, and to remain in the public eye so as to be at the service of all both at home and abroad. **7** Doesn't Aristotle also agree that he[43] is the sort not only to formulate and teach whatever relates to practical action, but also, since he decrees the laws for all, to preside over whatever's relevant to contemplation?[44] For he both sees to it that devotees of learning exist within the state, and sets a certain measure and limit for all branches of study. **8** Among the Romans, too, the sons of senators would be sent by public ordinance to Etruria to learn all about the science of augury,[45] and it was Persian practice for all young men to apply themselves to studying;[46] in both cases, a man of action managing the affairs of state was the one giving orders. For that reason, since the man of action has regulatory control over engagement in contemplation, he should doubtless be thought superior. **9** On this matter Cicero can be seen to have had excellent ideas. Since he'd located every mental operation and thought process either in deliberating on matters of moral rectitude that are relevant to living a good and happy life, or in studying particular branches of investigative knowledge, he related each of the two to action; for though he says that a person should thoroughly learn the skills involved in the exploration of truth, he nevertheless thinks that it is a violation of duty to be diverted, through devotion to those skills, from engaging in practical affairs. Hence the praiseworthiness of virtue, he says, lies entirely in action.[47]

---

[43] The man of action.
[44] The practical wisdom of the statesman is inferior to philosophical wisdom (Arist. *EN* 6.12 1143b34, 6.13 1145a6-11); but while the philosopher is self-sufficient (10.7 1177b1), he nevertheless needs the necessities of life (10.7 1177a28-9; cf. 10.8 1178a23-8, 1178b3-7, 33-5) in a social context where legislation facilitates and promotes philosophical training (10.9 1179b31-81b22).
[45] See V. Max. 1.1.1 with Wardle 2006: 325-7 on Cic. *Div.* 1.92.
[46] Barbaro means the ethical guidance that was by reputation encoded in the Persian education (cf. Xen. *Cyr.* 1.2.3, 6-9). Cyrus the Great (*c.* 600–530 BCE) exemplified the ideals of this education (cf. Cic. *Rep.* 1.43.2), but the primary goal remained to produce effective soldiers; further, Whidden 2007.
[47] A close adaptation of *Off.* 1.19, in a sequence of argument derived from the Stoic Panaetius (see Intro. pp. 18–19). In the immediate context Cicero presents the first of the four 'parts' of the honourable (*honestum*, 1.15), 'the knowledge of truth' (*veri cognitio*, 1.18).

10 Haec atque alia ex eisdem fontibus [11r] derivata adduci solent ab iis qui illud vivendi genus, quod graeci [πρακτικόν⁴⁸] seu [μηχανικόν] vocant, nos activum administrativum aut negotiativum dicimus, [θεωρητικῷ] hoc est contemplativo anteponendum putent. Occurrendum autem a nobis his est atque in hunc maxime modum particulatim respondendum. Facile id autem assequemur si prius sententiae nostrae rationem subiiciemus.

11 Vitae negotiativae finem Peripatetici, quorum inexpugnabiles rationes sunt, honestam actionem posuerunt, contemplativae vero summum et simplicissimum bonum, cognitionem. Contemplatores autem illos existimari voluerunt, non qui se intra domesticos parietes lucem et radium formidantes continerent aut qui vitam in tenebris et latebris⁴⁹ more ferarum exigerent, [11v] sed qui se a popularibus auris secernentes et curis gravioribus liberarentur et veritatis solicita inquisitione beatius et felicius viverent. **12** Intolerabile siquidem esset et inhumanum si coetus hominum odissemus et opem aliquam honestam petenti negaremus. Ast unum id hac in re ab iis est requirendum: ne se rerum privatarum publicarumve ministeriis obligent si contemplari perfecte voluerint.

His ita distinctis facile obiecta purgantur.

[4] De solutione eorum quae sunt obiecta in vitam contemplativam.

4.1 Hominem ais ad convivendum procreatum quando praesertim natura civile animal est: contemplativum ab hac consuetudine abhorrere: non esse igitur hominum numero aggregandum.

---

⁴⁸ Here and below, Br.'s proposals (62 n. 2) to fill the blanks in the MS.
⁴⁹ *lateribus* MS.

10 These and other arguments drawn from the same sources are usually adduced by the sort who think that that mode of life – a mode the Greeks call [*praktikon*] or [*mēchanikon*], while we term it 'active', 'practical', or 'engaged' – is to be preferred to [*theōrētikon*], i.e., the contemplative mode. But these arguments are to be countered by me, and to be answered one-by-one very much in the following manner. I shall easily achieve as much if I first set out the reasoning behind my viewpoint.

11 The Peripatetics, whose theories are unassailable, have posited virtuous action as the end-goal of the engaged existence, but pure knowledge, that highest and most unqualified good, as the end-goal of the contemplative life.[50] But those whom they wanted to be thought of as contemplatives were not the sort to confine themselves within their own four walls at home, dreading any ray of sunlight, or to spend their lives in dark lairs like burrowing animals; but rather the type who, by separating themselves from the breezes of popular opinion, both found freedom from weightier responsibilities and lived happier, more prosperous lives in the restless investigation of truth. **12** It would certainly be intolerable and less than human if we loathed social intercourse and said no to someone asking for some respectable form of help.[51] But in this matter the one thing to be demanded of them is this: if they want the fullest experience of contemplation, let them not bind themselves to the service-like duties of domestic or public affairs.

With these distinctions so made, the objections [to the contemplative life] are easily cleared away.

[4] On resolving the objections to the contemplative life.

4.1 You say that man was created to live in companionship, particularly since he is by nature a social animal; that the contemplative shrinks from this companionship; and that he's therefore not to be included in the count of humankind.[52]

---

[50] For the Aristotelian/Peripatetic primacy of happiness in the contemplative life, cf. Arist. *EN* 10.7 1177a12-78a8, 10.8 1178a22-79a32, Cic. *Fin.* 5.11.

[51] Already in Aristotle the contemplative need not be a recluse. So *EN* 10.7 1177a32-5: '...the philosopher, even when by himself, can contemplate truth, and the better the wiser he is; *he can perhaps do so better if he has fellow workers*, but still he is the most self-sufficient' (tr. Ross 1980: 264, my emphasis; cf. 10.8 1178b5-7, 1178b33-79a5). But the wide currency of the ideas Barbaro invokes here is reflected in, e.g., Seneca's Stoicizing portrayal of the contemplative sage as engaging in social intercourse (*Ep.* 9.1, 8, 15, 17-18, etc.) and helping others (*Dial.* 8.3.5, 8.6.4-5, *Ep.* 85.38) even as that sage thrives in self-sufficiency.

[52] If Cicero is implicitly addressed in 'You say' (cf. 1.4.8), Barbaro offers a pithy but unnuanced condensation of Ciceronian ideas in portraying the contemplative as an outsider to 'natural' human fellowship (for such fellowship cf. *Fin.* 5.66, *Off.* 1.12, 22, 50, etc.) and, by extension, to the active life (cf. *Off.* 1.19, 28, 71). But for nuance to Cicero's own position see n. 57 below.

2 Quod adeo verum est ut, dum te fortissima [**12r**] usum ratione arbitraris, pro me omnia concludantur. Deo nanque non homini comparandus est is qui se ab humana hac perturbatione separavit. Nam et mentem a sensibus sequestrasse et affectuum omnium insidias effugisse divina quaedam est virtus et supra hominis conditionem. **3** Quod si etiam hoc ad hominem pertinere videatur, certe magis id erit homini proprium quod maxime naturam contingit humanam. Veri autem cognitio iccirco est maxime homini peculiaris, quoniam ea virtus est una qua homines differunt a natura animantium reliquarum.

4 Soluta est etiam ratio illa, quae quod esset homini proprium, benefacere scilicet et opem ferre, contemplantibus auferebat. Dictum est enim nemini, quom possit, defuturum eum qui se ad sapientiae studia contulit. Quis enim est qui pietatem [**12v**] plus colat et iustitiae partes sciat quam qui semper in altissima sit rerum consideratione versatus? **5** Vir enim bonus sit est necesse qui se huiuscemodi studio alligavit. Nam et vacare omni vitio mentis debet et animi perturbatione qui in unam hanc curam secessit et neminem solicitius imitari quam eum ipsum quoius fruitur intellectu, Deum optimum maximum. Ille siquidem clementissimus[53] quom sit mundi fabricator et princeps singulari providentia, praesentissima pietate, maturissimo favore atque praesidio rerum humanarum consulit incolumitati.

---

[53] *claem-* MS.

2 This is true to the extent that, while you think you are deploying a very effective argument, everything gets decided in my favour. Why? One who has detached himself from this human state of disquiet is to be compared to God, not a mortal. For to have separated the mind from the senses and to have escaped the snares of all our feelings amount to a certain godlike excellence that transcends the human condition.[54] **3** But if even this [godliness] should seem relevant to humankind, surely more special to a human will be that which most affects what it is to be human. For this reason, knowledge of truth is humankind's most defining characteristic,[55] since that is the sole quality of excellence by which humans differ in nature from all other animals.[56]

4 Also dispelled is that argument which robbed contemplatives of that quality special to humankind, namely to benefit and bring help [to others]; for it's been said that the devoted student of wisdom will never, as long as he is able, fail to be of service to anyone. For who is there more to respect dutifulness and to understand the role of justice than one who has always been engaged in the deepest contemplation of such matters?[57] **5** Someone who has committed himself to intellectual activity of this sort is necessarily a good man; for a man who has withdrawn into this one form of study in particular must necessarily be free of any imperfection of judgment and disturbance of mind, and imitate no one more attentively than that very being whom he delights in comprehending – God most good, most great. *He* is certainly most kindly: since He is the world's maker and ordainer, He attends to keeping human circumstances safe and sound through His matchless foresight, His most immediate devotedness, His very timely support and protection.

---

[54] Christianizing adaptation of the familiar Stoic idea that the sage is godlike in serene detachment from ordinary human distractions, perturbation, etc. (see, e.g., Sen. *Dial.* 1.1.5, 2.8.2, *Ep.* 59.14; D. L. 7.119).

[55] Modeled directly on Cic. *Off.* 1.18: *primus ille* [sc. *locus*, the first of the four headings under which the honourable/*honestum* is considered; cf. n. 47 above], *qui in veri cognitione consistit, maxime naturam attingit humanam* ('The first of these [headings], that consisting of the learning of truth, most closely relates to human nature'; tr. Griffin and Atkins 1991: 8).

[56] I.e., participation in reason separates humans from all other animals (1.1.2 and n. 11); but transcendence through contemplation ('knowledge of truth') is still more elevating, separating the contemplative from 'the count of humankind' in an ennobling way that instantly disarms the critique launched in 1.4.1.

[57] Barbaro again appears to follow Cicero's *Off.* 1 closely, now reverting to 1.19 (cf. n. 47 above): 'The second fault [contrary to the learning of truth] is that some men bestow excessive devotion and effort upon matters that are both abstruse and difficult, and unnecessary ... It is, however, contrary to duty to be drawn by such a devotion away from practical achievements: all the praise that belongs to virtue lies in action' (tr. Griffin and Atkins 1991: 8–9). If Barbaro is seen implicitly to critique Cicero here (cf. n. 52), that critique (i) makes no allowance for Cicero's less uncompromising stance on the *vita activa* vs. *contemplativa* later in *Off.* 1 (esp. 1.71), and (ii) heralds the social utility of the contemplative's understanding of justice in terms that are in fact reminiscent of Cicero's *own* argument in this direction in *Off.* 1.155-6 (see further 1.4.19 and n. 83 with Intro. pp. 18–19).

6 Obiicitur rursus non esse id bonum quod bonum non sit semper et omnibus: contemplari autem ununquenque pernitiosum esse et ad interitum, si fiat id, esse quodlibet protinus perventurum. Naturae necessitatem non vitae illius ignobilitatem probare se [**13r**] sciat is qui sententiam suam eo argumento confirmat: ut enim est opportune obiici solitum, vitae necessitas facit ut ea quae natura desyderaret consequi sine aliis atque efficere non possimus, iccirco istam sotietatem[58] videri non nullis esse studiis omnibus anteponendam consuevit. **7** Quod si omnia, ut Cicero nititur confutare, quae ad victum cultumque pertinent quasi virgula divina, ut aiunt, nobis suppeditarentur, tum optimo quisque ingenio negotiis omnibus omissis totum se in cognitione et scientia collocaret. Adversum haec ponam Ciceronis ipsius verba, quia et hoc soleo mihi libenter usurpare ut clarius pateat id quod impraesentia quaeritur. Non est, inquit, ita: nam et solitudinem[59] fugeret et socium quaereret studiorum: tum docere, tum discere, tum dicere, tum audire vellet.

---

[58] *soti-* MS; *soci-* Br.
[59] *solicitud-* MS.

6 Again, the objection goes that that is not a good that isn't always a good, and for everyone; moreover, that it would be ruinous for each and everyone to be a contemplative, and that, if such were to happen, anything at all would be set on the path to destruction right away.[60] But one who shores up his own opinion by that line of reasoning should realize that he's demonstrating a requirement of nature, not the baseness of the contemplative life. As the usual reproach conveniently has it, it's an inescapable fact of life that we can't acquire or produce nature's wants without others;[61] hence some people customarily suppose that that state of communal fellowship is to be esteemed more highly than all intellectual pursuits. **7** But if – as Cicero strives to refute[62] – everything needed for our sustenance and upkeep were provided to us by a magic wand, so to speak, then everyone of the highest abilities would abandon all his busy responsibilities and completely devote himself to learning and knowledge. In answer to this, I'll state the words of Cicero himself, because it's my habit gladly to apply this method as well,[63] so as to give clearer exposure to the matter being examined in the moment. But that isn't so, he says: such a person would avoid being alone by seeking companionship for his studies; he would want sometimes to teach, at other times to learn, to talk at one moment, then to listen.

---

[60] In advance of directly citing Cicero in 1.4.7, Barbaro here varies the 'departure-from-life' argument made at *Off.* 1.153 (albeit there with weaknesses of exposition: Dyck 1996: 341): given humankind's natural sociability, devotion to theoretical study in isolation from one's fellow beings would lead one to 'depart from life' (*excedat e vita*). Cf. also 1.157 (directly before the Ciceronian passage on which Barbaro draws in 1.4.7): '... unless learning is accompanied by the virtue that consists in protecting men, that is to say in the fellowship of the human race, it would seem solitary and barren' (tr. Griffin and Atkins 1991: 61).

[61] This is in line with the familiar theory that humans first formed societies to meet common needs: see further Dyck 1996: 350 on *Off.* 1.158, where Cicero qualifies this theory by asserting that communal fellowship was motivated not solely for the securing of shared needs, but also because humankind is social by nature. Far from disputing this last point, Barbaro appropriates it in 1.4.7 'In answer ... listen'; but he departs from Cicero by focusing primarily in 1.4.6-10 *not* on the matter of human sociability per se (whether motivated by natural urge or strategic utility), but on contemplation as a 'natural' vocation if that social need (however motivated) were removed or non-existent.

[62] Almost a verbatim quotation of *Off.* 1.158 in Barbaro's *Quod si omnia ... collocaret* and then *Non est, inquit, ita ... vellet*.

[63] I.e., refuting the likes of Cicero by using their own words against them.

8 Sed eodem [**13v**] revolveris, vir clarissime, pace tua et aliorum venia dictum sit. Nihil est aliud quod nos ad eam, quam dicis, societatem revocaret, quam vitae necessitas. Ea est quae solos nos esse non sinit, quae et ad dicendum et ad audiendum et ad docendum discendumque ab aliis, quibuscum versemur, impellit. **9** Quod si eam tollas funditus necessitatem, sequentur omnia quae supra dixi; et si fieri queat ut ex admirabili quodam casu sapientiam quisque sectetur partitisque inter se naturae offitiis, quibus carere humana non potest infirmitas, totos se ad speculandum altissima illa naturae et divinitatis archana convertant, non essent utique Homeri ullius carmina aut Myronis et Praxitelis manus expetendae, quibus hominum facta et imagines memoriae posteritatis mandarentur. **10** Nam rerum illarum usus, ad gloriam aut [**14r**] delicias proculdubio excogitatus et ad movendos incitandosque ad bene vivendum animos aut ad aliud quippiam introductus, quem esset locum habiturus, ubi et voluptatem et gloriam unusquisque contemneret et nulla ad colendas servandasque virtutes hortatione aut ad vitia fugienda consilio indigeret? Nullus item armorum usus esse posset si aequa ubique pax atque concordia tam domi quam foris, intentis in unam rem tantum hominibus, toto orbe vigeret.

8 But, my most distinguished sir,[64] with all due respect to you, and with no offence to others, let it be said: you're coming back round to the same point.[65] What would summon us back to what you term communal fellowship is none other than a life-requirement. It's *that* which doesn't allow us to be alone, and drives us to talk and listen, and to teach and be taught by others we spend time with. **9** But if you completely remove that requirement, all that I mentioned above will ensue;[66] and if it could happen that, as a result of some remarkable eventuality, everyone pursues wisdom, and, dividing among themselves the duties of nature that human weakness can't do without,[67] they focus all their concentration on exploring those deepest secrets of nature and the divine, there would be absolutely no need to seek out the poems of any Homer or the masterpieces of Myron and Praxiteles,[68] so that by those means the deeds and likenesses of humankind could be transmitted to the memory of future generations. **10** Why? Because the practice of such things was doubtless devised to achieve glory or pleasure, and instituted to rouse and stimulate minds to the good life, or for some other goal; but what place would it be destined to have when each and everyone would disregard both pleasure and renown and need no encouragement to cultivate and uphold virtuous conduct or advice to avoid faults? Similarly, there could be no experience of arms if an unruffled state of peace and harmony prevailed at home and abroad everywhere in the entire world, with humankind preoccupied with only one thing alone.

---

[64] In hypothetical answer to Cicero.
[65] Return to 1.4.6: 'he's demonstrating a requirement of nature, not the baseness of the contemplative life.'
[66] I.e., the pull to the contemplative life described in 1.4.7 'But if . . . knowledge.'
[67] In effect, a concession to the point (1.4.6) that 'it's an inescapable fact of life that we can't acquire or produce nature's wants without others.'
[68] The sculptors Myron of Eleutherae (*fl.* 480–440 BCE) and Praxiteles of Athens (*fl.* 370–330 BCE; also mentioned at 2.4.5).

11 Verum ita compositi natura sumus, ut alios alia in diversum trahant, neque in unam coiri sententiam possit. Quare, cum propter naturae tum etiam propter vitae necessitatem, impossibilium maximum est ullam esse futuram aetatem quae ita studio sapientiae sit incensa ut contemplari solum singuli velint et universi possint ab omni [**14v**] actione abhorrere. **12** Quod si ita est, quae debet esse tanta temeritas, ut putemus studii illius vitium esse, non humanae necessitatis? Haec enim, ut diximus, diversas hominem vias coegit excogitare, ut quam[69] sibi quisque munierit, ea scilicet, iter ingressus, tendat ad finem.

13 Quae vero de fine utriusque vitae opposita sunt manifestam habere contumeliam videntur. Nam, ut perspicue palam est, quis est tantum ab inertia et desidia alienus, quam is qui nihil aliud efficit quam ne iaceat et torpeat ea pars animi quae solertissima est? **14** Nonne etiam longe praestantius et admirabilius aliquanto ad sempiterna illa ordinum et causarum omnium principia mentem attollere et ad naturam omnis divinitatis accedere quam intra humanae cuiusdam vilitatis terminos, tametsi et hoc laudabile vivendi genus, probata negotiandi discur[**15r**]rendique huc illuc molestia contineri? Ut enim haec plerunque offitia infra hominis potestatem sunt constituta, ita illa rerum cognoscendarum cura supra hominem esse videtur collocata. **15** Nisi forte accusandus iccirco sit contemplator, non quia[70] hominum studia ita fastidiat ut mentem a sensibus revocet et, quod magni esse ingenii Cicero demonstravit, cogitationes suas a consuetudine caeterorum abducat, sed quia supra modum conditionis humanae se tollat.

---

[69] *quas* MS, *qua* Br; but see p. 48 above.
[70] *contemplatur quod se non quia* MS, Br.; but for *quod se* excised as redundant to the sense, Br. 65 n. 2.

11 But we are naturally constituted in such a way that different interests draw different people in different directions, and there can be no shared agreement on a single viewpoint.[71] Hence, because of this necessary requirement not just of nature but also of life, there's no greater impossibility than the existence of any future generation so impassioned with the pursuit of wisdom that individuals would want *only* to engage in contemplation, and that all without exception would be able to shun *every* kind of action. **12** If this is so, how very reckless must it be for us to suppose that the fault lies in that pursuit of wisdom, not in human requirement[72]? For as I've said,[73] that requirement has forced humankind to devise different paths so that, when each embarks on his journey, he naturally reaches for his end-goal by the path that he'll have paved for himself.

13 But the opposed viewpoints about the end-goal of each of these two existences seem to imply a clear insult. For (as is patently well known) who is as much a stranger to slothful idleness as one who focuses all his effort on not letting that part of his mind that is very resourceful become inert with sluggishness? **14** Surely it's also far more impressive and considerably worthier of admiration to raise the mind to those eternal first principles of all systems and causes, and to draw near to the nature of the divine in its entirety, than to be confined within the limits of a certain human baseness, as if this too were a praiseworthy sort of existence in which the nuisance of preoccupation and of busily running about in all directions was viewed approvingly? For just as such duties are generally set below a man's capabilities, so that concern for grasping the reality of things seems to be pitched above the ordinary human level.[74] **15** Unless, perhaps, the contemplative is to be charged, not because he scorns the pursuits of humankind in such a way that he summons the mind back from the senses and (what Cicero showed to be the mark of great intelligence) distances his own thought-processes from the conventional ways of everyone else,[75] but precisely because he raises himself above the limits of the human condition.

---

[71] A corollary to the diversity of aptitudes/life-trajectories featured in 1.1.5-11: given the inevitability of such diversity ('because ... life' below), it is in practical terms impossible that all would seek to be contemplatives.

[72] I.e., the requirement of an inevitable diversity of human aptitudes and life-goals – including, for some, the vocation of contemplative celibacy.

[73] 1.1.5.

[74] In 1.4.13-14 as a whole, a fusion of at least three familiar classical ideas: (i) the energized mind rises above human torpor (13 'For ... sluggishness?'; cf., e.g., Sall. *Iug.* 1.1-4, Cic. *Fin.* 5.57); (ii) it approaches the divine by surpassing ordinary human limitations (14 'Surely ... baseness'; cf., e.g., Sen. *Ep.* 65.15-16, *Q. Nat.* 1 pref. 4-6, 9-11, 3 pref. 11, 18); and (iii) it thereby renders contemplation truly a form of serviceable 'action' (e.g., Sen. *Dial.* 8.5.6-8, esp. 8: 'even contemplation entails action'). The irreconcilable difference between contemplation and action as portrayed in 1.4.13 'But ... insult' is resolved by this stress on 'active' contemplation – itself a theme of central importance in the work (see Intro. pp. 18–19, 21, 23–4).

[75] A close adaptation of *Tusc.* 1.38: the un-philosophical mind cannot conceive of the soul as apart from the body; the idea was first grasped by intellects powerful enough 'to abstract the mind from the senses and separate thought from the force of habit' (tr. King 1945: 45).

16 Quod si sequi volueris, insectabimur[76] etiam illos qui humili loco nati stare intra maiorum suorum limites dedignantur. Incusabimus rerum maximarum repertores quia, non contenti iis quae a prioribus accepissent, conati sunt maiora quaedam perscruptari; vituperabimus quoque clarissimos imperatores et duces quia angustos rei publicae ter[15v]minos aspernati longe lateque imperium propagarunt. Quae si concedi non possunt, ut non sunt concedenda, extorquere etiam licebit eos esse reliquis anteponendos qui reliquis praestare voluerunt.

17 Neque verum est illud quod supra obiectum est, duce Aristotele: iccirco esse actionis finem quam contemplationis praestantiorem, quia ii qui civilibus implicantur rebus et quorum vita tota est in actionibus posita, curam gerentes disciplinarum, praeesse etiam contemplandi studio videantur. **18** Non enim scientiis quas praescribunt praefecti sunt, sed homini, qui tunc est imperitus quom legum latoribus subiacet: verum, quom iam evaserit egregius rerum humanarum et divinarum extimator, tum nullo indiget civitatis instituto, nullius imperio, nullius subiacet voluntati. Id enim est [16r] philosophi proprium, ut quemadmodum Aristippus dixit, ita sine legibus atque cum legibus vivat. Quare neque studium contemplandi neque ipse[77] contemplator subiectus esse cuiquam potest.

19 Ex his etiam facile Ciceroni respondemus: quod[78] si de eo homine intellexit, qui esset in re publica versaturus, plane accedo; si vero interdixit ne quis se a rebus gerendis abduceret, aperte dissentio. Si enim vita aliqua, quae in negotio sit, deligenda esset iis omnibus qui contemplatione rerum maximarum et veri cognitione delectantur, existimandum est aut finem sciendi debere esse actionem aut actionem esse quavis cognitione praestantiorem. Quorum utrunque manifeste falsum esse monstravimus et Cicero etiam ipse forsitan non negasset. Quo evenit ut neque virtutis laus omnis in ac[16v]tione consistat, neque agere quam cogitare sit pluris.

---

[76] *insert-* MS.
[77] *-ae* MS.
[78] *quor* MS.

16 If you want to pursue this point, I'll also go after those who were born of lowly rank and disdain to remain within the bounds of their forebears. I'll reproach those who made the greatest discoveries because, not satisfied with what they'd inherited from their predecessors, they made an attempt at certain more ambitious investigations. I'll also find fault with the most distinguished rulers and leaders because they rejected the narrow limits of the state and extended its power far and wide. If these things cannot be permitted (as if necessarily *not* to be permitted), it will still be possible to win this concession: those who wanted to do better than all the rest are to be more highly esteemed than all the rest.

17 Nor is there any truth to the objection lodged above under Aristotle's guidance:[79] that the end-goal of action is superior to that of contemplation because those involved in government, whose entire existence is lodged in practical activities and overseeing what gets taught, apparently control the pursuit of contemplation as well. **18** Why? Because they are in charge not of the branches of knowledge they prescribe, but of a person who is inexperienced when he is subordinate to the legislators. But once he emerges as an outstanding appraiser of matters human and divine, he at that point requires no ordinance from the state; he's subject to no one's authority, and to the will of no one. For the mark of the philosopher is such that, as Aristippus said, he thus lives without laws, and yet with laws.[80] Accordingly, neither devotion to contemplation nor the contemplative himself can be subject to anyone.

19 As a result of this, Cicero is easily answered as well.[81] If he understood his position [as solely] about a person destined for public life, I obviously agree; but if he's prohibited anyone from withdrawing from engagement in state affairs, I patently disagree. Why? If some kind of busy, practical existence were to be chosen by all those who delight in contemplating the greatest matters and in the investigation of truth, we have to suppose either that the end-goal of knowledge must be action or that action is superior to any mental investigation whatsoever.[82] I've shown that each of these options is clearly false, and even Cicero himself would perhaps not have denied as much.[83] Hence the result is that neither virtue's claim to praiseworthiness lies entirely in action, nor does being active have greater value than mental reflection.

---

[79] See 1.3.7 and n. 44.
[80] Aristippus of Cyrene (c. 435–356 BCE) was one of Socrates' followers and founder of the Cyrenaic school of hedonism (for which 3.5.14 and n. 82). Cf. D. L. 2.68: 'When asked one day what advantage philosophers enjoyed, he said, "If all the laws are repealed, we will live just as we do now"' (tr. Mensch 2018: 96).
[81] I.e., in his stress on the primacy of the active over the contemplative life (cf. 1.3.9 and n. 47).
[82] 'Action' in both cases here in the sense of practical, administrative engagement, as opposed to 'active' contemplation: see n. 74 above.
[83] Despite the superiority claimed for the active over the contemplative life at *Off.* 1.19, Cicero is less uncompromising towards the *vita contemplativa* at 1.71 and 155-6 (cf. nn. 57, 92, and see Intro. pp. 18–19); but Barbaro may also have in mind the intrinsic merits of philosophical study heralded by Cicero at, e.g., *Fin.* 5.48-54, *Tusc.* 5.9.

20 Calumniatoribus itaque iam pro virili nostra responsum est. Nos rursus paucis sententiam nostram confirmemus sic.

21 Animi nostri vim quemadmodum et Dei ex operibus eius elicimus. Quamvis enim Hunc neque videamus unquam neque sentiamus, ex rerum tamen memoria plurimarum et inventione motusque celeritate divinam quandam potestatem inesse nobis et virtutem agnoscimus. Ex quo etiam, quom multiplex sit illius vis, eam esse praecipuam existimandum est quae, quom nos a beluis separet, rerum omnium naturas discendo aut inveniendo, ut Aristoteli videtur, potest amplecti; vel, ut Platoni placet, insitas et consignatas in animis rationes et occulta vestigia recordatur: mentem dico atque illam ipsam animi sublimitatem quae ratio[**17r**]nis eiusdem diis nos immortalibus sotios fecit.[84] **22** Nam caetera quidem, corporis magnitudo, vires, firmitas, patientia, velocitas, praestantiora longe in mutis esse quam in hominibus iudicantur, adeo ut solo hoc a reliquis animantibus differamus, quia eam animi partem sumus assequuti quae nos in rerum maximarum cognitionem atque illius ipsius causae immortalis intellectum ducit. **23** Quae quom ita sint, palam esse quis dubitet[85] eam esse anteponendam vitam quae praestantiorem sibi animi partem vendicaverit? Nam activi hominis virtus in appetitu, qui cum ratione est,[86] et sensu, qui rationi paret, proculdubio

---

[84] Originally *rationis eiusdem cum diis immortalibus sotios esse nos fecit* MS, but interlinear *nos* added between *diis* and *immortalibus* and *cum* marked for deletion; *rationis eiusdem diis nos immortalibus sotios fecit* Br.
[85] *-at* MS, but interlinear *e* added above *a*.
[86] *non est* MS; but for *non* excised (Br. 67 n. 4) see my n. 88 ad loc.

20 And so my carping critics have now been answered to the best of my ability. In turn, let's consolidate my way of thinking in a few words as follows. **21** We infer our power of mind just as we do that of God as well from His works. For although we never see nor directly experience Him, we nevertheless recognize from the recollection and discovery of very many things, and from our quickness of mental operation, that a certain godlike capacity and quality of goodness reside within us. Hence also, given the versatility of that force of mind, it has to be considered exceptional – a force which, since it differentiates us from wild animals, can in Aristotle's view comprehend the essences of all things through learning or discovery; or, as Plato holds, it recalls faculties of reasoning that are planted and sealed within souls, and [recalls] hidden traces [of knowledge].[87] I mean the mind, and that very heightening of the soul that allies us with the immortal gods as sharers of the same faculty of reason. **22** For all the other attributes – body size, strength, robustness, endurance, speed – are adjudged to be far more impressive in dumb animals than in humankind, to the extent that we differ from all other creatures in this alone: we have acquired that component of the mind that guides us to comprehension of the greatest matters, and to an understanding of that immortal causal agency itself. **23** Since this is so, who would doubt the obvious point that the life that claims for itself this superior component of mind is to be preferred? Again, the quality of excellence in the active man doubtless necessarily resides in impulse, which co-exists with reason,[88] and in feeling, which is obedient to

---

[87] Barbaro here invokes the fundamental difference between (i) Plato's theory of knowledge, with learning as the 'recollection' (*anamnēsis*; cf. Barbaro's *recordatur*) of innate knowledge, and the abstract Forms or Ideas as the only reality outside time and space – the absolutely perfect exemplars of particular objects in the sensible world, and accessible only through the mind; and (ii) in rejection of the Platonic Ideas, Aristotle's view that stable ideas/forms do not exist independently of things but are immanent and comprehensible in particulars (see in overview Guthrie 1981: 100–5). Through this contrast Barbaro touches on the fundamental question of (in Frank's nice formulation, 1940: 35) 'whether the true being, God, is beyond this world and therefore also beyond the being of the philosopher himself or whether it is within himself, adequately intelligible to his own thought and intuition.' But the divine heightening of the mind in 'I mean ... reason' below is suggestively reminiscent of the climax of Arist. *EN* in particular, in anticipation of Barbaro's explicit reference to that work in 1.4.23; cf. 10.7 1177b26–78a8 with Guthrie 392–3, and esp. 1177b30–1: 'If reason is divine, then, in comparison with man, the life according to it is divine in comparison with human life' (tr. Ross 1980: 265).

[88] For *appetitus* vs. *ratio* cf. esp. Cic. *Off.* 1.101–2 ('For the power of the spirit ... is twofold: one part of it consists of impulse, called in Greek *hormē*, which snatches a man this way and that; the other of reason, which teaches and explains what should be done and what avoided. Reason therefore commands, and impulse obeys'; tr. Griffin and Atkins 1991: 39–40), 132, 141. See further n. 91 below, and cf. 3.5.10 and n. 74.

consistat est necesse. Hoc enim et a Peripateticis maxime et ab eorum, ut aiunt, coryphaeo et principe, in his libris quos ad Nicomachum de moribus scripsit, multis in locis approbatur. [17v] Contemplativi vero mens omnis atque opus in intelligendo et sciendo consumitur. Quare concluditur ratio: quanto inferior est appetitus ratione tanto activus[89] vincitur a contemplativo.

24 Quod si quandoque ratione aut cogitatione utitur is qui est in actione positus, non facit id ut activus sed ut contemplativus. Nam quemadmodum actionem plerunque et eas virtutes, quae sunt in appetitu collocatae, ab activo sumit contemplativus, ita et activus a contemplativo cogitationem mutuatur. **25** Neutrum enim sine altero esse potest vivendi genus: qualem fuisse fortassis Ciceronis sententiam est putandum, non eam quae se prima facie offert legentibus. Verum tamen alius modus est quo actione utitur contemplator, alius quo is qui agit contemplatione. **26** Nam ei, qui contemplatur, iccirco actione [18r] aliqua opus est quia fieri non potest ut earum rerum, quae tractantur, perficiatur quippiam, nisi intersit omnibus ratio et cogitatio, quibus efficitur ut prudenter agantur omnia et considerate.[90] Quare contemplativus actione utitur aliquando, activus vero contemplatione semper: et contemplativus quidem dum contemplabitur aget nihil, activus vero dum aget contemplabitur.

---

[89] *actius* MS.
[90] *-atae* MS.

reason; for this position is endorsed in many passages both by the Peripatetics in particular, and by their chorus leader (as it were) and head, in those books he wrote to Nicomachus about ethics.[91] In the contemplative's case, however, his entire mind and effort are spent on gaining knowledge and understanding. Hence the principle inferred: impulse is inferior to reason to the extent of the contemplative's superiority over the active man.

24 But if one who is established in [a life of] action ever exercises reason or reflection, he does so not as a man of action but as a contemplative; for just as the contemplative very often adopts from the active man action and those qualities of virtue that are lodged in our force of desire, so too the man of action borrows reflection from the contemplative. **25** For neither life-mode can exist without the other – the sort of opinion that we should perhaps think was Cicero's, as opposed to that which presents itself to his readers at first sight.[92] But there's nevertheless one way in which the contemplative engages in action, another in which the man of action engages in contemplation. **26** For the contemplative needs some kind of action because it can't happen that anything of the matters he deals with is carried out *unless* reason and reflection are involved in all the processes that ensure that everything is done thoughtfully and with due consideration.[93] Hence the contemplative occasionally engages in action, but the active man always in contemplation; and the contemplative will in no way be active while he contemplates, but the active man will contemplate while being engaged in action.

---

[91] So, e.g., *EN* 1.13 1102b13-1103a10, on the obedience of impulse to reason, esp. 1102b28-31: 'Therefore the irrational element also appears to be twofold. For the vegetative element in no way shares in a rational principle, but *the appetitive and in general the desiring element in a sense shares in it, in so far as it listens to and obeys it*' (tr. Ross 1980: 26-7; my emphasis).

[92] I.e., the superiority of the active over the contemplative life at *Off.* 1.19 eventually gives way to a less uncompromising position at 1.71 and 155-6 (cf. nn. 57, 83; Intro. pp. 18-19); and already at 1.19 the pursuit of learning complements *actio* by providing a break (*intermissio*) from that exertion.

[93] Barbaro's train of thought is very compressed in this sentence – unless, as Branca suspects (1969: 68 n. 2), the MS omits a phrase in the original after *opus est* to the effect of: 'For the contemplative needs some kind of action, *and the active man needs contemplation*, because ...'; 'he' just below would then refer to the active man, not the contemplative.

[5] Utra sit vita iocundior, eorumne qui in coelibatu vivunt an qui uxorem ducunt.

5.1 Hactenus haec. Nunc ordine et eam quaestionem aggrediar qua dubitari solet, utra sit iocundior vita, eorumne qui in coelibatu vivunt an qui cum uxore versantur. Primum quidem quid sit coniugium et quot et quanta exigantur brevissime aperiemus. Coniugium est viri et uxo[18v]ris ad comparandam sobolem legitime instituta coniunctio. 2 Antequam autem uxor ducenda sit inspicienda sunt quinque: mores, aetas, forma, genus, opes. Horum diligens ratio habenda est ne, si unius alicuius cura negligatur, poenitentiae et dedecoris molestiam subeamus. Uxorium vero munus tria solet requirere: mutuam perpetuamque charitatem, rei familiaris honestam curam et diligentem, vitae modestiam et probitatem. Modestia vero vultu, gestu, verbis, ornatu, victu, congressuque constat. Haec omnia latissime collegit avus meus in libris iis quos de re uxoria composuit.

3 His hunc in modum compendio praenotatis, reliquum est ut sciamus caelibum quoque duo esse genera: unum eorum qui, quom se[94] uxoriis compedibus alligari non patiantur, ad omnia impietatis flagitia proni scelerosa licentia coinquinantur; alterum eorum qui, [19r] ne ab eminentissimarum rerum contemplatione sevocetur animus aut exturbetur, eam sibi vitam delegerunt, quae ab omni molestia, praesertim uxoria, multum abesset.

---

[94] *sit* MS.

[5] Which existence is the more pleasant, that of celibates or of those who marry.

5.1 That's enough of that. Now in due sequence I'll also broach the familiar problem that considers which existence is the more pleasant, that of celibates or of those who marry. First, I'll very briefly clarify what marriage is, and the number and scale of its demands. Marriage is a lawfully sanctioned union of man and wife for the producing of offspring.[95] **2** Before a wife is to be taken, five factors warrant scrutiny: character, age, beauty, descent, and wealth. Careful consideration should be given to these so that we don't undergo the distress of regretful shame if our concern on any one of these counts is ignored.[96] Moreover, wifely duty usually has three requirements: a permanent state of shared affection; a respectable and committed devotion to family management; and a disciplined integrity in the manner of life.[97] As for that integrity, it consists in one's expression, carriage, words, attire, food and drink, and marital relations.[98] My grandfather covered all these features very extensively in those books he wrote on marriage.

3 Now that these points have been made in this concise fashion at the outset, it remains for us to know that there are also two classes of celibate. One consists of those who, since they don't allow themselves to be bound by the fetters of marriage, are disposed to all the scandals of ungodly behaviour and stained by their wicked licentiousness. The other consists of those who, to ensure that the mind is not called away from contemplating the loftiest matters or thrown into confusion, have chosen for themselves the sort of existence that's far removed from all disturbance, especially of the marital kind.

---

[95] Barbaro directly echoes the definition in his grandfather Francesco's *De re uxoria* (II.1 Griggio 2021: 180 [Gnesotto 1915-16: 28.7-8]): *est igitur coniugium viri et uxoris perpetua coniunctio procreand[a]e sobolis vel vitand[a]e fornicationis causa legitime instituta* ('Marriage, then, is the perpetual conjunction of man and wife, lawfully instituted for the procreation of offspring or for the avoidance of fornication'; tr. King 2015: 67).

[96] Barbaro replicates Francesco's listing early in *De re uxoria* of five criteria for choosing a wife (III.1 Griggio 2021: 188 [Gnesotto 1915-16: 32.14-17]): 'The ancients ... thought that a prospective wife should be judged for her character (*mores*), age ([*a*]*etatem*), descent (*genus*), beauty (*formam*), and wealth (*opes*), and that if any of these is neglected, we will certainly bring dishonour and sorrow to our families, and often grief to ourselves' (tr. King 2015: 71). See on the striking ordering of these criteria Intro. p. 16.

[97] Modeled on the three requirements listed by Francesco at *De re uxoria* X.2 Griggio 2021: 234 (Gnesotto 1915-16: 63.7-9): 'Three things, then, are required of a wife to make a marriage praiseworthy and admirable: that she love her husband; that she live virtuously; and that she manage domestic affairs soberly and diligently' (tr. King 2015: 96).

[98] Again modeled on Francesco's wording: wifely moderation 'is evident principally in a wife's expression (*vultu*), gestures (*gestu*), speech (*verbis*), dress (*ornatu*), eating (*victu*), and lovemaking (*congressu*)' (XII.1 Griggio 2021: 248 [Gnesotto 1915-16: 72.10-11]; tr. King 2015: 103).

4 Hunc postremum a nobis his libris institui putandum est, quippe qui ad bonam aliquam atque honestam consuetudinem ingenia hominum ducere pulcherrimum arbitremur. Illius vitam et mores usque adeo iocundos fore existimamus, ut cum nulla sint voluptate conferendi. **5** Nam ut reliqua vivendi genera gravissimis casibus et creberrimis fortunae incommodis obnoxia proculdubio sunt, ita noster iste caelibatus omni infestatione vacaverit, si ita se ad illum componere homines voluerint, ut a nobis per singula discurrentibus maiorumque auctoritate nitentibus erit institutum. Nihil est enim a nobis aut admonendum aut praecipiendum quod non [**19v**] sit a summis illis viris et in omni virtutum genere et scientiarum praestantissimis institutum.

6 Contra igitur sic nituntur ii qui uxoriam praeferunt voluptatem. Manifestum est, inquiunt, nihil esse generi humano commodius quam ut iunctis copulatisque mare et foemina perpetuae successionis ratio habeatur. Id enim est provisum a natura et veluti maxime cautum ne species ulla esset tam infoelix quae deficere aliquando posset. **7** Quapropter et a Platone immortales quaedam formae, quas numeros appellabat, et corpore et sensu seiunctae caelo sunt collocatae, et ab Aristotele subtiliter, ut caetera omnia, multis in locis est conclusum sempiterna esse genera oportere.

4 In sum, this latter type is to be considered my object of instruction in these books, inasmuch as I think it very beautiful to guide the human intellect to some good and respectable norms of behaviour. His existence and ways will, I think, be agreeable to the point that they defy comparison with any other source of pleasure. **5** For just as the other modes of existence[99] are doubtless vulnerable to the harshest misfortunes and to chance troubles coming thick and fast, so that state of celibacy of ours will be free of all vexation if people will want to form themselves on its model just as I shall prescribe as I range over every detail of it and rely on the guiding influence of my forebears. For no piece of advice or instruction is to be given by me that hasn't been taught by those men of the very highest distinction who are absolutely outstanding in every kind of moral excellence and branch of knowledge.

6 Conversely, then, those who prefer the pleasures of marriage argue as follows. It's clear, they say, that nothing is more in the interests of the human race than that the workings of ongoing generational succession are preserved through the union and physical coupling of male and female.[100] Nature made provision for this, as if the greatest precautions were taken to prevent any class of being from becoming so infertile that it could one day die out. **7** Hence certain everlasting forms, which he termed 'numbers,' were located by Plato in the heavens, completely set apart from the body and from sensory capacity; and Aristotle, with the same acuteness he shows in all else, drew the inference in many passages that there must be eternal orders of being.[101]

---

[99] I.e., married life and the active as opposed to the contemplative life.
[100] See 1.3.3 and n. 37. Of the voices in 'they say,' cf. after Cic. *Off.* 1.11 Francesco Barbaro early in *De re uxoria*: 'nature ... has instilled in every living species a desire for coition for the sake of reproduction, and a belief that its success consists in having reproduced' (II.2 Griggio 2021: 182 [Gnesotto 1915–16: 28.15-18]; tr. King 2015: 68).
[101] See n. 87 above. The Platonic association between Forms and numbers is fraught with challenges and complications (e.g., numbers as mathematical intermediaries between Platonic Ideas and sensible particulars, or as Ideas themselves?) that were acutely perceived by Aristotle: see Mohr 1981, esp. 622, with Rist 1989: 59–74 (on 'Forms, Numbers, and Aristotelian Development') and Guthrie 1978: 436-7.

8 Haec autem nos adeo esse concessa volumus, ut aperte fateamur necessarium esse hanc curam adhibere eos [**20r**] qui civitatibus praesunt quique ad gubernandum rei publicae statum et amplificandum imperium principes deliguntur. Nos autem non id quaerimus impraesentia ut utra sit[102] utilior sed ut utra iocundior vita et alacrior sit sciamus. **9** Quis enim nescit id esse civitati commodius quod latiorem rempublicam facit? Et nos supra confessi sumus propter vitae necessitatem fieri pleraque oportere quae minus expetuntur. Quare non de utilitate quae ad necessitatem pertinet, sed de voluptate quaerimus atque praestantia.

10 Sed iterum alii urgent, nullam esse foeliciorem dicentes vitam quam eam in qua laborum quisque suorum fructus et praemia quodammodo recognoscit; esse autem non posse expressius hanc animi voluptatem nisi cum uxore vivamus. Dubitare nemo debet: hinc enim laeta illa atque exul[**20v**]tans soboles procreatur, hinc illi ante ora parentum dulces et faceti lusus et iocundi circunquaque[103] discursus parvulorum, hinc aptae et simplices illae ridentium et balbutientium voculae plausu circunstantium atque oculis[104] parentum[105] exceptae. **11** Mox quom e cunabulis exiere, honesta quaedam indoles[106] et liberalis crescentis aetatulae ita saturat et reficit animum, ut nihil esse tam amplum aut tam honorificum et voluptuosum possit, quod spei suae, quam de liberis conceperunt, parentes anteponant. Spes enim, ut Bianti placet, rerum humanarum dulcis est comes, sed tum multo magis, ut mihi videtur, delectat quom timore vacat et metu: quod accidit in iis parentibus qui multum de liberis sperare coeperunt. **12** Illi enim ex ephebis excedentes, si expectationi responderint, non solum tranquillitatem parentibus afferunt et quie[**21r**]tem, quae proxima est ad omnem felicitatem via, verumetiam[107] et propinquorum omnium satisfaciunt votis, quibus assidue onerare solemus deos pro iis qui futuri sunt ea re tantum ornamento

---

[102] *sit sit* MS.
[103] *circun-* MS; *circum-* Br.
[104] *occ-* MS.
[105] *-um* MS; *-ium* Br., but see p. 48 above.
[106] *-is* MS.
[107] *verumetiam* MS; *verum etiam* Br.

8 I want to acknowledge these points to the extent of openly conceding that it's essential for this concern to be addressed by those who are in charge of communities and who are chosen as leaders to manage the affairs of state and to enlarge its power. But the goal of my present inquiry is not for us to know which of the two forms of existence brings more advantage, but to know which is the more agreeable and happy. **9** For who isn't well aware that what enlarges the state is more advantageous to the body politic? And I've granted above[108] that a great many things that are not very desirable have to be done because of life-necessity. Hence my inquiry is not about practical advantage, which relates to necessity, but about pleasure and preeminence.

10 But, again, others keep pressing, saying that there's no happier existence than that in which each individual in some fashion realizes the fruits and rewards of his own hard efforts; and that this mental pleasure can't be more distinctly felt unless we marry. No one should be in any doubt: it's from this that that beaming and bouncing brood of offspring is produced; from this [arise] the little ones' jovial and jocose jestings and their pleasant patterings all around before their parents' eyes; from this, the smiling and stammering children's suitably unvarnished voicings that are greeted with applause from the onlookers, and by their parents' watchful gaze. **11** Later, when they've left the cradle, a certain uprightness and nobility of disposition so abundantly fill and reinvigorate their minds as they grow into their coming-of-age that nothing can be so impressive, or bring so much honour or pleasure, that parents would prioritize it over their own hopes that they have formed for their children. For hope, as Bias thinks, is the sweet companion of human affairs;[109] but it brings much more pleasure, it seems to me, when it's free of fear and apprehension – which [sc. state of fearfulness] happens in the case of those parents who begin to form great expectations of their children. **12** For those emerging from adolescence, if they measure up to the expectations held of them,[110] not only bring their parents a calm serenity, which is the shortest path to complete happiness; but they also answer the prayers of all their relatives as well – prayers with which we're in the habit of always burdening the gods on behalf of those who are set to be a source of luster and distinction to us just because they are either related to us or as closely attached

---

[108] See 1.4.6, 8-9.
[109] Bias of Priene (first half of the sixth century BCE), one of the Seven Sages; his utterance is reported by D. L. 1.87, but with no contextualization.
[110] Perhaps gently teasing, as Zaccaria Barbaro beholds his precocious son's ambition for the celibate life.

nobis et decori, quod aut affines aut quam coniunctissimi nobis sint. **13** Quanta etiam et illa quidem maiora gaudia, quom filiorum honoribus fruimur, ex quibus alios ob singularem virtutis opinionem per ora hominum volitare, alios decreto aliquo civitatis et publico instituto in foro et in rostris statuas aut tabulas, postremo ornamentum aliquod et praerogativam meruisse videamus.

14 Qualem licet existimare Metellum illum quatuor filiis honoratum fuisse. Is enim ex iugali ista copula tanta est usus fortunae benignitate, ut praetorios et consulares filios viderit; honoribus vero, quantos conferre populus romanus[111] poterat, functus e vita migraverit. Post [**21v**] obitum quoque neque ea mediocris felicitas fuerit quod filii filiaeque nepotes et neptes in rogum honestissime[112] collachrymatum imposuerunt supervixeruntque diutissime. **15** Quare tantus est huiuscemodi consuetudinis et vitae fructus, ut ii qui ultro eo carere volunt, de hac ipsa luce, qua fruuntur, male mereri videantur. Odere nimirum se ipsos ii, quibus beatis esse quom liceat, vivere infelices velint orbati coniuge et liberis, quae praetiosissima etiam apud barbaras nationes existimantur.

[6] Solutio obiectorum.

6.1 Sed revocanda iam est oratio et veritas conquirenda, quae falsis, et tamen verisimillimis, rationibus plerumque obumbrata prope cadere de gradu solet. Nos illam, ut poterimus, in pristinam vendicabimus dignitatem.

---

[111] *-o ... -o* MS.
[112] *-ae* MS.

to us as possible. **13** How great also is that still higher pitch of joy when we delight in the distinctions conferred on our sons! Some of them we see flying about on people's lips because of their matchless reputation for excellence; we see that others have earned, by some decree of state and by official ordinance, statues or inscriptions in public places and platforms – in short, some special mark of honour and privilege.

14 We may consider the famous Metellus to have been of this sort in the distinction conferred through his four sons.[113] From that marital bond of his he experienced such a generous bounty of fortune that he saw his sons become praetors and consuls; moreover, he departed from life after enjoying the highest distinctions that the Roman people could bestow. In death, too, he enjoyed no ordinary degree of happy fortune, because his sons and daughters, grandsons and granddaughters, wept together for him in the most becoming fashion when they laid him on his funeral pyre, and they lived on after him for a very long time. **15** So great, therefore, is the reward of this sort of companionship and mode of existence that those who want of their own accord to do without it seem to deserve ill of this very life they're blessed with. They are evidently self-loathing, those who, though they are allowed to be happy, prefer to live wretchedly because they are deprived of a wife and children – assets that are thought to be most precious even among uncivilized peoples.

[6] Answering the objections.

6.1 But now my discussion is to be taken up again, and the truth sought out – a truth often obscured by misguided and yet very plausible arguments, and so it is used to being all but thrown from its proper footing. But I shall restore it to its former standing as best I can.

---

[113] The statesman and general Q. Caecilius Metellus Macedonicus, cos. 143, censor 131 BCE. For his legendary good fortune see also 1.6.7, and cf. Cic. *Fin.* 5.82, *Tusc.* 1.85, V. Max. 7.1.1.

2 Iocundam esse coniugis honestissimae et liberorum quamlibet in[**22r**]genuorum consuetudinem affirmamus; facere etiam ad parentum felicitatem bonam filiorum fortunam consentimus. Quid ni? Nam vel propinquorum secundae res delectare nos plurimum solent, sed et eorum plerunque benefactis gaudemus et calamitatibus permovemur, quos neque vidimus unquam neque cognovimus. **3** Quid? nonne et in theatro, ubi etiam ficta sunt omnia, quom Euripidis Polydorus aut Sophoclis Aiax populo recitatur, Hecubam, Teucrum et Telamonem ita plerunque misereremur ut etiam cum illis lachrymare videamur? Gladiatores quoque in arena quom manus conserere coeperunt, protinus studia spectantium scinduntur: et hi quidem acrius insistentem ignotum sibi prorsus neque visum prius in caelum laudibus tollunt eiusque virtutem et robur ultro admirantur, illi loco graviter pulsos et [**22v**] iam iam aperturos[114] hosti iugulum cum magna doloris significatione miserantur, queruntur,[115] obsecrant, clamant: veniam oppressus petat et populi clementiam imprecetur. Atque ita fit ut omne studium et amorem[116] praecipue parentum in filios magnum habere momentum nemo ire inficias audeat.

4 Sed hoc ipsum id est quod extorquere conabamur. Nihil enim est quod deterrere animum illius, qui est in maximarum rerum cogitatione versandus, a nuptiis tantum debeat quam haec tanta et tam vehemens amoris vis et benivolentiae, quae in iis accidere potissimum solet qui maxime felices ab omnibus iudicantur. Quare non solum a Stoicis, qui externa haec et quasi

---

[114] *aperit-* MS, Br.
[115] *quaer-* MS.
[116] *-em* Wi.; *amor* MS, Br., but see pp. 48–9 above.

2 I maintain that intimate companionship with a wife of the greatest respectability and with children however wellborn is a pleasant thing; I also agree that the good fortune of our sons makes for parental happiness. Why wouldn't it be so? For the success even of our relatives usually gives us the greatest pleasure, but we also often rejoice in the good deeds of people we've never seen or ever come to know, and are much upset by their misfortunes. **3** Again, even in the theater, where everything is also make-believe, when Euripides' *Polydorus* is presented to the public, or Sophocles' *Ajax*, don't we generally take pity on Hecuba, Teucer, and Telamon in such a way that we seem even to cry with them?[117] When gladiators, too, start to engage in combat in the arena, the spectators' loyalties are instantly torn.[118] Some praise to the skies a fighter who presses on more forcefully, even though he's totally unknown to them and they've never seen him before, and they spontaneously show their admiration for his manly courage and strength. Others show many outward signs of grief as they pity, protest, plead, and proclaim for those violently driven from their position and all but on the point of opening their throats to their adversary; may the beaten party seek pardon and pray for leniency from the crowd! So it is that no one would dare deny that all the devotion and love especially of parents towards their children carry great importance.

4 But this is precisely the point that I was trying to bring out forcefully. For nothing should discourage from marriage the mind of one who ought to be engaged in reflection on the highest matters as much as this force, so great and so powerful, of love and kindness – a force that usually affects those most of all who are adjudged by the world to be especially blessed.[119] Hence that

---

[117] The Euripidean play is *Hecuba*, but Barbaro's implied title stresses the tragedy of Polydorus' murder when, the youngest son of Priam and Hecuba, he was entrusted to the treacherous Thracian king Polymestor for safekeeping during the Trojan War; in revenge for Polymestor's killing of Polydorus, Hecuba blinded him. The Polydorus–Hecuba allusion thus anticipates Barbaro's stress below on 'the devotion and love especially of parents towards their children.' Then Sophocles' *Ajax*, on the tragic circumstances of Ajax's suicide and its aftermath: Teucer, Ajax's half-brother, figures in the play, but Telamon, their father, is mentioned but takes no part in the drama. In naming Telamon here, Barbaro again goes out of his way to assert the parent-child bond (cf. *Aj.* 462-6); and Teucer also stresses that bond in having Ajax's young son, Eurysaces, attend his father's body before burial (cf. 1171-81).

[118] On the anachronism of this gladiatorial allusion see Intro. p. 10.

[119] A very strained argument in its syllogistic underpinnings: (i) marital love brings what is commonly adjudged to be great prosperity (*felicitas*); but (ii) the sage disdains all such felicitous gifts of fortune as 'externals' that are irrelevant to true happiness (for the Stoic background, Long and Sedley 1987: 1.354-9); and so (iii) the sage will avoid marriage.

peregrina existimabant, verumetiam et a Potamone[120] Alexandrino, quem sequuti Peripatetici sunt, quia locum aliquem fortunae bonis assignavit, nimia illa prosperitas [23r] a vita sapientis est abacta. 5 Qua in re sapiens illud Amasis regis consilium, quod Polycrati Samiorum tyranno dedit, ad nostram usque memoriam prudentissimum perduravit. Is, quom veteri amicitia Polycrati iungeretur, per epistolam monuisse eum dicitur ne secundis rebus, quibus abundare supra modum Polycrates videbatur, nimium fideret; sibi suspectam esse tantam felicitatem et periculosam omnino videri; quare assuesceret rebus adversis, ne repentino fortunae impulsu frangeretur. Quamvis enim mali nihil unquam esset passus, tamen quom eandem ubique et semper haberet fortuna potestatem, ab usu tantum decidisse illam, non potestate putandum esse.

---

[120] *Potumene* MS.

excessive pitch of prosperity was made incompatible with the sage's existence not only by the Stoics, who viewed such things as external and as if foreign entities,[121] but also by Potamo of Alexandria, whom the Peripatetics followed because he assigned some special place to the goods of fortune.[122] **5** On this matter, that sound advice that King Amasis gave to Polycrates, tyrant of Samos, has endured in all its great wisdom right down to being remembered in our own time. Since he was bound to Polycrates by a longstanding alliance, Amasis is said to have advised him by letter not to trust too much in the prosperity that Polycrates appeared to abound in beyond measure; that so much good fortune aroused his own mistrust and seemed altogether dangerous; and that Polycrates should therefore get used to adversity, so that he wouldn't be crushed by a sudden blow of fortune. For [Amasis advised that] although he'd never experienced any hardship at all, fortune nevertheless in all cases and at all times retained the same power; hence the need to believe that she'd lapsed only from her usual practice [of whimsically changing], not from her capacity to change.[123]

---

[121] See, e.g., Cic. *Off.* 1.66 with Dyck 1996: 195–6; Sen. *Dial.* 1.6.1, *Ep.* 66.35, 74.6, 82.5 (the soul impregnable 'if it has given up external things').

[122] Potamo is described by D. L. 1.21 as the founder of an Eclectic school of philosophy, but whether that Potamo (late first/early second century CE?) is to be reconciled with a namesake located by the *Suda* in the Augustan age remains controversial (see Hatzimichali 2011: 67–72 for tentative acceptance of the identification, but cf. now Dorandi 2016). According to Diogenes, 'The end to which [Potamo] refers all things is a life made perfect in all virtue, which cannot be attained without external advantages and a body free of natural defects' (tr. Mensch 2018: 12). The distinction in Barbaro between the Stoic position on 'externals' and that of Potamo appears to hinge on the ongoing controversy in the first century BCE over (i) the Stoic sufficiency of virtue *alone* for happiness, and (ii) the further contribution to happiness made by 'external' goods (so the Peripatetics: see, e.g., Cic. *Fin.* 2.68 with Hatzimichali 132–3, and cf. 2.4.1 and nn. 76–7). Barbaro's finer point in invoking Potamo is that, even if 'externals' *are* allowed to contribute to individual happiness, that 'external' contribution is limited in extent (hence *aliquem* carries restrictive force in denoting only 'some' special place for fortune's gifts).

[123] Polycrates: tyrant of Samos *c.* 535–522 BCE; Amasis: Egyptian pharaoh of the twenty-sixth dynasty, reigning 570–526 BCE. Barbaro pointedly omits the well-known (and all too predictable) denouement of Polycrates' story when his legendary luck runs out: he was duped and horribly crucified by Oroetes, the Persian satrap of Sardis (cf. Hdt. 3.39-43, 120–5, Cic. *Fin.* 5.92, V. Max. 6.9 ext. 5).

6 Mihi vero semper eorum felicitati timendum videtur qui citra fortunam adversam repente beatissimi evaserunt. Ea nanque facillime permutantur quae sine[124] ullo labore [**23v**] adipiscuntur: difficillimum[125] siquidem ea tenere aut tueri, quae ultro quom volunt et accedunt et recedunt. **7** Quod si Metelli sibi quisque fortunam speret, (audiat Ciceronem), non cogitat ea sibi omnia posse accidere, quae si non acciderunt, non tamen de sua decidit fortuna potestate. Haec autem dici solent ab his, perinde quasi aut plures fortunati sint quam infelices, aut certi quicquam sit in rebus humanis, unde sperare prudentius sit quam timere. **8** Sed iis quoque, qui mihi Metellum obiecerunt, Priamum et P. Aemylium reiectabo: quorum alter, si Homero credimus, quinquaginta liberos nactus, e quibus septem et decem iusta uxore procreavit, infelicissimos eorum obitus et neces ante oculos foedissimas vidit; alter, quom Macedonico[126] bello consul victor rediisset, maiorem natu filium biduo ante triumphum amisit, post [**24r**] triumphum quoque secundum alterius filii funus eodem spatio interiecto extulit.

---

[124] *sint* MS.
[125] *-illime* MS; but for *-illimum* (Br. 73 n. 2) see p. 49 above.
[126] *Mac-* MS; *mac-* Br.

6 Unquestionably, it seems to me that we should always fear for the luckiness of those who, without any stroke of misfortune, have suddenly turned out very blessed. For what they acquire without any effort is very easily transformed; certainly, it's very hard to hold on to or preserve what comes and goes of its own accord when it wishes. **7** But if each hopes for himself the good fortune of Metellus[127] (let him heed Cicero),[128] he doesn't think it possible for all those accidents of chance to befall himself; if those accidents haven't yet happened, fortune nevertheless hasn't lapsed from her natural capacity [to change]. Such things[129] are usually said by these types[130] – just as if either more folk are lucky than ill starred, or there's any certainty in human affairs to make it better sense to harbor hope rather than fear! **8** But as for those too who've cited Metellus in objection to me, I'll also cast back at them Priam and Publius Aemilius.[131] The former, if we believe Homer, had fifty sons,[132] fathering seventeen in lawful wedlock,[133] but he witnessed the extreme misfortune of their deaths and their most heinous murders before his eyes. The latter, when as consul he'd returned in victory from the Macedonian War, lost his elder son two days before his triumph; after the triumph, too, and after another two-day interval, he carried to the grave his other son in a second funeral.[134]

---

[127] See 1.5.14 and n. 113.
[128] Cf. *Tusc.* 1.85, where Metellus' example is followed, as in 1.6.8 below, by the contrasting case of Priam; Cicero argues that, though people may be anguished by the prospect of being deprived in death of the good things in life (witness Metellus' happy fortune), death in fact 'removes us from evil, not from good' (1.83).
[129] I.e., wishing for Metellus' luck.
[130] I.e., the sort who 'don't think it possible for all those accidents of chance to befall themselves.'
[131] The wrong Aemilius. The true referent is L. Aemilius Paulus Macedonicus (*c.* 229–160 BCE), conqueror of King Perseus of Macedon (*c.* 212–166 BCE) at the battle of Pydna that ended the Third Macedonian War in 168 BCE ('when ... Macedonian War' below); see further n. 134 below.
[132] *Il.* 6.243-6, whence Virg. *Aen.* 2.503.
[133] Barbaro follows Cic. *Tusc.* 1.85, but cf. Hom. *Il.* 24.496 (nineteen sons so born), Theoc. *Id.* 15.139 (twenty).
[134] Barbaro modifies the Metellus–Priam contrast at *Tusc.* 1.85 to balance Metellus' four surviving sons (cf. 1.5.14) with Aemilius' loss of four sons, two by death as described here, two by adoption into other families (cf. Cic. *Tusc.* 3.70, Liv. 45.40.7, V. Max. 5.10.2, Vell. Pat. 1.10.3-5, Plut. *Aem.* 5.5, 35.1-3).

9 Plura et quotidiana, immo infinita adduci possent exempla, quibus, si persuaderi quemquam oporteret, miserrima esse huiuscemodi vita omnibus videretur. Ex iis quae sequentur maiora quaedam et propriora tractabuntur, quibus apertissimum fiet longe esse inferiorem vitam uxoriam ea, quae nunc est a nobis maxime approbata. **10** In qua re admonendos esse illos existimo, qui contrariae favent opinioni, ne sibi auxilium ullum ab exemplis petant. Non solum enim haec ratio non adiuvabit, sed etiam oberit, quom retorqueri idem in sese iaculum vehementius sentient. Et fortuna alioqui tametsi in utramque partem et varia sit et mobilissima, adversas tamen plerunque intulit calamitates, sive rei signum id sit sive ita naturae placuerit, [**24v**] ut longior esset malorum recordatio quam bonorum. Meminisse nanque ea solemus frequenter quae nobis adversa evenerunt: tenax enim tunc vel maxime memoria redditur, quom crebris fortunae impulsibus vapulamus.

11 Quamobrem et ad rem, de qua sermo erat, quandoque revertamur: optime mereri de ipsa luce qua fruuntur existimandi sunt ii qui, quo vegetior animi vis atque integrior ad contemplandam opificis illius Platonici[135] naturam et potestatem esset, uxoriam perturbationem despexerunt, neque rursus orbati coniuge et liberis et illa ipsa tam grandi et manifesta voluptate iudicandi, si et maiorem fructum ex hac vitae solitudine capiunt: et si molesti esse velint, non recte dictum putabunt orbatos se esse rerum earum quas neque unquam experti sunt et, quod pulchrius est, ultro contempserunt.

12 Deiecimus satis, ut arbitror, rationes illorum [**25r**] qui nostrae sententiae repugnabant. Nunc ad reliqua pergamus.

---

[135] *Plat-* MS; *plat-* Br.

9 Lots more everyday instances, even countless more, could be summoned by which to make it apparent to all (if anyone should need persuading) that this kind of existence is very wretched. Of the instances to follow, certain ones of greater weight and relevance will be dealt with; it will be made very clear by them that married life is far inferior to the existence that's now very much endorsed by me. **10** In this matter, I think that those favouring an opposite view should be advised not to seek any help for themselves from examples. For not only will this strategy be of no help to them, but it will even work against them, since they will experience the same shaft being hurled back at them still more forcefully.[136] And fortune, though otherwise inconstant and very capable of shifting in either direction, has nevertheless inflicted harmful disasters for the most part (whether that's the special mark of the phenomenon, or nature has so intended); and so we remember bad things longer than good ones. Certainly, it's usual for us often to recall the misfortunes that have befallen us; for the memory is caused to be even at its most retentive just when we're being thrashed by repeated blows of fortune.

11 At this point, then, let's return to the topic of our discussion. *They* are to be thought of as deserving very well of the actual life they enjoy – they who've scorned the disquiet caused by marriage so that their force of mind would be more energized and unimpaired for reflecting on the nature and capabilities of that famous Platonic demiurge.[137] Nor, on the other hand, are they to be thought of as sadly bereft of a wife and children, and of that very state of such profound and palpable pleasure, if they derive even greater gratification from this state of aloneness in life. And if they'd want to be annoying, they'll think it incorrectly said that they are *bereft* of the things that they've never experienced and – nobler still – disregarded of their own accord.

12 I've demolished well enough, I think, the arguments of those opposed to my way of thinking. Let's now hasten on to the matters that remain.

---

[136] I.e., examples of happy, fruitful marriage will always be vulnerable to the 'surfeit of prosperity' argument as deployed in 1.6.4-8; and happy examples (e.g., Metellus) are so easily countered by their opposite (e.g., Priam, Aemilius Paulus).

[137] In Plato's *Timaeus*; the lofty allusion intensifies by bathetic contrast 'the disquiet caused by marriage'.

Secundus liber incipit

[1] Prologus.

1.1 Postquam itaque duas explicavimus quaestiones, reliquum est ut ad propositum opus accingamur, et iam de ipsis vitae caelibum institutis, ad quae dudum festinat oratio, quaecunque sunt a maioribus tradita ordine universis et singulis pertractemus. **2** In quo, quemadmodum non pudebit fateri ea esse ab aliis fortasse non praetermissa, ita etiam illud ingenue audebimus polliceri, nos esse rem his libris tractaturos quae a nemine, quod sciam, in titulum operis sit unquam assumpta. In quo id me esse assequuturum credo, ut, quae partim a graecis scripta partim a latinis facere ad hanc rem videbantur palantia[1] **[25v]** atque dispersa, in corpus unum et locum veluti membra redigerem et nervis suis astricta fluere non amplius sinerem. Quod si pro viribus efficere sumus conati, mereri aliquam saltem laudem ex diligentia dubitare non possumus, non quod optime aut consummate[2] et, ut dici solet, ad unguem a nobis illa sint tradita (id enim temerarium est credere), sed quia laboris nostri, qualecunque futurum sit, praemium aliquod et fructum expectare libenter consuevimus. Sed iam rem ipsam aggrediamur.

---

[1] *pall-* MS.
[2] *consum-* MS, Br., but cf. Br.'s *consumm-* for MS *consum-* at 3.2.6, 4.1.1.

Book Two begins

[1] Prologue.

1.1 And so, now that I've clarified the two issues,[3] it remains for me to gird myself for my appointed task, and now to examine in sequence whatever has been passed down by our forebears about the actual practices (as a whole and individually) of the celibate existence – practices that my discourse has long been impatient to reach. 2 In this matter, just as there'll be no shame in admitting that such themes have perhaps not been overlooked by others, so too I shall venture candidly to affirm that I shall handle in these books a subject that, as far as I know, has never been taken up by anyone as the identifying title of a work.[4] In this, I believe my achievement will be to reduce into a single body and place the limb-like materials which, partly written by the Greeks and partly by the Latins, and scattered far and wide, seemed to fit this topic; and no longer to allow them to exist in a state of flux, held in place as they [now] are by their own sinews. If I've tried to achieve this to the extent that my abilities allow, I can't doubt that I deserve at least a modicum of praise for my efforts; not because such matters have been recorded by me very well or exhaustively and, as the saying goes, with perfect finish (for it's rash to believe that!), but because I've cheerfully got used to anticipating some reward and return, of whatever sort it may prove to be, for my hard work. But let's now set about the matter at hand.

---

[3] I.e., which life is superior, that of the active man or the contemplative? And which the more pleasant, the married or the celibate life?

[4] But titular *De coelibatu* was hardly unprecedented in combination with other phrasing, esp. in writings on clerical celibacy such as (e.g.) the exhortation *De coelibatu sacerdotum/On the celibacy of priests, c.* 1058) addressed by the reformist Benedictine Peter Damian (d. 1072/73) to Pope Nicholas II; or the 1423 *Dialogus de coelibatu ecclesiasticorum/Dialogue on the celibacy of churchmen* of the French church reformer Jean Gerson (1363–1429), itself in response to the 1417/18 *Lamentatio ob coelibatum sacerdotum/Lamentation for the celibacy of priests* of the French jurist Guillaume Saignet (*c.* 1365–1444). See further Parish 2010: 108–12 (on Damian), 136–7 (Gerson).

[2] Quid sit vita[5] caelebs et quae illius diffinitio et claritudo.

2.1 Primum autem quid sit caelebs vita diligentius perscruptantes repetamus, deinde suo quaeque ordine explicemus.

2 Caelibatus est viri boni ab omni[6] coniugii et congressus genere constans et voluntaria [**26r**] cautio ad contemplandam sine molestia naturae potestatem inventa. Quare, quia caelestis quaedam est virtus eorum et maxime divina, [eos ἠϊθέους][7] graeci, hoc est deo similes, appellaverunt. Quam rem si diligenter extimare et iuste iudicare velimus, tanta videbitur dignitas a sapientissimis illis viris caelibi attributa, ut explicari non possit quantum illorum auctoritati credendum sit, quibus hac nominis derivatione placuit vitam caelibis illustrare. **3** Aperte enim intelligi potest primos illos loquendi institutores, quibus fidem habere non mediocrem Stoici consueverunt, eius fuisse sententiae, ut ea, quae uxore careret et liberis, vita diis immortalibus conveniret. Nisi forte rerum ipsarum nomina, ut Platoni placet, naturalem habere significationem arbitremur: quod tamen et ipsum caelibatus nostri dignitatem et decus [**26v**] attestatur.

---

[5] *-ae* MS.
[6] *-is* MS, but see p. 49 above.
[7] So Br. 76 n. 1 to fill the blank in the MS.

[2] What the celibate life is, and what its definition is, and its claim to distinction.

2.1 Let's first revisit, through a rather thorough examination, just what the celibate life is, and then set out its every feature in its due sequence.
2 Celibacy is the good man's steadfast and voluntary avoidance of every kind of marriage and sexual union, devised for the purpose of pondering nature's power without vexation.[8] Hence, because theirs is a certain celestial virtuousness that is especially characteristic of a god, the Greeks called [them *ēitheous*], i.e., godlike.[9] If I'd want to consider this matter carefully and properly to assess it, the prestige accorded to the celibate by those wisest of men will be seen to be so great that it's impossible to articulate just how much faith must be placed in the weighty opinion of those who decided to give luster to the celibate life by this derivation of the term. **3** For it can be clearly understood that those first teachers of eloquence, in whom the Stoics customarily had considerable confidence, held the view that an existence free of a wife and children was fitting for the immortal gods.[10] Unless, perhaps, we're to imagine that the names of particular things have, as Plato holds, a meaning that is naturally appropriate [to the given thing] – a position that nevertheless also itself bears witness to the prestige and distinction of our state of celibacy.[11]

---

[8] For the importance of definition see 1.2.6 and n. 31.
[9] Branca 1969: 76 n. 1 invokes ἠϊθέους (properly 'unmarried youths,' LSJ ἤϊθεος 1) after Quint. *Inst.* 1.6.36, where the Gavius who is Quintilian's named source is probably the late Republican grammarian Gavius Bassus; Quintilian states that Gavius linked *caelibes* 'bachelors' with *caelites* 'gods' by analogy with ἠϊθεοι/*ēitheoi* 'young men' and θεοί/*theoi* 'gods'. Cf. also Fest. *De verb. sign.* Lindsay 1913: 38.21, Isid. *Etym.* 10.34. In a neat form of ring-composition Barbaro takes up the play on *caelebs/caelibatus* and *caelestis* late in the book (see 2.6.18 and n. 174).
[10] Cf. again Quint. *Inst.* 1.6.36: *caelibes* related to *caelites* because both bachelors and gods 'are free of the weightiest burden.' Barbaro's reference to the Stoics is presumably prompted here by their notorious zeal for etymology (see Allen 2005 with Schenkeveld and Barnes 1999: 182, and also n. 11 below).
[11] In Plato's *Cratylus* Hermogenes holds a conventionalist view of names/naming, i.e., that the assigning of names to things is arbitrary and governed by convention and agreement (see 384c-d with Sedley 2003: 51–4); by contrast, Cratylus urges naturalism, i.e., that a genuine name naturally resembles what it represents (383a-b). Plato's Socrates rejects both the conventionalist and naturalist approaches, but the dialogue nevertheless upholds certain propositions about language without challenge, among them that 'a correct name indicates the true nature of the thing named' (cf. 422d, 423e, 428e with Modrak 2001: 14–19). In the course of the proceedings, the 'science' of etymology is applied to the task of decoding names that imitate (430a) or offer a concealed description of (433a) the underlying reality. Hence Barbaro here attributes the naturalist position to Plato – one that attests to 'the prestige and distinction' of celibacy because *caelebs* is now seen to bear a pure and 'natural' etymological relation to *caelestis*.

4 Nam sive a natura, ut Achademici voluerunt, sive prudentissimorum hominum institutione, ut Peripatetici, nomina deriventur, magnae nimirum in utranque partem auctoritatis ipsa vox caelibatus est futura. Non solum autem hoc vivendi genus appellatione est a veteribus illustratum, verumetiam re ipsa atque opere mirifice est excultum. **5** Nam, ut mediocres et plebeios philosophos omittamus, Thalem Milesium et Platonem Atheniensem accepimus eam sibi vitam delegisse, quam, ut nos arbitramur, honestiorem et liberiorem esse sunt suspicati, maxime vero ad cognoscendam veritatem idoneam et opportunam. **6** Horum alter, quom assiduis propinquorum precibus sollicitaretur, adduci nunquam potuit ut animum ad nuptias applicaret; alter vero non solum uxorem non duxit, sed etiam, ut plerique[12] censuerunt, [**27r**] perpetuam pudicitiam conservavit: quo fit ut viri duo[13] praestantissimi, quom nulli se vinculo alligassent, plurimam attulerint[14] suis temporibus et posteris etiam utilitatem. **7** Nam Thales fuisse primus dicitur qui de rerum naturae principiis disserere coeperit et solis et lunae deliquium investigare; Plato vero tanta vir praestantia fuit ut non minus ingenii quam doctrinae desiderari nihil in eo homine possit: quamquam scio esse non nullos[15] qui Alexim Phoedronemque et nescio quem alium Astera Platoni

---

[12] *-isque* MS.
[13] *duo* MS; omitted by Br.
[14] *-erint* MS; *-erunt* Br.
[15] *non nullos* MS, Wi.; *nonnullos* Br., but see p. 49 above.

4 Why? Because, whether names are derived from the intrinsic nature [of a thing], as the Academics[16] wanted, or from the guiding instruction of the wisest people, as the Peripatetics have it,[17] the word 'celibacy' is itself evidently going to be of great prestige either way. But not only was this mode of life given luster by the ancients through its naming, but it was also wonderfully ennobled in actual fact and deed. **5** For, to say nothing of minor, run-of-the-mill philosophers, we're told that Thales of Miletus and Plato of Athens chose such an existence for themselves[18] – one, I think, that they surmised to be more creditable and unencumbered, but particularly suitable and convenient for the investigation of truth. **6** Of these, the one, though constantly harassed by his relatives' entreaties, could never be influenced to apply his mind to marriage.[19] The other, however, not only never married but also, in the opinion of most, remained chaste throughout his life.[20] The result is that two men of such outstanding character, since they hadn't shackled themselves to anyone, conferred the greatest possible benefit on their own and also later times. **7** For Thales is said to have been the first to begin to expound on the first principles of the natural order and to search into the solar and lunar eclipse;[21] but as for Plato, he was a figure of such preeminence that nothing could be found wanting in that man in terms as much of intellect as of learning. Admittedly, I know there are some who cite against Plato Alexis and Phoedron and someone else called Aster,[22] and there's also no shortage of people to claim that Thales was conjoined in marriage and even begat from

---

[16] Platonists; the Academy was founded in Athens by Plato in c. 387 BCE.
[17] In contrast to Academic naturalism above, Barbaro imputes a conventionalist position to the Peripatetics (for whom 1.2.6 and n. 30), but Aristotle's own position is less clear-cut. See Modrak 2001: 19 on Aristotle's advocacy of conventionalism in *Int.* 1, in that he 'grants that the relation between the written word and the spoken word and the relation between the spoken word and the psychological state (*pathēma*) the word signifies is determined by social practice ... By contrast, the relation between the notion and the thing it represents is natural; a mark of its being a natural relation is that this relation is the same for all humans.'
[18] The primacy of the celibate state is underscored by the pre-eminence of Thales (c. 624/20–548/45), in Greek tradition the first philosopher (cf. Arist. *Metaph.* 1.3 983b20-1: founder of the school of Ionian monists), and of Plato, first among philosophers (cf. 2.2.7).
[19] See for Thales Plut. *Sol.* 7.1, *Mor.* 654c, D. L. 1.26.
[20] But D. L. 3.31 alleges one Archeanassa, a courtesan of Colophon, as Plato's mistress. For male lovers also alleged, 2.2.7 and n. 22.
[21] For Thales' researches in these areas, D. L. 1.23; but there is good reason to doubt the tradition of his groundbreaking prediction of a solar eclipse in the early sixth century (cf. Hdt. 1.74.2 with Mosshammer 1981; Cic. *Div.* 1.112 with Wardle 2006: 377–9; Plin. *NH* 2.53).
[22] Cf. Apul. *Apol.* 10.8-9, D. L. 3.29, 31, both referring to Φαῖδρος/Phaedrus (miscast as Phoedron in our text).

obiiciant, non deesse etiam qui Thalem affirment coniugio copulatum atque ex uxore etiam filium Calistum nomine procreasse. Verum apud me pluris est semper eorum auctoritas qui bene de viris illustribus quam qui male scripserunt: bene enim consulunt ii qui, quom de fama aliquoius et vita contrariae sententiae circunferuntur, haerendum iis putant [**27v**] quae minus laedere quempiam videantur. **8** Sed afferre alia exempla possem quibus facile appareret quantum iis sit ab antiquitate tributum, qui ad honestum aliquem finem carere uxore voluissent. Nam de Misone minus mirum est, quem quom Apollo sapientissimum iudicasset, memoriae proditum est ita solitudinem adamasse ut non solum a coniugio deterreretur, verumetiam et studia hominum varia demiratus omnem sotietatem[23] effugeret. Quod profecto faceret unusquisque, nisi mutare consilium cogerentur.

9 Coniugia enim, ut diximus, et ad perpetuandum genus et amplificandam reipublicae gloriam et propagandam imperii successionem a philosophis atque illo ipso Platone sunt instituta, non quod aut felicior vita iugalis sit aut praestantior, sed quod ad civitatis statum idonea magis atque utilior videbatur. Neque [**28r**] putandum est ob id sensisse Platonem esse omnibus ducendas uxores, sed iis solum qui forensibus negotiis et publicis muneribus student; sicut neque Aristotelem existimare debemus caelibatum improbasse quod, quom de optimo rei publicae statu loqueretur, abigendos eos omnis[24] a

---

[23] *sot-* MS; *soc-* Br.
[24] *-es* MS, but interlinear *i* added above *e*.

his wife a son named Calistus.[25] For me, however, the authority of those who've written favourably of distinguished men is always worth more than that of ill-disposed writers: good counsel is shown by those who, when contrasting opinions about a person's reputation and life are doing the rounds, think they should stick to those opinions that seem to do a person less harm. **8** But I could bring to bear other illustrations by which it would easily be made clear how much regard the ancients paid to those who'd wanted to be free of a wife for some respectable end. For instance, there's no great surprise about Mison's case:[26] since Apollo had adjudged him the wisest of all, tradition has it that he was so enamored of being alone that he was not only put off marriage, but also avoided all communal fellowship in his wonderment at the motley enthusiasms of humankind. This is undoubtedly what each and everyone would do, were they not forced into a change of plan.

9 Marital unions, as I've said,[27] were established by philosophers and by that vaunted Plato himself for perpetuating the race, for enlarging the state's renown, and for the continuation of imperial power through generational succession – not because married life is either happier or superior, but because it seemed better suited and more advantageous to the state's circumstances.[28] Nor should you imagine on that account that Plato felt that everyone should take a wife, but only those devoted to public business and state service[29] – just as we shouldn't suppose that Aristotle condemned

---

[25] Cf. the conflicting reports in D. L. 1.26, the one that Thales married and had a son Cybisthus, the other that he remained unmarried (so 2.2.6 and n. 19) but adopted his nephew (named as Cybisthus also by Plut. *Sol*. 7.2).

[26] Myson of Chen or Chenae (*fl*. sixth century BCE), one of the Seven Sages (cf. Pl. *Prt*. 343a). If Barbaro draws here on D. L. 1.106-8, he grafts, in an approving way, the topic of non-marriage on to Diogenes' account of Myson's misanthropy. But why *Misōn* in the MS, as opposed to *Mysōn* from Gk. Μύσων? Perhaps because, in his original, Barbaro wanted to spell out the man's misanthropy in his name (cf. D. L. 1.107 μισανθρωπεῖν/*misanthrōpein*).

[27] Cf. 1.3.3, 1.5.1, 6.

[28] A likely distillation of the societal benefits of procreation in marriage as surveyed in Francesco Barbaro's *De re uxoria* (II.1-8 Griggio 2021: 180-6 [Gnesotto 1915-16: 28.1-31.15]; tr. King 2015: 67-70) – an account that itself reflects traditional ideas on the good of marriage lying 'not merely in the procreation of children, but also in the natural compact itself between the sexes' (August. *De bon. coni*. 3; tr. Walsh 2001: 7). Augustine is implicated in Ermolao's *philosophis* here, but the Platonic reference-point is surely *Republic* 5, where male-female unions in the Guardian class are carefully regulated on eugenic principles designed to produce the strongest possible next generation (see 457c-461e with Taylor 2012, esp. 76-81; for the imperative of marriage benefitting the state first and foremost cf. *Leg*. 773b-e). In the *Republic* conventional marriage within the individuated household gives way to short-term unions among the Guardians, with children held in common: part of the Platonic appeal for Barbaro here is that, since Platonic 'marriage' is itself a radical departure from Greek norms (see Taylor 81), Plato offers no endorsement of conventional marriage per se.

[29] Barbaro appears to mean here the special terms of 'marriage' that apply solely to Plato's Guardian class in *Republic* 5 (see n. 28 above).

civitate dixerit qui vel orbati et carentes liberis vel ad procreandam sobolem minus apti aut inutiles viderentur. **10** Quom enim aliquid philosophi tractant, non id in ea re quaerunt quod rebus omnibus bonum sit, sed quod ad id quod tradunt aut commodum aut necessarium videatur. Quare aperte nobis ostenditur, quom coniugia sint in re publica a maioribus instituta non ut sibi ipsis homines consulant, sed ut alienae provideant voluptati, necessitate non nobilitate rem uxoriam fuisse introductam.

11 Nam est in hac re illud tempestive dictum: aliis vivere qui uxore [**28v**] non careant, sibi ipsis vero qui careant. Et si rei ipsius naturam inspexeris, animadvertes virum, quom mulieri congreditur, de gradu prope suo decidere et, ut dici solet de iis qui se ipsis[30] minora pertractant, in abiectam quandam descendere vilitatem: foeminam contra coeundo sexus sui parvitatem excedere et perfectiori naturae coniunctam congressu virili fieri perfectiorem. **12** Unde et illud est observatum quam saepissime, eas mulieres odisse maxime solere impuros adolescentes a quibus primum sibi pudorem sublatum sciunt: e diverso autem, eos plurimum a foeminis amari consuevisse quibuscum pudicitiam primo solverunt. **13** Usque adeo efficax est huiuscemodi experimentum, ut palam omnino fiat quemadmodum foeminas ex viri congressu utilitatem capere, ita cum viris ex foeminae coniunctione male agi: quorum alterum ex [**29r**] mira illa cupiditate coeundi, quae foeminis inest, alterum ex tacita illa atque latentissima abominatione, quae turpitudinem in viro sequitur, natura videtur significasse.

---

[30] *-os* MS, Br., but see p. 49 above.

celibacy because, when speaking of the best order of the state, he said that all those were to be driven from the body politic who were seen to have lost children or never to have had them, or to be less equipped or unfit for producing offspring.[31] **10** For when philosophers deal with a given topic, they don't seek to establish in that particular case what is good for all cases, but what seems either beneficial or necessary for what they are talking about. Hence we are clearly shown that, since marital unions were established in the state by our forebears not for people to attend to their own interests but to provide for the pleasurable circumstances of others,[32] marriage was brought in by force of need, not by highness of principle.

11 Moreover, on this matter there's that opportune saying: the married live for others, but the unmarried for themselves. And if you look into the true character of the matter, you'll notice that a man, when he goes with a woman, more or less falls from his own station[33] and, as is usually said of those who deal with matters that are beneath them, he lowers himself into a certain state of sordid baseness. A woman, on the other hand, moves through intercourse beyond the slightness of her own sex; and because she is sexually conjoined with a more developed nature, she becomes more developed through union with a man. **12** Hence also the observation that's been made on every possible occasion: that unchaste young men usually have the greatest dislike for the women by whom they know their sexual innocence was first removed; by contrast, however, those men tend to be very much adored by the women with whom they first gave release to their sexual reserve. **13** Putting matters to this sort of test yields results so powerful that it's altogether common knowledge: just as women derive advantage from intercourse with a man, so men fare badly from union with a women. Of these two tendencies, nature seems to have signaled the former from that remarkable desire for intercourse that resides in women, and the latter from that quiet, very hidden sense of loathing that accompanies shameful behaviour in a man.

---

[31] Barbaro presumably refers in 'when ... state' to the *Politics*, but with imprecision: Aristotle's coverage in 7.16 of how marriage and reproduction should be regulated (1334b29-36a2) in accordance with the natural male and female impulse for procreation (cf. 1.2 1252a26-31; hence reproduction is a public service, 7.16 1335b26-9) contains none of the punitive measures that Barbaro (all too melodramatically?) attributes to him here.

[32] I.e., for the common good as articulated in 2.2.9 'Marital unions ... circumstances.'

[33] On this male 'superiority' see 1.2.5 and n. 29.

14 Verum, ut dixi, plurimum necessitas facit, ut minus etiam animadverti possit quantum ex illa coniunctione utriusque sexus virilis dignitas et excellentia minuatur. **15** Praeclaram Metelli Numidici orationem hunc in modum ad populum habitam ferunt: 'Si sine uxoribus esse possemus, Quirites, omnes equidem ea molestia libenter careremus: sed quoniam ita est a natura institutum ut neque cum illis commode neque sine illis vivere liceat, saluti perpetuae potius quam brevi voluptati consulendum est.'

16 Quae verba etiam coniugii necessitatem non praestantiam ostenderunt quemadmodum et illae Lycurgi leges quibus ignominia notabantur ii qui septem et tri[29v]ginta annos nacti sine uxore vixissent. Apud Romanos ad multam aetatem ea duravit consuetudo, ut nemini caelibem vitam ducere concessum esset, quin etiam publicis muneribus anteferebantur ii qui uxorem haberent quique liberos procreassent. Nam et Iulia lege institutum et cautum erat ut, quoniam sobole opus esse videbatur, ei qui ex consulibus prior esset sumere fasces liceret: prior autem dicebatur non qui plures annos nactus esset, sed qui aut maritus non caelebs esset aut qui plures liberos quam collega educavisset. **17** Quae omnia iccirco fuere introducta ut civitates, quae opibus et multitudine tenues admodum videbantur, liberis hominibus ampliores honestioresque redderentur. At Romanis fortasse aliud consilium fuit,

14 But, as I've said,[34] compelling need [for reproduction] very much means that it can be even less appreciated just how much a man's pre-eminent standing is reduced as a result of that union of the two sexes. 15 Metellus Numidicus is said to have made an excellent speech in this fashion before the people: 'If we could be without wives, Romans, we would indeed all gladly be free of that nuisance. But since nature has ordained that it is not permitted to live agreeably either with or without them, thought should be given to our lasting wellbeing rather than to our short-lived pleasure.'[35]

16 These words also demonstrate the need for marriage, not its superiority, as also do those laws of Lycurgus that branded with disgrace those who reached thirty-seven without marrying.[36] Among the Romans, for a considerable span of time the practice had lasted of allowing no man to lead a celibate existence; yes, and those who were married and had produced children were given precedence in offices of state. By the Julian law provision was formally made that, since there was seen to be a need for offspring, the right to carry the fasces was granted to the senior of the consuls; but the one called senior wasn't the older in years, but the one who was either married and not a bachelor, or who had reared more children than his colleague.[37] 17 All these initiatives were brought in precisely so that states that seemed rather weak in resources and population would be rendered larger in the number of their free-born people, and of better standing. But the Romans perhaps had an additional purpose: they were afraid that, if at some point the Sabines wanted to claim back their wives (after being robbed of their women and

---

[34] Cf. 2.2.9 and n. 27.
[35] I.e., the long-term wellbeing of humankind as opposed to the short-term 'pleasure' of non-marriage. For the anecdote told of Q. Caecilius Metellus Numidicus, cos. 109 BCE, censor 102, cf. Gell. 1.6.1-6. Misattribution by Gellius has been suspected (hence Manuwald 2019: 74–5 fr. 6 includes the anecdote under Q. Caecilius Metellus Macedonicus, for whom 1.5.14 and n. 113); but for Numidicus powerfully vindicated as Gellius' reference-point see already McDonnell 1987. The anecdote is recounted after Gellius by Francesco Barbaro early in *De re uxoria* (II.10 Griggio 2021: 186 [Gnesotto 1915–16: 31.26-32.3]; tr. King 2015: 70–1). Francesco offers it as one of '[m]any other rejoinders to those skeptical of marriage [that] can be adduced' (II.9 Griggio 186 [Gnesotto 31.20-1]; tr. King 70); but Ermolao modifies his grandfather's emphasis to play up instead the hint of resignation to marriage in Numidicus' words.
[36] So at least Francesco Barbaro on the legendary Spartan lawgiver Lycurgus (*fl.* seventh century BCE?) in *De re uxoria* II.3 Griggio 2021: 182 (Gnesotto 1915–16: 29.2-4); tr. King 2015: 68. For Lycurgus' incentivizing of marriage and stigmatization of bachelors cf. Plut. *Lyc.* 15.1-2, *Mor.* 227f; but it was Aristotle, *not* Lycurgus (despite Francesco's claim at *De re uxoria* IV.4 Griggio 198 [Gnesotto 39.6-9; tr. King 77]), who specified thirty-seven as the marital age for men that was most conducive to procreation (*Pol.* 7.16 1335a29).
[37] The Julian legislation was introduced in 18 BCE as part of the emperor Augustus' moral reforms to curb adultery and promote childbirth (see Frank 1975 with Lefkowitz and Fant 2005: 102–11); fundamental to it was that marriage was incumbent on Roman males aged between twenty-five and sixty, and on women aged between twenty and fifty.

verentibus ne, si quando Sabini suas repetere uxores voluissent, privati sexu et sobole, [**30r**] vim rursus inferre finitimis cogerentur.

18 Ex his omnibus perspici facillime potest maiorum nostrorum eam fuisse sententiam, ut ii qui in re publica versarentur uxorem ducerent et filios alerent: qui vero maritalem copulam attingere noluissent, a cura civilium rerum abducerentur utpote qui inutiles[38] et sint et habeantur.

19 Esse autem longe praestantiorem et pulchriorem contemplandi rationem nemo sapiens dubitavit: id autem praestare nemo perfecte potest, nisi qui se molestiis omnibus uxoriis praesertim eripiat. Neque Socratis exemplo moveri debemus, qui non solum matrimonii vinculis se addixit, verum et duas subinde eodem tempore uxores habuit. Quod tamen facilius, ut alii quoque identidem facerent, concedere potuissem, dum non[39] Xantippem alteram fuisse non ignorassem. **20** Ea, ut perhibent, [**30v**] usque adeo molesta viro fuit, ut non incommode liceat dicere ea de causa plurimarum rerum oblitum Socratem naturae perscruptationem deserere voluisse animumque ad morum et iustitiae investigationem, velut ad faciliorem quandam viam et rudiorem disciplinam, transtulisse. Is enim, quom pauca admodum sciri posse existimaret, quia perpetuae mutationi subiecta esse omnia videbat, relicta ea parte philosophiae quae [φυσική[40]] dicebatur, Archelai praeceptoris sui pauca, quae de bono et aequo primus excogitaverat, summa diligentia perquisivit in eamque potissimum curam studium omne suum contulit.

---

[38] *qui ad in-* MS.
[39] *dum non* MS, but Br. 79 n. 2 conjectures *dummodo*: see p. 49 above.
[40] Proposed by Br. 80 n. 1 to fill the blank in the MS.

offspring), they [the Romans] would be forced once again to inflict violence on their neighbors.[41]

18 From all this it can be very easily appreciated that our forebears took the view that those who engaged in public life married and raised children; but that the sort who wanted nothing to do with the marital bond would be diverted away from managing the affairs of state as being – and regarded as being – unfit for service.

19 No sage has doubted that to concern oneself with contemplation is far more distinguished and more beautiful; but no one can fully practice as much unless he rescues himself above all from all wifely annoyances. Nor should we be swayed by the example of Socrates, who not only surrendered himself to the chains of wedlock but even had two wives at one and the same time;[42] that others too would habitually do the same I could, however, have more easily granted as long as I'd known that Xanthippe wasn't one of the two. **20** She, they maintain, was so thoroughly irksome to her husband[43] that it can quite appropriately be said that, because he'd for that reason forgotten a great many things, Socrates had wanted to abandon his investigation of nature, and had turned his mind instead to examining ethical behaviour and justice, as if [turning] to a certain easier path and a more basic branch of study. For since he thought that very few things could be known because he saw that everything was subject to constant change, he abandoned the area of philosophy termed natural, and studied with the greatest attention the few ideas of his teacher Archelaus that the latter had been the first to formulate about goodness and justice; Socrates devoted the whole of his energies to this concern above all.[44]

---

[41] This allusion to the legend of the Sabine women's abduction so as to grow Rome's population soon after the city's foundation in 753 BCE is ironically charged in (i) quietly contrasting the ideals of the Julian legislation with Romulus' 'rather crude plan' (*subagreste consilium*, Cic. *Rep.* 2.12) for proto-unions in Rome; and (ii) imagining an ongoing threat of Sabine retaliation even centuries after the original outrage.

[42] Plato and Xenophon suppose one wife (Xanthippe), but the divergent tradition of two wives at once (the other reportedly Myrto, a descendant – possibly a daughter – of Aristides the Just) later in the fourth century BCE is reflected in D. L. 2.26 (cf. Arist. *De nob.* fr. 3 Ross 1955: 58–9) and Jer. *Adv. Iovinian.* 1.48 (*PL* 23.291 §316). Barbaro combats the implication (via Socrates' two wives) that philosophical contemplation is compatible with marriage by (i) asserting in 2.2.19-20 just how extremely disruptive Xanthippe was to Socrates' philosophical endeavours; and (ii) reporting in deadpan fashion the 'two wives' story that, we suspect, he already took to be an obvious fiction, on which see Woodbury 1973.

[43] The many anecdotes of Xanthippe's shrewishness (see, e.g., D. L. 2.36-7 with Saxonhouse 2018, and cf. Francesco Barbaro's *De re uxoria* II.9 Griggio 2021: 186 [Gnesotto 1915–16: 31.16-17, 20-6]; tr. King 2015: 70) were generated not least to affirm Socrates' very different tendencies (Woodbury 1973: 7 n. 1).

[44] Barbaro seemingly elaborates on D. L.'s report that natural philosophy ended with Archelaus (*fl.* fifth century) 'after Socrates had introduced ethics. Yet Archelaus seems also to have touched on ethics... But Socrates, who received the subject from him and advanced it to its <pinnacle,> was thought to be its inventor' (2.16; tr. Mensch 2018: 69). But the further implication is that Barbaro's Socrates gave up natural philosophy partly through disillusionment: Xanthippe's temperament defies the rule that 'everything [is] subject to constant change.'

21 Quod ne accidat iis, quos altiora et sublimiora tractare volumus, vitam uxoriam inprimis abegimus. Haec enim sive iocunda sit sive, ut credimus, permolesta, non multum nocere non potest eorum studio, qui se ad rerum divinissimarum [**31r**] cogitationem ab actionibus et negotiis seiunxerunt.[45] Feceris superiorem, feceris parem inferioremque quam ducturus uxorem sis: suas sibi illa vult partis, sua tempora, suas voluptates. **22** Adde, si optata proles advenerit, si natae filiorum filiarumque centuriae sint, si familia torrentis instar accreverit, quantum aversionis, quantum curarum debeatur. Abrumpitur illa vis animi et remissa mentis intentio: ita studiis omnibus detrahit, ut exhaustis ingenii viribus atque in diversa et aliena disiectis acumen, quodcunque vel arte vel natura sit partum, abeat prorsus omne atque dispereat. **23** Vix uni arti sufficere singulos experimur et abiectissimae quaeque actiones totum hominem requirere consueverunt, ut non sit difficile iudicare vacandum fuisse alienis omnibus curis eis[46] qui se ad unam illam, quam eminentissimam esse probavimus, [**31v**] componere voluerunt.

24 Quid sit itaque caelibatus, quae dignitas, quis fructus, quae veterum opinio diximus. Nunc eam partem aggrediemur quae quot et quanta caelibem vitam agentibus necessaria esse sumus arbitrati facillime declarabit.

[3] De iis quae in eo puero requiruntur qui se ad coelibatum accinget.

3.1 Quoniam vero duo sunt tempora, quibus vita omnis eorum qui sine uxore victuri sunt continetur, unum quom sub cura parentum aut propinquorum erunt, alterum quom sui iuris esse coeperunt, utrunque a nobis est pertractandum, priore quidem loco quod prius est, posteriore vero quod consequens.

2 Cogitantibus itaque nobis illud occurrit: ei, qui futurus est caelebs, in prima statim infantia parentum cura, patrimonii quantum sufficiat, corporis [**32r**] robore, ingenii felicitate opus esse. Quatuor haec, tametsi ex iis aliqua sint quae per totam vitam requirantur, quia tamen necessaria etiam in puero visa sunt, non duximus relinquenda. Sed ordine singula percurremus, donec ad eam partem, quae offitia latissime coelibis continebit, perventum fuerit.

---

[45] *se vinx-* MS.
[46] *ei* MS.

21 To prevent such a thing happening to those whom we want to be dealing with higher and loftier matters, I've ruled out married life first and foremost; for whether this is enjoyable or (as I believe) full of trouble, it cannot but significantly harm the intellectual pursuits of those who've distanced themselves from the engagements of the active life to reflect on the most divine matters. Regard the wife you're set to marry as your better, regard her as your equal or below you: she still wants her own role for herself, time to be set aside for her, pleasures to be hers. **22** Moreover, if the offspring you pray for come along, if hundreds of sons and daughters are born, if your household grows like a torrent, how much distraction there's bound to be, and how much anxiety! That power of thought of yours is shattered, and your mental concentration slackened; it takes away from all your pursuits in such a way that your mental energies are all used up and squandered in different directions and on the concerns of others, and whatever sharpness you've acquired by design or nature completely vanishes right away, and it's done for. **23** Experience tells us that individuals are scarcely equal to a single skilled pursuit, and all the most humble activities usually call for a person's undivided attention; so it's not hard to decide that those wanting to organize themselves for that one concern that we've agreed to be of the greatest distinction should steer well clear of all the concerns that are unrelated to it.

24 And so I have spoken of what celibacy is, what standing it has, what reward, and what the ancients said about it. I shall now proceed to the section that will very easily show the number and scale of the qualities that I've considered essential in those leading a celibate existence.

[3] On the qualities looked for in the boy who will ready himself for celibacy.

3.1 Since, however, there are two phases that circumscribe the entire existence of those set to live without marrying – the one when they will be cared for by parents or relatives, the other when they begin to be their own master – I must examine each of them in detail, the earlier phase in the first section, the subsequent phase in the later part.

2 Accordingly, the following presents itself to me as I reflect on the matter: right from the very start of childhood, the celibate-to-be needs the devoted attention of his parents, adequate familial resources, physical robustness, and the good fortune of having natural ability. Though some of these attributes are the kind looked for throughout an entire life, all four of them have nevertheless also seemed essential in boyhood, and so I thought they weren't to be ignored. But I shall go through them individually in sequence, until we get to the section that will offer very broad coverage of the celibate's responsibilities.

3 Dicimus autem parentum seu necessariorum operam esse maxime desyderandam iis, qui se ad coelibatus nostri puritatem accingunt. Nam si carendum esset iis dumtaxat uxore, quod impurissimorum est hominum, facile id quidem assequerentur, neque ullius auxilium expectarent: verum quia non solum id volumus, quod tamen scio quam sit difficile impetrare, iccirco ea a parentibus diligentia est exigenda sine qua parum proficere huic spei destinatus possit. [**32v**] Nisi forte divinitus nobis quispiam offeratur, qui vel sine praeceptore et duce possit ad eam, quam optamus, felicitatem emergere. **4** Quod si sperandum est, dicamus etiam nasci aliquem sapientem posse usque adeo fortunatum, ut neque ulla nutrice neque uberibus ullis illi sit opus. Quae si natura non admittit, demus parentes eam adhibere solicitudinem oportere qua pueri honestis moribus imbuantur et liberaliter educentur.

5 Nostro autem caelibi tanto id impensius praestent quanto ad difficiliora longe et spetiosiora[47] natus est. Sciant se unum ex liberis Deo similem reddituros, si neque < ... neque> in primo statim limine deterreri, quod iis solet accidere qui aut molestiam reformidant aut fieri posse desperant ut finem laboris adipiscantur: quorum utrunque parvi animi et abiectae mentis signum est. **6** Hos ego parentes mihi dari nolim, quippe qui non solum omnia [**33r**] referre ad voluptatem videantur, quae res a vita quam instituimus alienissima esse debet, sed etiam vim animi omnem ne magna atque excelsa contempletur ita tollant, ut et sibi ipsis noceant et iis qui illorum mores imitentur. Facillime autem ea discunt pueri atque imbibunt quae fieri a parentibus vident, quippe quae impune etiam facere ipsi possint.

---

[47] *-sora* MS.

3 I maintain that those readying themselves for the pure state of celibacy as we envisage it require above all the devoted efforts of their parents or close relatives. For if all they had to do without were a wife (which is characteristic of the most unchaste of men), they would easily achieve that goal, and wouldn't wait for anyone's help. But because we want not just what I nevertheless know to be so hard to attain, close attention is for that reason to be demanded from parents; without it, the boy set for this anticipated future couldn't sufficiently advance – unless, perchance, someone were revealed to us by divine agency who could rise to our desired state of bliss even without a teacher and guide. **4** If that is to be hoped for, let's also say that someone could be born wise to such a pitch of blessedness that he wouldn't need any breast-milk from any wet nurse. If nature doesn't allow such things, let's grant that parents ought to provide the sort of watchful care that would imbue their children with upright values and rear them in noble fashion.

5 The far more difficult and more impressive the goals to which he was born, the more zealously they should provide our celibate with this support. They should realize that they will cause one of their children to be like God, if neither <... nor>[48] to be put off right at the very threshold, which usually happens to those who either shrink from trouble or give up hope of possibly attaining the goal of their hard work. Each of these two attitudes signals little willpower and a despondent mindset. **6** I wouldn't want to be granted such parents, inasmuch as they not only seem to judge everything in terms of pleasure[49] (a tendency that ought to be wholly incompatible with the existence I'm prescribing); but they also do away with our entire force of mind, preventing it from contemplating great and lofty ideas in such a way that they harm both themselves and those who copy their behaviour. Children very easily learn and absorb what they see their parents doing, inasmuch as they themselves could also do those things without adverse consequences.

---

[48] The MS reading ... *si neque in primo* ... is surely incomplete, 'neither' (*neque*) requiring a complementary 'nor.' If with Branca 1969: 81 n. 2 a second *neque* is duly posited, the first *neque* clause then presupposes a missing main verb governing (i) an infinitival phrase in that first *neque* clause (to the effect of, e.g., 'they neither allow themselves to be distracted from their goal nor ...') and (ii) *deterreri* in the second *neque* clause.

[49] The phrase *omnia ... voluptatem* is Ciceronian in colour, pejorative in implication (cf., e.g., *Am.* 32, *Fin.* 2.58, 85, 90, *Nat. D.* 1.113, *Sen.* 43), imputing to such parents a negative form of Epicurean self-indulgence.

7 Quis enim nescit, ut ad id unde discessimus revertamur, fieri praeclarum aut admirabile nihil repente posse sine studio et sudore? nihil sine labore, ut inquit Sophocles, excelsum et praestans esse? Quod siquis huiuscemodi difficultatem pertimescat, existimare saltem debet uberiores fructus se esse relaturos, si ab opere et opera non cessarint. **8** Si quem ex parentibus perconcteris velitne liberos suos Persarum reges decerni, 'Quid ni?' scio responderet. [**33v**] Atqui certum esse illis potest quanto cum vitae discrimine sint istuc perventuri. Quin immo, nemo omnium erit qui sit pericula omnia detrectaturus ut filii facultatibus, et quidem non satis amplis, abundent, nedum opulentissimo regno potiantur. **9** Dubitabimus pro eo laborare qui non solum sit regibus anteponendus sed, ut saepius diximus, caelitibus et diis annumerandus? Nam et Aristippus (neque is quidem plene perfectus neque eius generis adhuc quem volumus) sese regibus praeferebat, quia solam et nudam disciplinam esset labore et vigiliis consequutus.

10 Nobis vero audendum est etiam magis qui virum bonum eundemque sapientem ab omnis congressus impuritate seiungimus: quod minime praestare voluit Aristippus. Nam habuit aetas illa, quae post Socratem est subsequuta, maximos scelerum [**34r**] et libidinis fautores: quo fit ut mirari interdum soleam eos fuisse philosophos publice[50] nuncupatos, qui a nulla re tantum quam a sapientia abhorrerent quique ab exoletis et ebrietate tantum haberentur ut studere nulli virtuti possent. **11** Ut autem verbo complectar, usque adeo depravati illius temporis mores sunt, ut sive a Theodori scholis, quem [ἄθεον[51]] appellabant, defluxisse ea vitia videantur, sive ab illo ipso Socrate praeceptore, ut minus culpa vacante, initium sumpserit voluptatis

---

[50] *-ae* MS.
[51] ἄθεον or θεόν proposed by Br. 82 n. 1 to fill the blank in the MS; see my n. 58 ad loc.

7 But to return to the point from which I digressed: who doesn't know that nothing outstanding or remarkable can all of a sudden come about without the sweat of dedicated effort? That, as Sophocles puts it, there's no lofty distinction without hard work?[52] But if anyone quails before this sort of tough challenge, he should at least consider that richer rewards will be the return if there's no holding back from work and effort. **8** If you asked a parent whether he'd want his children to be appointed kings of Persia, I know the answer would be 'Of course!' And yet they can be sure of just how much risk to life will be involved in them reaching that goal.[53] Moreover, there's no one at all who would shy away from all manner of dangers so that their children would have plenty of opportunities (opportunities that wouldn't be plentiful enough at that!), not to speak of reigning over a kingdom of extreme affluence. **9** Will we hesitate to exert ourselves for one who is not only to be esteemed more highly than kings, but, as I've said more than once,[54] is to be regarded as equal to the celestial gods? For Aristippus too – not the fully finished article, it's true, and not yet the sort of person we want[55] – exalted himself above kings on the grounds that, through hard work and watchfulness, he had achieved a unique form of unadorned knowledge.[56]

10 But we must act even more boldly in distancing the good man, and wise besides, from the sordidness of all sexual intercourse – something Aristippus didn't in the least want to bring about. For the generation that followed after Socrates had the greatest proponents of villainy and wantonness. Hence it's my habit sometimes to marvel that *they* had been publicly anointed as philosophers – the sort who were disinclined to nothing as much as to wisdom, and who were so held in the grip of debauchery and drunkenness that they couldn't apply themselves to any virtue. **11** To sum up in a word, standards of behaviour at that time were perverted to the point that, whether those vices are thought to have emanated from the followers of Theodorus (whom they called 'godless'), or from the famous teacher Socrates

---

[52] *El.* 945, Electra to her sister Chrysothemis, trying to enlist her help for the task of avenging their father Agamemnon by killing Aegisthus, his murderer (947-89).
[53] For but one sample of the ruthlessness of Persian succession see Waters 2014: 158: '[The assassinated] Xerxes [*c*. 518–465 BCE] had (at least) three sons: Darius, Artaxerxes, and Hystaspes. Artabanus [minister under Xerxes] managed to convince Artaxerxes that Darius was responsible for the assassination. Darius was brought before Artaxerxes, who put Darius to death. Artaxerxes then foiled Artabanus' plan to kill him as well; Artabanus was slain instead.'
[54] Cf. 1.4.2, 5, 14, 21; 2.2.2; 2.3.5.
[55] For Aristippus, 1.4.18 and n. 80; the dim view of him taken here recurs in 3.5.14.
[56] He 'exalted himself above kings' despite earning the soubriquet 'the royal poodle' because of his opportunistic favour-seeking in the court of Dionysius II of Syracuse (cf. D. L. 2.66).

assertio, nihil minus a graecis expectetur quam virtutis et probitatis exemplum. **12** Pudet referre quantum in perdocendo vitam cuiusque coinquinarit philosophorum impuritas, adeo nullus omnium vitio vacare et impietate visus est. Quo minus mirum esse debet si paucos invenire potuimus, et illos quidem non citra calumniam et suspitionem, [**34v**] qui aut in coniugio modeste aut in coelibatu vixerint moderate; ut Bioni Boristhenio filios et nuptias improbanti non facile dixerim quantum sit succensendum. **13** Is, tametsi sapientem se interrogante qualis esset Antigono profiteretur, scelestissimae se tamen turpitudini[57] alligavit. Taceo Archesilaum, Speusippum, Aristotelem, quorum memoriam Graecia omnis veneratur.

14 Foedum esse scio et crudele invehi in mortuos, sed bili et stomacho obtemperandum fuit. Quid erit tandem pertimescendum, aut quor non magno animo asseramus graecorum doctrinam, non mores, et verba, non facta, imitari oportere?

15 Sed quantum, dii boni, aberravimus! Aut quor non potius ad viam revertamur? Suscipiendam itaque liberorum educationem parentes boni sibi ipsis putent efficiantque ut, quemadmodum ut illi essent laborarunt, ita ut bene beateque vivant [**35r**] nullo labore deterreantur. In coelibatu autem victuris suam imprimis opem non denegent, sed ad comprimendas vitiorum omnium foeditates, praecipue vero ad contemnendam voluptatem, monitis et exemplis animent et hortentur; quibus rebus assuefactos ad capescendas

---

[57] *-pidini* MS.

himself,[58] wrongdoing became more active, pleasure began to be vindicated, and nothing was less anticipated from the Greeks than a model of virtuous uprightness. **12** It's shameful to report just how much, in their thorough teaching, the sordidness of philosophers befouled everyone's life – so true is it that no one at all seemed to be free of depravity and ungodliness. It should therefore be no wonder if we could find few cases – and those not free from malicious accusation and distrust – of those who lived either with propriety in wedlock or with restraint in celibacy; so that I can't easily express just how indignant we should be at Bion of Borysthenes when he objects to children and marriage.[59] **13** Though he declared himself a sage when Antigonus asked what sort of man he was,[60] he nevertheless devoted himself to the most abominable shamefulness.[61] I say nothing of Arc[h]esilaus, Speusippus, and Aristotle, whose memory the whole of Greece reveres.[62]

14 I know it's horribly cruel to attack the dead, but I had to submit to my splenetic vexation. What, after all, is there to be scared of, or why shouldn't we boldly assert the need to imitate the learning of the Greeks but not their behaviour, their words but not their deeds?

15 But good God! How we've gone astray! Or why not rather get us back on the proper path? Accordingly, good parents should believe that they themselves are to undertake the training of their children, and ensure that, just as they made an effort to bring them into life, so they shouldn't be deterred from making every effort for them to live good and happy lives. They shouldn't refuse their own help above all to those who are destined for the celibate life, but through their advice and example they should inspire

---

[58] Given the charge of 'depravity and ungodliness' in 2.3.12, Theodorus and Socrates both illustrate the irreligiousness that Barbaro implicitly associates with moral corruption here. Heterodoxy in terms of state religion was one of the two charges (along with corrupting the young) for which Socrates was condemned to death in 399 BCE (cf. Pl. *Ap.* 24b). For Theodorus of Cyrene (*c.* 340–250 BCE), a pupil of Aristippus the younger (grandson of the Aristippus mentioned in 2.3.9, 10), see Cic. *Nat. D.* 1.2, 63, 117, D. L. 2.86 ('Aristippus' student was Theodorus the Godless, later nicknamed God'; tr. Mensch 2018: 104), 97. Barbaro's stress on impiety suggests that the Greek word omitted in the MS was 'godless' (ἄθεον/*atheon*) – unless he preferred the more sarcastic barb of 'god' (θεόν/*theon*, as also entertained by Branca 1969: 82 n. 1; cf. D. L. 2.100).

[59] The philosopher Bion (*c.* 325–250 BCE) is fittingly adduced here through association with Theodorus and his atheistic leanings (cf. D. L. 4.52, 54); for his sardonic view of marriage, D. L. 4.48, and cf. also 3.4.3 and n. 52.

[60] Apparently extrapolated from D. L. 4.46; in old age Bion became a court philosopher of the Macedonian king Antigonus II Gonatas (*c.* 320–239 BCE).

[61] See for illustration D. L. 4.53-4.

[62] A damning silence: strong hedonistic impulses are reported of Arcesilaus (315/4–241/40 BCE, the sixth head of the Platonic Academy and founder of Academic skepticism; see D. L. 4.40-1); of Speusippus (d. 339/8, the second head of the Platonic Academy; D. L. 4.1); and even of Aristotle (D. L. 5.3-4).

disciplinas promptiores habebunt et patientiores. **16** Et ne in singulis morer, ea omnia sibi parentes proponere debebunt in hac cura, quae de liberis optime educandis sunt a veteribus pertractata. Inde enim sibi illa uberius petent, et nos, quia caeteris quoque communis est institutio, libenter alienis partibus concedemus, ea tamen conditione ut tria prius memorentur, quae observari maxime a parentibus in hac cura velim.

17 Primum est ut, a puero, liberi, qui vitam coelibem amabunt, religiosorum et proborum hominum consuetudine utantur: a quibus [**35v**] non modo nihil neque dictu neque factu turpe proveniat, sed etiam multa de Deo et eius cultu dicantur. Quorum exemplo in prima statim infantia Deum vereri assuescant imbibantque eam de omni religione et sanctimonia opinionem, quam vel sine ulla ratione firmissimam habeant et tueantur. **18** Qua propter, ut pleraque alia, in nostra civitate praeclare viget apud quosdam parentes mos, qui, quom a studiis vacandum liberis est, eos aut in urbe aut extra urbem secum ad templum aliquod, quod spatiosum et amplum sit, advehunt, ubi et iocundissime[63] cum sanctis hominibus diversentur et voluptate simul aliqua, quae aetati illi egrediendo et expatiando vel maxima est, abunde perfruantur. **19** Fit enim hoc pacto ut ab ea maxime, quam improbamus, vivendi luxurie[64] declinare animus possit et ad temperantiam pudicitiamque [**36r**] amplectendam incendi. Cavendum est enim iis ante omnia, ne luxu et deliciis praepediti a vitae innocentia et puritate abducantur. **20** Nulla nanque res est, nullum vivendi genus quod despicientiam voluptatum plus quaerat quam coelibatus: contra coelibatum nihil tantum expostulat quam despicientia voluptatum.[65] Hae obsistentibus adversantibusque tandem cedunt, quos veluti sui contemptores primum impugnare coeperant: quo fit ut si semel iis dederis manus, facile expugnari possis.

---

[63] *-ae* MS.
[64] *-ae* MS.
[65] *contra coelibatus ... despicientiam* MS, but see Br. 84 n. 2: the MS reading merely repeats the point of *nulla ... coelibatus* above.

and encourage them to stifle the abominations of every moral defect, but especially to despise pleasure. When they've made their children used to such things, they will find them readier to take instruction, and more compliant. **16** And, so as not to linger on individual details, in meeting this responsibility parents will have to set before themselves all that the ancients thoroughly discussed about the best way of rearing children.⁶⁶ For they will then pursue those [best practices] more productively for themselves; and, because this line of instruction is shared with those other authors as well, I'll gladly defer to the standpoints of others – albeit with the stipulation that I first mention the three points that I would want most to be heeded by parents in this responsibility.

17 The first is that, from boyhood, children who are set to fall in love with the celibate life experience the company of devout, upright people – the sort not just from whom nothing shameful would ever arise in word or deed, but who also say much about God and his worship. Through their example, they would become used to revering God right from early childhood, and they would drink in ideas about every aspect of religious observance and probity – ideas they would hold on to and preserve most steadfastly, even without any rational justification. **18** Hence, as in many other things, in our state some parents uphold the admirably thriving practice of taking their children with them, when they need a break from their studies, to some temple either in the city or beyond it that is impressively expansive in size; the aim is for them to spend a most agreeable time there as the guests of holy men, and at the same time to enjoy to the full a certain pleasure that that generation takes (even the greatest pleasure) in getting out and about beyond their normal bounds. **19** The result is that by this means the mind can turn its attention very much away from that indulgent mode of living I condemn, and be inspired to embrace sober chastity; for before all else they have to guard against being shackled by the comforts of luxury and drawn away from the blamelessness of an unsullied existence. **20** Certainly, there's no circumstance, no mode of living, that more seeks to despise pleasures than the celibate life; conversely, nothing demands celibacy as much as contempt for pleasures. In the end the latter give way to those who resist and oppose them – adversaries the pleasures had first begun to assail as being despisers of themselves [i.e., the pleasures]. Hence, if you once surrender to them, you could easily be swept aside by them.

---

⁶⁶ So, e.g., from different perspectives and with diverse priorities [Plut.] *De lib. educ.* (= *Mor.* 1a-14c) with Intro. pp. 13 and n. 78, 20 and n. 130; Quint. *Inst.* 1 and 2 with Bloomer 2011; Jer. *Ep.* 107 with Katz 2007.

21 Alterum, quod erat praecipiendum a nobis, est ut domi habeant praeceptorem, et illum quidem et senem et quam probatissimum. Nam doceri in scholis ad eos pertinet qui sunt inde ad forum traducendi; et alioqui multa in tanto caetu dicuntur, multa fiunt quibus adesse tuto non potest is[67] qui est vel a minima etiam turpi[**36v**]tudine revocandus. Domi quoque facilior cura morum erit et pauciores admonendi ne malo exemplo sint ei puero quem educabunt; in ludis vero publicis tot varia ingenia sunt ut necesse sit fieri aliqua inhoneste. **22** Demum peccare in scholis multi possunt; domi vero, ubi unus docendus est puer, unus tantum potest. Cum praeceptore vero neque dormiant unquam neque cum alio quopiam, sed vel cum patre vel etiam soli: nam romano quidem more neque cum soceris generi lavabantur. Scio quam notam infligam aetati nostrae, sed id quidem invitus facio. **23** Nihil enim obticendum ei fuit qui ad bene vivendum aliqua praecipiebat, in ea praesertim cura qua nihil est difficilius: verum, quia satis est quod intelligitur, non ultra quid facto opus sit explicabo, iuditio et id parentum relicturus quos esse prudentissimos volo. Tantum notasse locum et signum, [**37r**] ut aiunt, dedisse sufficiet.

24 Postremum quod est admonendum: quomodo pueri adolescere coeperunt,[68] quae aetas ad libidinem prona et accensa esse solet, curare parentes debent ne ancillae ad illorum ministeria adhibeantur. Id enim plurimi insipienter et stulte faciunt, neque ullam aetatis illius aut sexus, qui vel tum maxime virilis congressus appetentissimus est, rationem habent. **25** Qua propter famuli, et hi quidem et senes et domestici, quibus abundare

---

[67] *potestis* MS.
[68] *-erint* MS.

21 The second recommendation that I had to make is that they have a teacher at home, and for that teacher to be both elderly and as highly esteemed as possible.[69] For a school education applies to those who are to be steered from there into public life; and besides, much is said in such a large gathering-place, and much happens, that can't be safely witnessed by one who has to be summoned back from even the slightest trace of indecency. At home, too, supervising moral behaviour will be easier, and fewer will have to be warned not to set a bad example for the boy they will be rearing. In the public schools, however, there's such a motley collection of mindsets that some shameful incidents are bound to happen. **22** Finally, many can make mistakes in schools; at home, however, where only a single boy is to be taught, only that single boy can go wrong. But they should never sleep in the company of their teacher or anyone else, but either with their father or even alone; for by Roman custom sons-in-law wouldn't bathe with their fathers-in-law.[70] I know the slur I'm imposing on our times, but I do so reluctantly. **23** For nothing was to be passed over in silence by one offering a few words of instruction for living well, especially in that responsibility[71] that is unmatched in difficulty. But, because I've said enough to be understood,[72] I shall not expound further on what action is needed, set as I am on leaving that too to the judgment of parents, whom I want to exercise the greatest foresight.[73] It will be enough just to have marked the place and, as they say, to have given a signal.

24 Finally, a necessary piece of advice: as boys begin to come of age, a time that tends to be burningly bent on lust, parents should take care to ensure that maidservants aren't assigned to look after them. For very many [parents] do just that with mindless folly, paying no regard whatsoever to a maidservant's life-stage and gender, which even at that very moment has the greatest appetite for intercourse with a man. **25** For that reason, male servants should be assigned to this duty – and in fact those who are both elderly and from

---

[69] With time-honoured stress on the teacher's probity and expertise; cf. already [Plut.] *De lib. educ.* 7 (= *Mor.* 4a-b), Quint. *Inst.* 2.2.3-8 (see also 1.2 for the pros and cons of a private education at home as opposed to one at school, with all its attendant social dangers).

[70] For the custom (embarrassment thereby avoided at the display of nakedness), Cic. *Off.* 1.129; cf. *De or.* 2.224, Plut. *Cat. mai.* 20.5.

[71] Of nurturing the young celibate-to-be.

[72] I.e., about the dangers of a corrupt teacher's bad influence, a time-honoured caveat; see, e.g., Quint. *Inst.* 1.1.9 and Jer. *Ep.* 107.4 on the lingering habits instilled in the young Alexander by his *paidagōgos* Leonides.

[73] The kind of foresight memorably inculcated by [Plut.] through negative illustrations of parental conduct in *De lib. educ.* 7 (= *Mor.* 4c-5c).

familiae singulae solent, huic muneri deputentur, quibus semper haereat adolescens, a quo contra nunquam illi discedant. Sic enim illaesi servabuntur si diu senibus committantur, noctu vero parentum tutelae et fidei relinquantur. **26** Praeceptori quoque, tametsi moratissimo, voluntas peccandi, si concupiscet, et materies, si deerit occasio, abradetur: sed forte tales magistri nobis obvenient quibus [**37v**] credi liberi tuto possint. Meminisse tamen debemus cavere nemini nocuisse unquam, contra fidere profuisse raro. Parentum itaque ea inprimis[74] cura sit, ut ea, quae nobis nunc in mentem venere, praestare filiis non dedignentur.

27 Addidissem pluris rationes et exempla etiam fortiora, nisi, ut dixi, haec ut aliena pertractarem; satis fore ratus si signata haec et quasi decursa cognoscant ii qui ad beatitudinem componere liberos suos volent.

Diximus de cura a parentibus adhibenda.

[4] Quod necessariae sint facultates ei qui se a puero ad vitam coelibem comparabit.

4.1 Nunc quoniam neque satis illa proderit neque ad id quod quaerimus bonum sufficere videbitur, necessarias esse dicemus facultates iis qui se a puero huic vitae astruxerint: quamvis enim virtus sine ullo rerum externarum adminiculo suffi[**38r**]ciens sit ad bene beateque vivendum, non tamen praestare id quod volumus in coelibatu poterit quisquam nisi rebus iis affluat, quae sufficere saltem ad victum possint. **2** Neque tamen ea possidere velim

---

[74] *inprimis* MS; *in primis* Br.

within the household, the sort who are usually plentiful in each home establishment – so that the young man always stays close to them, while they, on the other hand, never depart from him. For in this way they will be kept unharmed, if they should be entrusted for a long time to the elderly, but left at night to the faithful guardianship of their parents. **26** As for their teacher as well, even though he may have a very civilized bearing, any disposition for wrongdoing (if he proves covetous) will be knocked out of him, as will any means of misbehaviour, if he's short of opportunity; but with luck we shall encounter the sort of teachers to whom children can be safely entrusted. We should nevertheless remember that being careful never harmed anyone, and, by contrast, that being trusting rarely brought advantage. And so it should be a primary parental responsibility to ensure that they don't disdain to provide their sons with the thoughts that have now entered my mind.

27 I would have added more arguments and even stronger illustrations, were it not, as I've said,[75] that I were examining these matters when they properly belong to others. I thought it would suffice if those who will want to prepare their children for happiness should get to know these points that I've marked out and (as it were) run through.

I've finished talking about the duty of care to be applied by parents.

[4] On the capacities needed by one who will prepare himself from boyhood for a celibate existence.

4.1 Now, since that [parental duty of care] will neither be sufficiently helpful nor seem adequate for the good we seek, I shall assert that there are capacities of vital importance to those who have applied themselves to this existence from boyhood. For although virtue without any support from external factors is adequate for living a good and happy life,[76] no one will be able to fulfill what we wish for in celibacy unless he abounds in the resources that can at least meet the needs of his way of life.[77] **2** I wouldn't want him, however, to

---

[75] 2.3.16.
[76] Essentially the Stoic position on despising external goods, virtue alone sufficing for happiness: see 1.6.4 and nn. 121–2.
[77] After the Stoic associations of 'For ... happy life,' Barbaro implicitly asserts the Peripatetic position on externals (cf. 2.4.3, and see 1.6.4 n. 122): the chief good of happiness (*eudaimonia*) is final (i.e., sought for its own sake: Arist. *EN* 1.7 1097a28-34) and self-sufficient (i.e., not improved by the supplementation of other goods: 1.7 1097b14-16), but happiness yet 'needs the external goods as well; for it is impossible, or not easy, to do noble acts without the proper equipment' (1.8 1099a31-3; tr. Ross 1980: 17). For this 'proper equipment' extending to life-necessities see 1.4.6 and n. 61, 1.4.8-9. Further on the attendant problems of the Aristotelian position on externals see Sharples 2007, esp. 627–33.

quae aut ipse paraverit aut lucratus fuerit, quippe qui neque mercaturae operam ullam det neque generi ulli quaestus addicatur: sed ea dumtaxat habeat quae aut patrimonii iure aut ab aliis quaesita per successionem aut quovis alio genere honestatis obvenerunt. Vacet enim necesse est omni molestia illius animus qui in unam hanc curam incumbit: nam ea quae ad virtutes et mores attinent etiam in paupere et negotioso reperies. Satis enim ii exercere videntur virtutis opera, si honeste degant.

3 Neque Peripateticis concedendum est qui virtutis nomen et gloriam ab inope auferunt quia abundare divitiis studiosos opor[**38v**]tere arbitrantur: ut enim si malus homo quid invitus egit, non est iccirco bonus putandus quia mentem non facta perpendimus, ita si vir bonus ex indigentia praestare non potest quae vellet non statim cadere a virtutis nomine est credendus. **4** Extrinsecus est enim quicquid operamur. Intrinsecus consilium et voluntas: [cuius[78]] ea laus est ut etiam si nulli effectus extent non desit tamen virtutis et probitatis nomen. Quod si munificum appellamus et liberalem non qui multa erogavit sed qui de sua facultate quod aequum sit impertiit, ut ei quidem qui plura possiderit plura etiam sint largienda, qui vero pauciora non tantundem sed ratam, ut inquiunt, partem et constitutam, quor etiam liberalem non dicamus eum qui si nihil habuerit nihil etiam dederit? Non desit tamen, si posset, benefaciendi voluntas. **5** Quam absurdum etiam illud et inhumanum est, [**39r**] quod aiunt, si is qui magnifice omnia faciebat, quom dives et locuples esset, opes et fortunas amiserit virtutem quoque debeat amisisse? Perinde quasi tum virtus sit in una quaque re, quom utilitatem capere ex ea possumus: non secus atque si Phydiae Minervam aut Praxitelis Iovem

---

[78] Conjectured by Br. 86 n. 1 to fill the blank in the MS.

have at his disposal assets that he has either obtained himself or acquired as profit, inasmuch as he puts no effort into commerce and isn't devoted to any kind of gainful occupation;[79] but he should at least have what has come his way by right of inheritance from his father or acquired from others through hereditary succession or in some other honourable way. For the mind of one who applies himself to this concern alone must necessarily be free of all vexation;[80] for you will find all that's connected with virtuous conduct also in a pauper, and in a man of affairs: they are seen to practice the tasks of virtue adequately, if they live respectably.[81]

3 Nor should we yield to the Peripatetics, who withhold from one who lacks resources any renown and distinction for virtue because they think that its devotees should be abounding in wealth.[82] For if a bad man's done something against his will, he's not for that reason to be thought of as good, because we weigh the intention, not the deeds; just so, if as a consequence of poverty a good man can't provide what he would wish, he isn't to be regarded as instantly forfeiting all reputation for virtue. 4 For whatever we busy ourselves with is external to us, but deliberation and choice are internal to us; such is [their] praiseworthiness that, even if no practical outcomes are forthcoming, a reputation for virtuous respectability nevertheless doesn't just cease to be. But if we call bountiful and generous not the man who's paid out a great deal but one who's shared what amounts to a fair proportion of his resources, to the effect that one who has more also has lavishly to give more, while the person who has less gives not the same amount but an assessed (as they say) and allotted share – why wouldn't we also call generous the person who, if he has nothing, has also given nothing?[83] His intention to do good wouldn't be wanting, however, if he had the means. 5 How ridiculous would it also be, and lacking all human feeling, so to speak, if a person who did everything on a lavish scale when he was richly affluent lost his wealth and property and necessarily forfeited his good character as well? It would be as if true excellence existed in each and every commodity only when we're able to benefit from that commodity – just as though we'd allow Phidias'

---

[79] In line with the celibate's devotion to the contemplative as opposed to the active life; cf. 1.1.9-10, 1.3.11, 1.5.3-5.
[80] Close to the wording of, and so reaffirming, 1.2.1 *Vacare autem illorum animos omni molestia et tumultu pernecessarium videbatur*.
[81] Yet for all their virtue, the pauper and the man of affairs are never free of vexation (cf. 2.4.7-8) – unlike Barbaro's contemplative celibate.
[82] A highly tendentious rendering of the Peripatetic view, for which see n. 77 above.
[83] Essentially an Aristotelian stance on liberality as defined not by the amount given but in relation to the giver's means and character (cf. *EN* 4.1 1120b7-11).

frustrari sua laude pateremur quia nullus sit illorum amplius usus et fructus, **6** aut si artificem optimum contemnamus quia aeris inopia nihil fingat, aut athletam aspernemur quia vel occupatus vel impeditus adesse olympicis certaminibus nequeat. Non sic Stilpo sensit, non sic Bias Priennaeus, quorum uterque non solum sprevere usum divitiarum, verumetiam a vita sapientis alienissimum putaverunt. In nostra enim potestate posita sunt animi bona neque ope ulla extrinsecus comparata egent.

7 Haec volui dixisse hoc loco maxime, non ab re esse [**39v**] ratus si fieret ex his manifestum non esse in coelibatu facultatibus ullis opus ad eas virtutes acquirendas, quae sunt in moribus collocatae, sed ob id esse dumtaxat expetendas opes ut nihil cogitationes illorum abduceret. Abducit autem maxime egestas et carentia facultatis. **8** Fieri enim non potest ut recte speculetur is qui victum et necessaria omnia quaeritat, quom nullam vacuam habeat vitae horam in qua possit sine molestia et mentis aversione contemplari, sed et turpe etiam est ab iis panem mendicare quibus te ipsum anteponas. Nam et eos quidem, qui negotiativam victuri sunt vitam, antequam virtutis habitum consequantur, optarem utique divites essent ne deesset iis quicquam quo fieri meliores possent. **9** Nam et praeceptores habendi sunt et hii a quibus utilitatis aliquid capiant: horum consuetudine, sine [**40r**] iis quae necessario erogantur, uti nemo poterit. Quom vero virtutem est quispiam nactus, vellem etiam adessent opes; sed si defuerint[84] nihilominus tamen de

---

[84] *-erint* MS; *-erunt* Br.

Minerva[85] or Praxiteles' Jupiter[86] to be done out of their proper praise because the original purpose and pleasure of them no longer apply; **6** or if we scorn an excellent artist because he sculpts nothing through a shortage of bronze, or we spurn an athlete because some prior commitment or obstacle means that he can't attend the Olympic games. Stilpo didn't think like this, or Bias of Priene, each of whom not only disdained the enjoyment of wealth but also thought it completely incompatible with the life of wisdom; for all the goods of the mind are placed in our power, and they need no help that's acquired from the outside.[87]

7 I very much wanted to have stated these thoughts in this context, as I felt it wouldn't be off the point if it became clear from them that, in celibacy, no particular means are needed for acquiring the good qualities found in proper behaviour, but that resources are to be looked for only to ensure that nothing distracts their thinking. Abject poverty and a complete lack of means are extremely distracting. **8** For proper mental investigation can't happen when someone is always on the lookout for food and all the bare essentials, and when he has no free hour in life when he can contemplate without vexation and any distraction of mind; but it's also shameful to go begging for bread from those you esteem less highly than yourself. Moreover, in the case of those as well who are destined for a busy life of action, before they take on the garb of virtue, I'd want them certainly to be wealthy so that they'd lack nothing that could help their improvement. **9** And teachers are needed as well, and these the sort from whom they might take some advantage; but no one will be able to benefit from interaction with such teachers unless the means are there to cover necessary expenditures. Certainly, when someone has achieved a level of merit, I'd want there to be resources at hand as well; but if they are in short supply, he'll still not fall in any way from his position

---

[85] The most celebrated of the numerous Athena/Minerva statues produced by Phidias (*fl. c.* 465–425 BCE) was the colossal Athena Parthenos on the Athenian Acropolis, for which Davison 2009: 1.69-272.

[86] No image of Zeus/Jupiter is attested for Praxiteles (for whom 1.4.9 and n. 68) – unless Barbaro alludes to Zeus' inclusion in The Twelve Gods (in the temple of Artemis Sōteira at Megara) that was 'said to be the work of Praxiteles' (Paus. 1.40.3). Barbaro may well balance Phidias with Praxiteles here to embroider his point; if so, he perhaps misattributes to Praxiteles Phidias' own famous Olympian Zeus (cf. Plin. *NH* 34.49) – a work coupled by Pliny with Phidias' Athena Parthenos at 34.54, 36.18.

[87] For Bias see 1.5.11 and n. 109. For the anecdote of him unflustered by any material loss after the capture of his native Priene because 'I carry all my possessions with me,' Cic. *Parad.* 8-9, V. Max. 7.2 ext. 3. But in the later tradition the anecdote is told of Stilpo (*c.* 360–280 BCE), the Greek philosopher of the Megarian school that prized self-sufficiency; so Sen. *Dial.* 2.5.6, *Ep.* 9.18, [Plut.] *De lib. educ.* 8 (= *Mor.* 5f), D. L. 2.115.

virtutis gradu non cadet. Perfecte vero contemplaturos hoc amplius abundare oportet ut nunquam ita deficiant res, ut dimoveri ab opere suo cogantur.

10 Quamobrem vel in hoc admonendi diligentiae studiosi parentes sunt, ut filiis hanc vitam eligentibus abunde suppeditentur omnia. Neque viventibus viventes praestare solum id velint, verumetiam et si forte prius sit sibi moriendum plurimum studere debent ut post mortem quoque sine molestia et lite filii relinquantur. **11** In hunc usum testamenta legum latores instituere ut controversiis omnibus liberati quiete viveremus: quae lex adeo viget in nostra civitate ut ii, qui intestato moriuntur, sciant se ma[**40v**]ribus partem haereditatis adempturos. Hoc enim diligens rei publicae moderator voluit ut aequa filiabus portio daretur, nisi parentes prius caverint testamento. **12** Sed quid moror in re tam facili? Neque enim parentes expecto usque adeo imprudentes ut tantae rei deesse velint: pertinere[88] ad suam vel mortuorum felicitatem filiorum secundas res arbitrentur.

13 Soleo enim libenter Aristoteli assentire praesertim quom bene sentit: haec ille dixit cui nos audacter accedimus. Sed quem potius sequar quam Homerum, omni genere disciplinarum totius Graeciae et tot etiam saeculorum consensu praestantissimum? quem imitari et nominare non solum esse utilissimum putaverunt sed etiam honorificum et gloriosum. **14** Quem sequar, inquam, potius quam Homerum quoius eam fuisse

---

[88] *-timere* MS.

of merit.[89] But those set for complete engagement in contemplation ought to be better supplied than this, so that they never experience a degree of want that forces their removal from their task.

10 Hence even in this matter parents who make every effort to be attentive need to be reminded that all resources be made plentifully available to sons who choose this existence. Nor should they want only to provide this much support to the living while they yet live; if they perchance have to die first, they must also make every possible effort to ensure that, after their death as well, their sons aren't left with any tiresome legal trouble. **11** For this purpose the legislators established wills, so that we could live in peace, with freedom from all disputes. This law is so effective in our state that those who die without making a will know they will deprive their male heirs of part of the inheritance; for the scrupulous state regulator wanted an equal share to be granted to daughters, unless parents had beforehand taken precautions against this in a will.[90] **12** But why do I linger on something so straightforward? For I don't anticipate that parents will be inadvertent to the extent of wanting to fail in so important a matter. They should reckon that their sons' prosperity is directly relevant to their own happy state even when they're gone.

13 I usually gladly agree with Aristotle, especially when he expresses a sound opinion: he said this,[91] and I confidently side with him. But whom would I sooner follow than Homer, that figure of the greatest pre-eminence in every branch of knowledge according to the general assent of Greece as a whole, and also of so many generations? To copy him and mention him by name were not only very beneficial, they thought, but also a mark of respect that enhanced their own renown. **14** Whom, I say, would I sooner follow than

---

[89] By qualifying the need for resources when positive progress has already been achieved, Barbaro reasserts the 'indifferent' status of wealth, esp. in the Stoic tradition. For poverty as an indifferent, e.g., Sen. *Ep.* 82.10-11; as no evil, *Dial.* 12.10.1-3, 12.1, *Ep.* 80.6, 123.16.

[90] If a father died intestate, Venetian statute allowed daughters to inherit, but with restrictions on the kinds of asset they could receive; there was also scope for judicial appeal if that inheritance was insufficient to provide a 'congruent' dowry equivalent to a full share in the patrimony (see Bellavitis 1998, esp. 149–50, albeit focusing on the Cinquecento merchant and bureaucratic class of *cittadini* below the patriciate). On the complex linkage between inheritance, dowries, and the problem of dowry inflation at Venice see Intro. pp. 12–13, 15–16, 27.

[91] The point distilled at 2.4.12 'They ... gone,' i.e., that the happiness of the dead is affected by the fortunes of their descendants. See *EN* 1.10-11 1100a10-1101b9 – a passage fraught with interpretational challenges, among them the problem of reconciling the popular view that the deceased are affected by the shifting fortunes of friends/descendants with the Aristotelian view that happiness is an activity (i.e., happiness is achieved through virtuous action in life) and that activities end at death (see concisely Dubois 2014).

sententiam verisimillimum est, ex iis versibus quibus mortuum Achillem apud [**41r**] inferos cum Ulixe loquentem induxit, et de Neoptolemi sui gloria diligentissime perconctantem ... Quom vero iam laudes amplissimas de filio audisset, usque adeo exultare visus est ut neque responsum quidem ullum amplius prae gaudio dederit, sed laetabundo simillimus alio se converterit surripueritque sermoni ...

15 Credo sapientissimum eruditissimumque philosophum (quor enim hoc nomine non appellem potius quam poetae?) quom gaudium patris exprimere pro dignitate non posset, responsum ademisse. **16** Cuius exemplo Thimantes ille Cy[**41v**]thnius, qui Hyphigeniae imolationem summa arte pinxit, patris caput velavit, quom nullos speraret affectus, quibus digne dolorem paternum exprimeret. Noverant enim viri prudentissimi nullam esse maiorem aut vehementiorem amoris vim, quam ea quae patris in filios est, quippe quam neque a viventium animo neque mortuorum seiungi posse iudicarent.

Homer, who had very probably been of that same opinion, to judge by the lines in which he presented the deceased Achilles talking with Ulysses in the underworld, and making the most painstaking enquiries about his own Neoptolemus' claim to glory? ...[92] Certainly, when he'd now heard the most complimentary praises of his son, he seemed so unrestrainedly overjoyed that, because of his delight, he didn't give any other reply at all, but looking very much like someone full of rejoicing, he turned elsewhere and stole himself away from the conversation ...[93]

15 I believe that the extremely wise and most learned philosopher (for why not call him by this name rather than that of poet?) dispensed with any reply because he couldn't articulate the father's joy with appropriate grandeur.[94] **16** Following his example, the well-known Timanthes of Cythnus, who depicted the sacrifice of Iphigenia with the greatest skill, veiled her father's head because he couldn't hope for any strong expressions of feeling by which appropriately to convey a father's grief.[95] For the most knowledgeable men knew that there's no greater or more powerful force of love than that of a father for his children, inasmuch as they reckoned that it could not be removed from the consciousness of either the living or the dead.

---

[92] Two-and-three-quarter lines are left blank in the MS, with 'gr.' written in the right margin, *Od.* 11.492-3 presupposed: 'But come now,/ tell me anything you have heard of my proud son, whether/ or not he went along to war to fight as a champion' (tr. Lattimore 1967: 180–1).

[93] Four lines are left blank in the MS, with 'gr.' written in the right margin, *Od.* 11.538-40 presupposed: 'So I spoke, and the soul of the swift-footed scion of Aiakos/ stalked away in long strides across the meadow of asphodel,/ happy for what I had said of his son, and how he was famous' (tr. Lattimore 1967: 182).

[94] The joyful pride that Achilles takes in Neoptolemus is by implication akin to that which the celibate's parents are to take in his achievement (and Barbaro's father in *his*?); the failure of even Homer to articulate Achilles' joy well articulates the elation to be felt at the celibate son.

[95] For Timanthes (*fl. c.* 400 BCE) and his rendering of Iphigenia's sacrifice at the hands of Agamemnon see Cic. *Orat.* 74, V. Max. 8.11 ext. 6, Quint. *Inst.* 2.13.13, and esp. Plin. *NH* 35.73-4 ('Timanthes is the only artist in whose works more is always implied than is depicted, and whose execution, though consummate, is always surpassed by his genius'; tr. Rackham 1952: 317) with O'Sullivan 2008, esp. 183–4. Barbaro's invocation of Timanthes here may be shaped in part by the contemporary humanist aesthetic of the 'veiled face' (*vultus velatus*); cf. Moffitt 2005 on the Netherlandish sculptor Claus Sluter (*c.* 1340–1406) viewed through a Timanthean lens.

17 Qua in re, ne multa fortasse exigere videar, eam esse in providendo liberis diligentiam hominibus velim quam reliquae animantes catulis suis adhibere consueverunt. Nam, ut multa et admirabilia quae in feris experimur paternae charitatis exempla omittantur, nullum est animae particeps tam inhumanum quoi[96] foetus sui non sint carissimi; neque ullum est tam ignobile et prope sensu carens animal quod rei ex se genitae curam non gerat maximam. **[42r]** Quid quod etiam in iis, quae sine motu sunt et prorsus inanima, hanc naturae providentiam deprehendimus, ut simile a similium corruptione non solum abstineat, verumetiam et conferre vim suam et opem adicere[97] videatur quo fortius sui quicque generis et validius fiat?

18 Sed et in iis, quae arte fiunt, servatur paternum nomen. Nullius enim artis est, ut aiunt, opus a se factum destruere aut delere: nam tametsi figurae[98] quam fecit pictor atramentum obducat, non tamen iccirco picturae detrahitur. Non enim delet ut pictor: idem enim vel imperitissimus quisque artis illius efficiet.

19 Plura quam instituta materia postulabat diximus, eo me hercle consilio, ut persuaderem id quod est potissimum in liberorum educatione requirendum; quod si erimus assequuti, satis superque in ea re laborasse videbimur.

---

[96] *quor* MS.
[97] *addic-* MS.
[98] *-am* MS.

17 On this matter – lest I perhaps seem to be demanding a lot – I'd want humans to show in providing for their children the attentiveness that the other animals habitually apply to their young.[99] To say nothing of many remarkable instances of fatherly affection that we find in wild animals, no living being is so heartless that his own offspring are not most precious to him; and no being is so base and all but devoid of feeling that it doesn't have the greatest concern for an entity produced from itself. Moreover, even in those creatures that lack motion and are quite lifeless, don't we detect this natural power of foresight that means that a given being not only refrains from doing harm to its own like, but also seems to exert its own energy and to apply its help so that each thing of its own kind is made stronger and more robust?[100]

18 But even among the products of craftsmanship the term 'father' still applies; for it's characteristic of no art form, they say, to destroy or efface a work produced by it. Why? Because even though a painter spreads black pigment over a drawing he's made, still there's no loss to the picture on that account. He doesn't efface it in his capacity as a painter; indeed, even all the least experienced in that craft will achieve the same result.[101]

19 I've said more than my appointed topic demanded, but with the intention, I assure you, of urging what is most needed in the rearing of children. If I'll have achieved that goal, I'll seem to have exerted myself on that subject more than adequately.

---

[99] Though Barbaro's focus is on paternal love, *animantes* is here fem. because the masculine noun commonly denotes humans, the feminine non-human animals (as also at, e.g., 1.1.3, 1.4.3, 3.6.6). The familiar idea that animals naturally feel affection for their young was importantly affirmed by Aristotle (e.g., *EN* 8.1 1155a16-21), and also by the Stoics in connection with their doctrine of 'affiliation' (*oikeiōsis*: see, e.g., Cic. *Off.* 1.11, 54 with Dyck 1996: 87 and 172-3, and cf. 3.5.1 n. 59).

[100] In Aristotelian terms, minerals are at the bottom of the *scala naturae* beneath plants; minerals and plants, because they cannot move, are distinguished from animals and humans; the capacity for growth and reproduction separates plants, animals, and (at the top of the *scala*) humans from minerals. In 'even ... lifeless,' Barbaro seemingly refers to plant reproduction for the continuity of the given species (cf. Arist. *De an.* 2.4 415a22-b2), albeit plants are distinguished from all but the simplest animals in having no function besides generation, and no association with their progeny (cf. *Hist. an.* 7[8] 588b22-589a3).

[101] I.e., in all cases the underlying design remains intact beneath the painted appearance, its intrinsic quality unaffected even if the painting process betrays a novice hand.

[5] [42v] Quod ad eum perficiendum hominem, qui caelebs sit futurus, valitudo inprimis[102] requiratur.

5.1 Nunc, quoniam satis est dictum de ea qua opus est caelibi[103] rerum affluentia, ea prosequemur quibus necessariam esse bonam valitudinem in puero ostendemus: quam rem persuaderi sibi quisque eo facilius sinet, quo latius videbit non solum iis, quos nunc instituimus, sed et aliam quampiam eligentibus vitam opus esse corporis firmitate. Sive enim in bellum profecturus, ad quem usum robur esse solet maxime requisitum, sive in re publica versaturus sis domi (nam et ea offitia quibus sibi quisque manu victum parat proculdubio incolumitatem artificis postulant) maximus erit ubique fructus sanitatis. 2 At Appius ille Claudius amissis oculis pacem cum Pyrrho dissuasurus in senatum venit et laudem est maximam hoc facto apud posteros consequ[43r]utus. Quid? si visu non caruisset nonne maiora et ampliora praeconia meruisset quod animum simul et corpus ad usum rei publicae praeservasset?

3 Nam quantum quibusdam civitatibus civium aegritudines obesse possint, hinc colligi debet, quod quom pes condoluit, ut aiunt, aut dens aut tactum aliquo dolore corpus sit, occlusis foribus domi continentur, rerum non modo privatarum sed etiam publicarum obliti et, ut dici solet, 'vel si caelum et terra consistat et ruat civitatis status non me hinc dimovebo.' 4 Quid putandum est fore, si vehementiore podagra aut ilium tormentis laborarent? Quod si tantum illud iis obest adhibendamque ob id vel magnam

---

[102] *inprimis* MS; *in primis* Br.
[103] *-ibu* MS.

[5] On good health as a primary requirement for fully fashioning a man destined for celibacy.

5.1 Now, since enough has been said about the abundant resources the celibate needs, I shall proceed to the points by which I'll show that good health is essential in the young boy. The wider the perspective with which everyone sees that it's not just those I'm now instructing who need physical robustness, but also those choosing any other sort of existence, the more easily he will allow himself to be persuaded of this matter. For whether you're set to go off to war, a deployment for which bodily strength is usually the most important requirement, or to serve in public life at home (because those services too by which each secures a livelihood for himself by his own efforts doubtless presuppose physical soundness in the skilled professional),[104] the benefits of good health will be very considerable on all fronts. **2** But[105] the famous Appius Claudius, after losing his sight, came into the senate to argue against any peace-deal with Pyrrhus, and among later generations he won very great praise for this action.[106] Well? Had he not lost his vision, would he not have earned greater plaudits, and more of them, because he'd safely preserved his mind together with his body for the state's benefit?

3 Moreover, the extent to which the illnesses of citizens can harm certain states should be inferred from the fact that, when there's foot-ache (so to speak) or toothache or the body is affected by any degree of pain, they remain cooped up at home with the doors firmly closed; they forget not just about their private affairs but also about their public ones and, as the saying goes,[107] 'Even if heaven and earth come to standstill and the state's political order collapses, I'm not budging from here.' **4** What should we imagine would happen if they were struggling with a more severe case of gout or agony in their privates? But if that does so much harm to *them* (and on that account

---

[104] After the options set out in the *sive . . . sive* clauses, the parenthesis generalizes the point beyond military and public service: *any* skilled pursuits/crafts producing a livelihood rely on a robust physical constitution.

[105] A hypothetical objection: does the example that follows of impairment overcome not suggest that physical robustness is *not* necessarily a prerequisite for success? Answer: freedom from impairment would have enhanced yet further the successes already achieved despite physical restriction.

[106] In *c*. 280 BCE Ap. Claudius Caecus (cos. 307 and 296), now aged and blind, famously persuaded the Roman senate not to make peace with Pyrrhus of Epirus after the Roman defeat at the Battle of Heraclea (see Cic. *Sen.* 16 with Powell 1988: 136 for other sources).

[107] 'If the sky falls in'; cf. Ter. *Haut.* 719, Hor. *Carm.* 3.3.7-8 with Nisbet and Rudd 2004: 40.

curam Antipater Stoicus putat iis qui viliora quam nos sunt tractaturi, ambigi non potest turbaturam etiam esse malam corporis valitudinem illius mentem et animum, qui [43v] se ad divina cogitanda cognoscendaque transferet, quando praesertim nihil esse illi cum corpore debeat, qui se a corpore, quantum fieri possit, abducat et revocet.

5 Nisi forte credendum est bonam habitudinem[108] nihil ad mentem illius pertinere, qui est ita victurus, ut cogitando dumtaxat et contemplando nihil egere sensuum offitio videatur. Quod utinam liceret concedere! Non enim illum ex hominum numero faceremus, sed, quod longe praestantius est, non Deo proximum amplius, sed Deum liberius atque honestius diceremus. **6** Verum, postquam huic addicta corporis carceri sapientis anima inexplicabilibus vinculis coercetur et veluti compedibus in custodia detinetur, multis demum modis praepeditur, necesse est uti naturae incommodis atque iis legibus subiacere,[109] quae perpe[**44r**]tua quadam potestate et sempiterna consuetudine sunt firmatae. **7** Quamvis enim in corpore animus ex se pati non possit, ea tamen quorum ministerio recordatur, extimat, imaginatur et iudicat, quia corporea sunt, laedi etiam possunt. Ex quo, quod sequens est, impeditur animi opus atque deseritur: ut enim instrumentis destituta suis ars nihil efficit, ita mens corpore perturbato suam desyderat actionem.

---

[108] Perhaps *valitud-* (Br. 90 n. 1)?
[109] *-ere* MS; *-eret* Br., but see p. 49 above.

the Stoic Antipater thinks that even a good deal of concern is to be shown to people likely to engage in far more trivial pursuits than we),[110] it can't be doubted that poor bodily health will also upset the mind and spirit of one who will apply himself to reflecting on and coming to know the divine[111] – especially since one who detaches and retrieves himself as much as he possibly can from the body ought to have nothing to do with his body.

5 Unless, perhaps, we're to believe that a good physical condition is of no concern at all to the mind of one who is set for an existence that appears to need no service of the senses, at least for reflection and contemplation. I wish it were possible to grant as much! I wouldn't count such a person as a human, but – a far greater distinction – I'd no longer call him closely cognate to God, but more freely and decorously term him God.[112] **6** However, after the sage's soul has been assigned to this bodily prison, it's bound with chains that cannot be loosened, held in confinement as if by fetters, and, in short, shackled in multiple ways.[113] It necessarily experiences nature's inconveniences and is inevitably subject to those natural rules that are reinforced by a kind of unremitting power and the customary hold of eternity. **7** For although the mind within the body can't suffer affliction from itself, those agencies that help it to remember, assess situations, conceive ideas, and make judgments are nevertheless bodily, and so they can also be injured.[114] Hence it follows that the mind's work is hampered and abandoned: for just as artistic skill that's deprived of its tools achieves nothing, so the mind falls short in its performance when the body's upset.

---

[110] I.e., 'we' contemplative types. Barbaro surely means Antipater of Tarsus (second century BCE), successor of Diogenes of Babylon as head of the Stoa at Athens, and not Antipater of Tyre (first century BCE); for given Barbaro's wider engagement in *De coelibatu* with Cicero's *De officiis* (see Intro. pp. 8, 18–19, 32), the text-book Stoic commitment to serving human fellowship that Cicero attributes to Antipater of Tarsus at *Off.* 3.52-3 is well reflected in the wide constituency for which Antipater has thought in 'even a good deal ... than we.'

[111] Essentially an Aristotelian position if the celibate contemplative's happiness presupposes the external good of bodily health (cf. *EN* 7.13 1153b17-19 with Cooper 1985, esp. 181, 188). The Stoic emphasis on virtue alone sufficing for happiness (cf. 1.6.4 and nn. 121–2; 2.4.1 and n. 76), with health then an indifferent (albeit a 'preferred' one; see Long and Sedley 1987: 1.354-9), departs from this Aristotelian view. Yet Barbaro subsequently veers in a Platonic/Stoic direction by advocating detachment from the body in 'since ... his body' immediately below (cf., e.g., Sen. *Ep.* 15.1-3, 65.22, 92.10).

[112] For the divine analogy see Intro. pp. 7, 8.

[113] For the familiar Platonic/Stoic vision of the soul's bodily incarceration cf. Pl. *Phd.* 62b, 67d, 82e; Sen. *Ep.* 65.16-17, 21, 79.12, 88.34.

[114] I.e., bodily/sensory impairment affects intellectual performance – a scenario that appears coordinated with the likely allusion to Arist. *De an.* in 2.5.8 (see n. 116 below).

8 Ipsa vero neque ob id quidem mancha est aut concisa, sed infatigabilis semper atque integrae potestatis: quanto enim altiora complectitur (non quemadmodum sensus quos excessus, ut inquit Aristoteles, effringit) tanto perfectior et absolutior redditur. **9** Quemadmodum ergo si virum fortem aut magnanimum imperatorem, quales Alexander et Themistocles et Hannibal fuisse memorantur, [**44v**] pedibus manibusque devinctis in vincula victor Darius aut Xerxes aut Scipio coniecissent, non fuerat iccirco putandum pristinae illorum virtuti aliquid fuisse detractum, sed vitam tum, aliena non sua imbecillitate, a rebus gerendis destitisse, existimandum etiam, si sui iuris esse incepissent, idem animi robur eandemque praestantiam fuisse revocaturos, ita de animo quoque sentiendum est, easdem esse illius vires ubique et potestatem, quae, si carceris onus posset excutere, mirabiles quasdam ac divinissimas ederet[115] actiones. **10** Verum, quom ita sit suo corpori alligata, ut nisi soluta compage ministerio alieno non multum egere non possit, adhibere hanc curam debemus ut corporis quaevis pars optime convalescat et sustentetur, ne praeclarissimum illud contemplandi intelligendique munus nostra negligentia praecidatur.

---

[115] *aed-* MS.

8 Yet the mind itself isn't enfeebled or crushed because of that, but is ever tireless and undiminished in power. For the loftier the ideas it embraces (unlike the senses which, as Aristotle says, are broken down by overload), the more complete it is rendered, and the more fully developed.[116] **9** If, therefore, a victorious Darius, Xerxes, or Scipio had bound hand-and-foot and thrown into chains a brave man or a greathearted leader such as Alexander, Themistocles, and Hannibal are said to have been,[117] there'd have been no need to suppose for that reason that their former courage had been diminished in any way; but rather that, at that moment, through an inability that wasn't their own but was due to outside factors, their existence ceased from managing events; and we'd also have to suppose that, if they'd begun to be their own master [again], they would have been set to recover the same strength of mind and the same preeminence. We should think of the mind, too, in the same way: its powers remain the same in all circumstances, as does its capacity, if it could throw off the burden of imprisonment, to exhibit certain modes of activity that are remarkable and most godlike in nature.[118] **10** But since the mind is bound to its body in such a way that – unless the composite structure breaks apart – it can't but have a great need of instrumental support from outside itself, we must take these pains to ensure that any part of the body whatsoever is in the very best health and very well maintained, to prevent that most distinguished calling of contemplation and gaining knowledge from being cut short through our own carelessness.

---

[116] Cf. *De an.* 3.4 429a29-b5: 'But that the perceptive and thinking faculties are not alike in their impassivity is obvious if we consider the sense organs and sensation. For the sense loses sensation under the stimulus of a too violent sensible object; e.g., *of sound immediately after loud sounds* ...; but when mind thinks the highly intelligible, it is not less able to think of slighter things, but even more able; *for the faculty of sense is not apart from the body, whereas the mind is separable*' (tr. Hett 1957: 165–7; my emphasis).

[117] A colourful sequence of pairings and hypothetical scenarios, but the historical reality is that Darius III of Persia (*c.* 380–330 BCE) was decisively defeated by Alexander the Great at the Battles of Issus (333) and Gaugamela (331); Themistocles (*c.* 524–459 BCE) led the allied Greek navy to victory at Salamis in 480 BCE over the Persians under Xerxes I; the Second Punic War ended in 201 BCE after P. Cornelius Scipio Africanus defeated Hannibal at the Battle of Zama in 202, forcing the Carthaginians to come to terms.

[118] The analogy drawn between the soul/mind undiminished during/despite its bodily imprisonment and Alexander, etc., undiminished in/despite their hypothetical captivity is diverting but hardly persuasive: whereas the emancipated soul emerges from its imprisonment fundamentally intact and unchanged, Barbaro presupposes that Alexander, etc., are immune during their incarceration to any processes of human change, deteriorating powers, or shifts of motivation and attitude over time.

11 Neque corpori [**45r**] hanc operam impendi sciamus (corporis enim parva est iactura), sed animo qui, ut inquit Empedocles, corporis habitum sequitur. Is quoque, ut meminit Aristoteles, corpore permutato prudentiam permutari dixit. Quantum Platonis ingenio favit membrorum integritas, quantum eius successoribus Lyconi Xenocratique, disciplinarum omnium instructissimis, opitulata est corporis firmitas? **12** Contra, quantum detraxit Archesilao Anaxagorae et Theodoro aegritudinis vis? Quantum Pherecydae Syri mentem concussisse verisimile est serpentum copiam ex eius toto corpore erumpentem? quo tandem morbo animam egisse illum memoriae proditum est. **13** Quid dicam de Heracleote[119]? qui, quom plurimos annos in speculando consumpsisset[120] ex renibusque, ut fit, acriter laboraret, de

---

[119] Br.'s conjecture (92 n. 1); *Heradocte* MS, but see my n. 129 ad loc.
[120] *-pissset* Br.

11 We should understand that this effort is being expended not for the body (for the loss of the body is trivial) but for the mind, which, as Empedocles says,[121] follows the condition of the body. He also said, as Aristotle recalls, that thought changes when the body undergoes change.[122] How much did Plato's soundness of body support his abilities of mind,[123] and how much did their bodily strength help his successors, Lyco and Xenocrates, the most learned exponents of all branches of knowledge?[124] **12** On the other hand, how much did the intense effect of illness take away from Arc[h]esilaus,[125] Anaxagoras,[126] and Theodorus?[127] What is the likely extent to which Pherecydes of Syros' mind was impaired by the abundance of maggots bursting forth from his entire body?[128] Tradition has it that he eventually breathed his last through that affliction. **13** What to say about the man from Heraclea?[129] He'd spent a

---

[121] See n. 122 below.

[122] Cf. Arist. *Metaph.* 4.5 1009b17-19: 'For Empedocles [*c.* 495–430 BCE] says that those who change their bodily condition change their thought: "For it is with regard to what is present that intelligence [*mētis*] grows in humans"' (D243 LM = B106 DK = T164 Graham 2010: 398-9; tr. Tredennick 1933: 185–7 with Laks and Most 2016: 567). For elucidation, Graham 429: 'Thought seems to be continuous with perception . . .; since all things are percipient, all have thought in some measure.'

[123] Cf. D. L. 3.4: originally named Aristocles, he 'studied gymnastics with Ariston the Argive wrestler, from whom he received the name Plato because of his robust constitution [from Gk. *platus* 'broad']' (tr. Mensch 2018: 135). For the legend of this derivation see also Sen. *Ep.* 58.30, Apul. *De dog. Plat.* 1.1.1 with Notopoulos 1939; cf. the Platonic relation between names and their referents in 2.2.3 and n. 11.

[124] For the athletic robustness of Lyco of Troas (*c.* 299–225 BCE; his teacher Strato of Lampsacus' successor as head of the Peripatetic school) see D. L. 5.67. Xenocrates of Chalcedon (396/5–314/13 BCE; head of the Platonic Academy from 339 to 314) was according to Diogenes 'dignified and grave of countenance' (4.6; tr. Mensch 2018: 181) and renowned for his self-restraint; his sexual continence may also commend his example to Barbaro here as elsewhere in *De coelibatu* (cf. 3.5.16 and n. 89).

[125] For whom 2.3.13 and n. 62; for his fragile health, D. L. 4.44.

[126] He lived *c.* 500–428 BCE, the first of the Presocratic philosophers to settle in Athens; charged with impiety, he is said by D. L. 2.14 to have come to court 'so weak and wasted by disease that he owed his acquittal more to pity than to the merits of his case' (tr. Mensch 2018: 68).

[127] See 2.3.11 and n. 58; but any traces of serious illness in Theodorus are hard to find in the literary record.

[128] For this version of the death of the philosopher Pherecydes (*fl.* 544 BCE; reputedly the first Greek prose writer), Plin. *NH* 7.172 with Beagon 2005: 389. Further on Pherecydes, 4.1.3 and n. 9.

[129] The Stoic Dionysius of Heraclea (*c.* 328–248 BCE), a pupil of Zeno of Citium, the school's founder. Barbaro draws here on Cic. *Tusc.* 2.60 for the story of Dionysius' abandonment, through acute illness, of the Stoic indifference to pain. He went over to the Cyrenaic view that pleasure/the absence of pain is the highest good; hence his nickname 'the turncoat' (cf. D. L. 7.37, 166; Diogenes specifies eye trouble, not kidney problems, as does Cic. *Fin.* 5.94).

sententia, quam a Zenone de dolore contemnendo didicerat, [45v] deiectus est protinus coactusque propter vim morbi de studio philosophiae male sentire. Nam quae de Possidonio et aliis compluribus memorantur, nulla aegritudine, nullo dolore, quo vel maximo articulorum distensionisque[130] laborabat, aut frangi aut a philosophando desistere potuisse, divina potius quam humana res est, neque ab omnibus ita expectanda, ut hoc exemplo nullam secundae valitudinis curam gerant. **14** Nam et is ipse, quem supra diximus[131] malorum omnium fuisse patientissimum, praeclariora longe praestantioraque edidisset[132] si nullo esset morbo afflictatus. Dolor enim, tametsi obrui virtute possit, animum tamen a vehementi[133] illa cogitationis intentione aliquantum abducit, fitque ut quandoque melius sit e vita migrare quam tot tantosque perpeti cruciatus. **15** Qua in re Cynicus[134] [46r] ille Diogenes obviam Speusippo[135] philosopho factus, qui lectica ob podagram vehebatur, salutatusque ut de via solet, salse fertur respondisse: 'At te, inquit, quor resalutem non habeo, nisi imprecer ut salvus esse non possis.'

---

[130] *distinti-* MS.
[131] *supradiximus* Br., but Br. separates off *supra* at 1.4.9, 3.6.26.
[132] *aed-* MS.
[133] *-is* MS; but for *-i* (Br. 92 n. 4) see p. 49 above.
[134] *Cycini-* MS.
[135] *Pseus-* MS.

great many years engaged in his investigations when, as tends to happen, he began to suffer intensely from kidney trouble. He was immediately thrown from the position on disregarding pain that he'd learnt from Zeno, and compelled because of the force of the disease to take a dim view of the pursuit of philosophy. As for what's said of Pos[s]idonius and several others, that they couldn't have been crushed in spirit or led to cease doing philosophy by any illness or pain (he suffered from quite the most painful swelling of his joints),[136] that's more a divine than a human property; and so there should be no expectation of it from everyone else, to the effect that, on this [divine-like] model, they show no concern for favourable health. **14** Moreover, even he himself, who I said above had been very capable of enduring all possible afflictions,[137] would have produced far more brilliant and distinguished works if he'd not been tormented by any disease. For physical pain, though it can be suppressed by courage, nevertheless diverts the mind somewhat from that energetic concentration of thought; hence it's sometimes better to depart this life than to keep putting up with so many torments of such severity.[138] **15** In this connection, the well-known Cynic Diogenes[139] ran into the philosopher Speusippus[140] when the latter was being carried in a litter because of his gout. Greeted in the usual way from the road, Diogenes is said to have wittily replied: 'But I've no reason to wish you well in return, except to pray that you can't be well.'[141]

---

[136] After invoking Cicero's Dionysius of Heraclea at *Tusc.* 2.60, Barbaro now draws on 2.61 for the contrasting example of the Stoic Posidonius of Apamea (*c.* 135–51 BCE), from an anecdote that the Roman statesman Pompey the Great (106–48 BCE) allegedly liked to tell of a visit he made in 62 to the painfully arthritic but indomitable philosopher.

[137] Cf. 2.5.13 'that they couldn't ... pain.'

[138] In line with Stoic suicide (see, e.g., Cic. *Fin.* 1.49, 3.60-1; Sen. *Ep.* 58.36, 98.16); but after drawing on *Tusc.* 2.60-1 in 2.5.13, Barbaro may here follow that source to its conclusion at 2.66-7 (death always available as a release from pains).

[139] Diogenes of Sinope, *c.* 404–323 BCE.

[140] For whom 2.3.13 and n. 62.

[141] I.e., Speusippus 'can't be well' in the sense that he is so ill that he will surely prefer to die. Speusippus indeed 'willingly ended his life'; so D. L. 4.3, rendering Diogenes' retort more straightforwardly: 'Well, I don't wish the same to you, if you can bear to stay alive in your present condition' (tr. Mensch 2018: 179).

16 Quod si ad omnes virtutes et munera obeunda incolumitas prodest, obest infirmitas, ad nos quoque pertinere arbitrabimur valitudinis curam non esse in postremis habendam. Quare partim vires exercendo, partim in victu cultuque continentiam retinendo reddendi erunt sensus validissimi et ad labores animi perferendos et ad res sine ulla molestia investigandas inveniendasque. **17** Motu enim est opus iis qui bene valere cupiunt, speculantium vero ea conditio est ut intentis nimium viribus durare parum queant in cogitando. Nam et maximus labor est [**46v**] semper contemplari, et quia immoti haec facimus et quiescentes, marcescere corpus oportebit, nisi aliqua voluptate vires reficerentur et assiduitas studiorum intermissione aliqua levaretur. Cogitantium enim pars una, et quidem quoad corpus inutiliter, exercetur; reliquae iacent suis muneribus spoliatae; quo fit ut suis offitiis exutae cogantur interire.

18 Sed plura, quam volebamus, egressi sumus paulum et quodammodo expatiati: sed quoniam et haec quoque erant utilia accomodataque ad eam partem, in qua de offitiis pertractabimus, visum est longius aliquanto provehi orationem oportere. **19** Nunc vero, ut multa in pauca conferam, qui filios in hanc spem tollent, curare debent ut quos sanos et integros susceperunt, dum suae curae credebantur, integriores, si fieri possit, efficiant. Interim crescet puer et quidem quam robustissimus, [**47r**] fietque ut sui iuris factus curam parentum imitetur sibique ipsi pater et custos sit, postremo talis evadat qualem optamus.

20 Diximus iam de cura parentum, de opibus, de valitudine, quae in prima statim aetatula adesse puero nostro debent.

16 But if physical soundness is beneficial for taking on all the qualities of excellence and our duties, and if frailty hampers us, it also matters to us, I think, that looking after our health isn't to be regarded as a lowly afterthought.[142] Hence, partly by working on our physical strength and partly by observing self-control in terms of diet and lifestyle, our faculties of perception will have to be rendered very strong both for supporting our strivings of mind and for the trouble-free exploration and discovery of things. **17** For movement is a necessity for those who wish to keep well; but for explorers of mind, their circumstances are such that, when their powers are overstretched, they are underequipped to persevere in their thinking. For constant reflection is a very great exertion,[143] and because we're motionless and at rest when we do this, the body will inevitably be enfeebled, unless its strength should be restored by some pleasurable means, and our constant engagement in our pursuits relieved by some amount of interruption. For thinkers engage only a single part of themselves, and uselessly so in terms of the body. All the other parts are idle and robbed of their functions; hence, because stripped of their duties, they are forced to fail.

18 But I've digressed somewhat in more respects than I'd wanted, going off on a certain tangent. But since even these matters, too, were beneficially suited to the section in which I'll be dealing with [the celibate's] duties,[144] it seemed necessary for my discourse to go on at somewhat greater length. **19** For now, however, to put a lot briefly, those who will raise their sons with this expectation [of celibacy] in view must take pains to ensure that they render still more vigorous (if such were possible) those they brought up healthy and vigorous while they were entrusted to their care. All the while the boy will grow, yes, and into the sturdiest possible state, to the effect that when he achieves independence he copies the devotion shown by his parents and acts as his own father and guardian to himself, and he ultimately turns out exactly as the sort we pray for.

20 I've now spoken of the parental attention, the resources, and the state of health that must attend our young boy in the very first stages of his life.

---

[142] Perhaps with a barb at the Stoic categorization of health as but a preferred indifferent (see n. 111 above).
[143] An emphasis underscoring the point that contemplation is truly 'active': see 1.4.14 n. 74 and Intro. pp. 18–19, 21, 23–4.
[144] In Book 3.

[6] Quale ingenium esse illius debeat qui caelebs sit futurus.

6.1 Age, nunc videamus quale ingenium esse illius debeat: in quo quamquam scio ea omnia esse requirenda quae a diligentissimis auctoribus sunt declarata, hoc tamen amplius illis addendum fuit, ut, quoniam difficiliorem quam ut negligentius aliqua pertractentur finem exigimus, accuratius quoque ea omnia, quae ad rem nostram faciebant, aut nondum plene praecepta aut obscurius tradita, in clariorem distinctioremque modum redigerentur. Sed de re iam agamus.

2 In iis, qui in re publica [**47v**] versari volunt, varium desideratur ingenium. Non modo enim natura mites et placidi intromittendi sunt, verum et severiores quosdam et propemodum asperos intermiscere[145] oportet: ex quorum facto veluti corpore civitas constet. Fit enim ut ex hac hominum varietate non solum augeatur, sed etiam illustretur atque splendescat. **3** Quapropter alios ad militiam promptos, alios domi utiliores futuros, plerosque[146] utrunque complexos invenies in magna et excellenti republica, ut si opus fortitudinis, si consilii fuerit, praesto sit qui navare operam possit, et si placabilitatis usus sit quispiam aut misericordiae domi habeas quos huic praeficias muneri, contra si gravitate aut supercilio sit utendum non desint qui et huic utilitati deserviant. Ita fit ut in omnem casum [**48r**] servare reipublicae maiestatem et custodire imperii gloriam possint. **4** Quam delectat non nullos illius temporis recordatio in quo Themistocles et Aristides diversis in eundem finem studiis in re publica versabantur! Ille quidem gloriosus et ad populi favorem inclinatus humanitate omnium animos sibi devinciebat, alter contra rigens et minime ambitiosus iustitia maxime nitebatur: atque

---

[145] *intro-* MS, but interlinear *e* added above *tr*.
[146] *plaer-* MS.

[6] The kind of disposition needed in the celibate-to-be.

6.1 Come, let's now consider the kind of natural disposition he must have. Although I know that all the qualities that have been set out by the most painstaking authors are to be sought in him, this further addition nevertheless had to be made to them for the following purpose: since I've set a goal that's too challenging for anything to be dealt with at all carelessly, all the factors that were useful to my topic – factors either not yet fully propounded or not very visible in their transmission – should also be brought with more precision into a clearer, better defined form. But let's now engage with the matter at hand.

2 Different kinds of disposition are needed in those who want to engage in public life.[147] For not only are those of a gentle and peaceful nature to be admitted, but certain harsher types and virtual ruffians should also be added to the mix so that the state consists of the body, as it were, formed from those [mixed natures]; for this diversity of types causes the state not just to grow stronger, but also to shine with a brilliant luster. **3** Hence you'll find in a powerful, preeminent state that one group will be at the ready for military service, another of greater use on the home front, and a considerable number who embrace both sides. The result is that if there's a task involving courageous action or deep deliberation, there's someone on hand with the ability energetically to perform it; and if there's some utility in a conciliatory approach or a show of compassion, you have at home the sort to put in charge of this kind of duty. If, by contrast, a weightier show of authority or sternness is to be applied, there's no shortage of people to devote themselves to this expediency as well. The result is that they can protect the state's sovereignty against every eventuality, and preserve the empire's glory. **4** What delight a good many people take in recalling the time when Themistocles and Aristides applied their different energies to the same end when they were in public life![148] Vainglorious and tending naturally to court popular favour, Themistocles united the minds of all in devotion to himself through his approachability. Aristides, by contrast, was inflexible: anything but eager to please, he was the

---

[147] Down to the end of 2.6.7, perhaps a loose adaptation of Cicero's survey of the diversity of human personality at *Off.* 1.107-9, esp. given Barbaro's recourse to Themistocles and Solon in 2.6.4 and 2.6.7 respectively (cf. *Off.* 1.108).

[148] Barbaro implies a harmonious balance of opposites that runs counter to the mainstream tradition of the cunning populist Themistocles (for whom 2.5.9 and n. 117) as a determined rival of the upstanding, aristocratic Aristides (*c.* 530–468 BCE); on their rivalry, Ostwald 1988: 343–4.

utrique tantum bono civitatis proficiebant, ut hoc quidem Athenienses ad coercendas iuvenum et perditorum hominum cupiditates et continendos intra aequitatem moderationemque appetitus, illo vero ad contrahendas cum finitimis amicitias sotietatesque conservandas et retinendos in fide animos subditorum uterentur. 5 Ex quo palam est posteritati factum multiplicia esse ingenia rempubli[**48v**]cam administrantium oportere, quorum ope civitatis status et decor diutissime perseveret. Neque solum hoc in diversis, verumetiam et in singulis, qui sedere in puppi velint, requiri ornamentum solet, ut unus idemque sibi ipsi repugnans interdum sit, et hic quidem doleat, illic vero laetetur, hic humanus sit, hic superbus, nunc asper, mox lenis, deiectus, elatus, remissus et torpens, audax et concitatus. 6 Inserviendum enim est tempori et consuetudini aliquid dandum et a vultu quam saepissime concidendum: ea demum omnia perquirenda quibus reipublicae dignitati et gloriae honestissime consulatur, neque Prothei illius homerici sit ulla tam discolour speties, quam pro temporis necessitate induere reipublicae gubernator erubescat. 7 Ad hoc enim natus est ut quid opus facto sit, quid civitati conducat, non [**49r**] solum optime sciat sed etiam audacter aggrediatur. Et Solonem non tantum leges, quas Atheniensibus dedit, quam quod se insanum simulaverit illustrare potuerunt; cuius exemplo L. Brutus, sicut ille tyrannidem Pysistrati debuit auferre, ita populum romanum

greatest stickler for the claims of justice.[149] Yet each of them was of such beneficial service to the state that the Athenians deployed Aristides to curb the enthusiasms of the young and the dissolute, and to keep appetites within fair limits of restraint; but Themistocles they deployed to establish ties of friendship with their neighbors and to preserve alliances, and to retain the continuing loyalty of those subject to their authority.[150] **5** From this it became clear to later generations that the temperaments of those running the country should be varied, so that by their help the state's standing and distinction would persist for the longest time. And this special characteristic tends to be looked for not just in different people, but also even in individuals who want to sit at the helm of the ship of state, so that one and the same person is sometimes at odds with himself: he's pained here but joyous there, now he's obliging, now arrogant, harsh at the moment but gentle soon after, subdued, carried away, relaxed and lethargic, brash and excited. **6** For attention must be paid to the needs of the moment and some concession made to interacting companionably, and you must cease as often as possible from any angry countenance:[151] in short, all paths are to be explored for acting in the most becoming way in the interests of the state's prestige and renown; nor should any appearance of Homer's famous Proteus[152] be so different in coloration that the state's ruler would blush to assume it according to the needs of the moment. **7** For he was born for the purpose not just of knowing very well what action is needed and what is to the state's advantage, but also of confidently undertaking as much. Even in Solon's case, it wasn't so much the laws he gave to Athens that were able to make him famous, as the fact that he pretended he was mad;[153] after his example, just as Solon had to do away with the tyranny of Pisistratus,[154] so

---

[149] Hence nicknamed 'the Just' (cf. 2.2.19 n. 42); so, e.g., Nep. *Arist.* 1.2, 4, Cic. *Off.* 3.16 (his scrupulousness is well illustrated by contrast with Themistocles at 3.49), Plut. *Arist.* 6.1, 7.6.

[150] A markedly one-sided picture that passes over (e.g.) Aristides' ostracism in 483/2 BCE, Themistocles' in the late 470s, Spartan allegations of Themistocles' complicity in intrigues with Persia, his eventual flight to Asia Minor, and his condemnation to death at Athens. Through this eloquent silence, Barbaro perhaps challenges the superficially attractive portrait of devotion to public service in 2.6.4 – an existence that is in any case off-limits to the celibate (cf. 2.6.8).

[151] Cf. for this nuance of *vultus* Cic. *Off.* 1.112, Hor. *Carm.* 3.3.3, *Serm.* 1.6.121, 2.7.44.

[152] See *Od.* 4.363-570, esp. 417-18 and 455-8 for Proteus' shifting forms (water, fire, serpent, leopard, etc.). For the divided tradition of positive and negative receptions of Proteus in Renaissance culture see Pesic 2010, esp. 61–3; Barbaro's allusion is seemingly positive in connotation – unless the more negative implications of public service in 2.6.2-7 (see nn. 148, 150 above) lend a pejorative shading here.

[153] When in the war against Megara for possession of Salamis (*c.* 600 BCE) it was forbidden at Athens to advocate the island's recovery, the Athenian politician and poet Solon (*c.* 630–560) allegedly feigned madness and publicly recited a poem of his own making that urged precisely that action (cf. Cic. *Off.* 1.108, Plut. *Sol.* 8.1-3, D. L. 1.46-7 with Leão 2019: 41–8).

sapientia dissimulata in libertatem asseruit. Horum autem ingeniis quid aeque versatile? Iure igitur nihil in re publica tantum laudari solet quam honesta haec et multiplex affectuum, ut ita dixerim, vicissitudo.

8 At in iis, quos ab ista cura in aliam et quidem praestantiorem abducimus, nihil minus expectandum est quam ista haec morum dissimilitudo; contra nihil tantum requirendum quam una et constans sententiae firmitas, quam vultus, quam persona et omnis habitus corporis cum animi stabilitate consentiens. In iis nihil volo nisi simplex, nisi perseverans, gravita[**49v**]tem et verecundiam maxime prae se ferant sintque in vita omni sibi ipsi neque repugnantes neque contrarii, sed et ab honorum et gloriae ambitione maxime abhorrentes. Hanc et spernere assuescant, hanc et suapte natura contemnant.

9 Sed quoniam duo sunt hominum genera, qui nulla gloriae cupiditate tanguntur, unum eorum qui quom timeant omnia et reformident se ipsos premunt et, ut in proverbio est, vocem tollere non audent, sed et metus sibi ipsis vanos fingunt et squalenti cuidam vitae se addicunt, honores vero et munera non modo petere verentur sed et praesumpta desperatione se indignos putant in quos beneficia ulla conferantur: hos quemadmodum

Lucius Brutus disguised his intelligence when he released the Roman people into freedom.[155] What can match the versatility of their temperaments? With good reason, therefore, nothing usually receives as much praise in public life as this respectable and multifaceted interchangeability of casts of mind, so to speak.

8 But in those I'm leading away from responsibilities of this sort to a different and, yes, superior concern, nothing is less to be hoped for than this variability of disposition.[156] On the contrary, nothing is to be sought as much as a single, unwavering stability of viewpoint – a countenance, a form of self-presentation, and an overall physical bearing that accords with a steady mind. In such people I want nothing except a quality of straightforward steadfastness – that they display to the fullest degree a serious-minded sense of restraint, and in every aspect of life they are neither at odds with themselves nor in self-conflict, but also with a very great aversion to any desire for advancement or renown. May they get used to disdaining such desire, and to despising it of their own true nature.[157] 9 But there are two kinds of people who are unaffected by any desire for high renown. One consists of those who, since they face everything with fearful apprehension, hold themselves in check and (as the saying goes) don't dare raise their voices; but they also conjure empty fears for themselves and surrender to a certain grubbiness of life, and in fact they're not only afraid to seek public office and appointments, but also take hopelessness for granted, thinking themselves unworthy of being granted any

---

[154] Barbaro reshapes history to facilitate the parallel between Solon and Brutus as anti-tyrannical liberators (see also n. 155 below). Pisistratus, tyrant of Athens (d. 527 BCE), first gained power in c. 560, allegedly through the ruse of whipping up popular sentiment by feigning injury from his political opponents. After the populace was won over, he sought and was awarded a bodyguard of fifty club bearers – a motion unsuccessfully opposed by Solon, who thereafter withdrew into retirement, only later to be courted once more by Pisistratus (cf. Hdt. 1.59; [Arist.] *Ath. Pol.* 14.1-2; Plut. *Sol.* 30.1-3, 5, 31.1). Barbaro greatly exaggerates Solon's resistance to Pisistratus – unless he alludes in 'just as ... Pisistratus' to Solon's (unsuccessful) opposition to the tyrant's seizure of power. He perhaps also compounds his account of Solon's feigned madness with a silent allusion to Pisistratus' feigned injury – another good example of shrewd pretense.

[155] In 509 BCE the semi-legendary L. Iunius Brutus reputedly expelled his uncle, L. Tarquinius Superbus, the seventh and last king of Rome, thereafter founding the Roman Republic. For his feigned idiocy in self-protection during Superbus' tyranny (hence the acquired surname *Brutus* = 'stupid'), Liv. 1.56.7-8, 59.2, 8, V. Max. 7.3.2, Ov. *Fast.* 2.717-18 with Smith 2007.

[156] Ciceronian phrasing (cf. *Off.* 1.109: *innumerabiles aliae <u>dissimilitudines</u> sunt naturae <u>morumque</u>, minime tamen vituperandorum* 'There are countless other dissimilarities of nature and conduct, which do not in the least deserve censure'; tr. Griffin and Atkins 1991: 43); such wording consolidates the broader case for Barbaro's dependence on *Off.* 1.107-9 in 2.6.2-7 (see n. 147 above).

[157] For this trueness to one's own nature cf. Cic. *Off.* 1.110, 114, 120 – part of what may be Barbaro's larger engagement with Cicero in this section (see nn. 147, 156 above).

natura ipsa frigidioribus praecordiis infamavit, ita et nos veluti censoria nota inustos a familia nostra reiicimus; **10** alte[**50r**]rum vero genus est huic contrarium et quam dissimillimum, sed quod esse in re aliqua nihilominus proximum videatur: uterque enim umbram hanc despicit, sed ille quidem ut quaerere non audeat, hic vero ut dedignetur; nobis autem ii placent ex omnibus maxime qui vilescere sese arbitrantur, quom rerum humanarum utpote humilium et caducarum curam ullam suscipiunt. In his et latum cor et patentissimae fibrae et animorum multitudo per totum corpus diffunduntur; ex quo efficitur ut ima haec et oculis subiecta omnia aspernentur et suprema atque sublimia semper cupiant attrectare. **11** Hos si capessere negotia iusseris, non modo non ferent sed aut negligenter rebus utentur publicis aut labore non sibi conveniente frangentur. Fit enim quam saepissime ut ea, [**50v**] quae nostro ingenio minora sunt, difficilius peragantur quam ea ad quae etiam si maiora sint, ultro tamen accedimus. **12** Effluit enim atque dilabitur animi vis, indignanturque inani studio fatigari, ut magna sit pars mentis ociosa iis qui a contemplatione ad aliud munus revocantur. Nam et ollae clepsydraeque ea natura est, ut reseratis oris ad dimidium oppletae quicquid infuderis statim emittant: ad summum vero refertae liquorem intra se teneant. **13** Intervertitur

shows of favour. Just as nature itself has dishonoured them through this chill of faintheartedness, so too I've banished them from our fellowship, as if branded with the stern stigma of disgrace. **10** The other kind is opposite to this first sort, and different to the fullest extent possible; but in a certain respect it nevertheless seems very similar. For each of them looks down on this empty form,[158] but the first kind to the effect of not daring to seek after it, the second of showing contempt for it. But the ones I approve of most of all are those who think they're cheapened when they take on any responsibility for human affairs, inasmuch as those affairs are unimportant and fleeting. In such people, a broad heart, a very far-reaching network of viscera, and a host of vital powers are widely spread throughout the entire body.[159] The result is that they spurn all these lowliest commodities that are set before their eyes, and always want to deal with the highest matters of lofty consideration. **11** If you order them to take on matters of business, not only will they not endure them, but they'll either treat public affairs carelessly or be broken by a task that doesn't suit them; for it happens all the time that the tasks that are below our abilities are accomplished with greater difficulty than those which, even if they're above us, we nevertheless undertake voluntarily. **12** For mental energy is drained away and vanishes, and people resent being exhausted by a trivial pursuit, so that those who are summoned back from mental study to some other task are largely disengaged in mind. Moreover, the natural property of pots and water clocks is such that, when filled to halfway with their openings unstopped, they immediately let out whatever you've poured in; but when full to the brim, they retain the liquid within them.[160] **13** In the

---

[158] Desire for public recognition.
[159] This expansiveness of the supra-human viewpoint is nicely expressed through a form of physiological expansiveness. In distinguishing the celibate's aversion to public life from that of the faint-hearted, and in portraying the celibate's disdain for human affairs, Barbaro differently channels two aspects of the Ciceronian man-of-action as drawn in *Off.* 1.72: 'But those who are equipped by nature to administer affairs *must abandon any hesitation over winning office* [cf. Barbaro at 2.6.9 'One consists . . . favour'] and engage in public life . . . No less than philosophers . . . must those who choose public life acquire *the magnificent disdain for human affairs that I stress* [cf. Barbaro at 2.6.10 'But . . . fleeting'], and tranquillity of mind and freedom from care. Otherwise, how will they live without anxiety, with seriousness and with constancy?' (tr. Griffin and Atkins 1991: 29; my emphasis).
[160] Of course with the stops now intact; by analogy, the engaged mind, as if with its own stops in place, fully retains its capacity for the task in hand.

quoque animae in speculando concitatus vigor, quum quis optime ad id natura compositus in inferiorem veluti gradum dignitatis retorquetur. Laborant procera corpora si in angustis et curtis ostiis[161] summittantur et capacissima quaeque domus paucis incolentibus squalorem ducit et situm. **14** Quare, quemadmodum omnes corporis partes ca[**51r**]rere suo alimento non possunt, sed nisi nutriantur torporem et vitium ducunt, ita marcescere animus poterit nisi excolatur totus et eo quo eget cibo saturetur. Maxime autem laedi solet ea pars quae praestantior est: nam videmus delicatis hominibus nocere plus ea quae parva et levia sunt, quam quae magna et gravia robustis et rusticanis. **15** Quod si ab opere suo deiectum agricolam vires et robur remittere aut etiam amittere plerunque[162] experimur, negabimus animum exturbari posse si ad studium aliud, quam id quod natura et sponte sua sequitur, transferatur? Omitto etiam id et concedo fieri posse ut in alieno munere aliquid quispiam praestet: verum illa alacritas, qua quisque in agendo ea quae diligit utitur, nonne abibit omnis? nonne voluptas illa in dolorem potius aegritudinemque vertetur? [**51v**] Quis haec nescit?

16 Quare haec erunt signa ingenii ad nostram rem facientis: dolebit si a studio suo moveatur, pigrescet in munere alieno. Quare utinam mihi puer is detur qui simplicissimus quum sit et magni animi gloriae nullius amore capiatur! Hunc seducens[163] a contemplando tantum se sciat pater sceleris admissurum, quantum si factum ex filio turpe mancipium saevissimae[164] genti venundaret. **17** Dignoscent autem huiuscemodi ingenium parentes

---

[161] *host-* MS; but for *ost-*, Br. 96 n. 1.
[162] *plaer-* MS.
[163] *-ere* MS; but for *-ens* (Br. 96 n. 3) see p. 49 above.
[164] *-issime* MS, but see p. 49 above.

case of the mind, too, the force of energy that's stirred in contemplation is misapplied when someone who's naturally very well made for such contemplation is redirected as if to a lower degree of prestige.[165] Tall bodies get into difficulties if they're made to stoop lower in cramped and compressed doorways, and all the most spacious homes invariably become filthy through disuse if only a few people live in them. **14** Hence, just as all parts of the body can't do without their nourishment, but take on a lethargic unhealthiness if they're not fed, so the mind could be enfeebled unless it's well tended in its entirety, and abundantly furnished with the food it needs. The more superior part is usually damaged the most; for we see that petty insignificances do more harm to delicate types than large-scale burdens do to sturdy, rustic types. **15** But if we generally find that a farmer who is ousted from his work compromises or even loses his vigor and strength, shall we refuse to accept that the mind can be thrown into disorder if it's reassigned to a pursuit different from that which it naturally follows of its own accord? I also pass over the point – and grant it – that it can happen that someone makes a worthwhile contribution in a task that's foreign to his nature.[166] But that briskness that everyone brings to bear in discharging those responsibilities that are held dear – won't it completely disappear? Won't that sense of pleasure be turned instead into pained distress? Who doesn't know this?

16 These, therefore, will be the marks of the temperament that suits my topic: he will be upset if he's ousted from his own favoured pursuit, and prove sluggish in a task that's foreign to him. Hence I wish I were granted the sort of boy who is very unaffected and lofty of spirit, and therefore not captivated by any passion for glory![167] A father should know that, in drawing such a boy away from contemplation, he's going to be committing as great a crime as if he made a vile slave out of his son and sold him to a very savage people. **17** Parents will recognize a temperament of this sort as easily as possible,

---

[165] A weak analogical point because of its strained dependence on 'lower' (*inferiorem*): after the vision of rapid water outflow through a lower opening in 2.6.12, the celibate's half-store of energy for non-contemplative duty is soon dissipated via swift efflux through a task of 'lower' prestige.

[166] A concession perhaps influenced by the comparable Ciceronian point made at *Off.* 1.114.

[167] Barbaro's stress on unaffectedness (*simplicissimus*; cf. 2.6.17 *simplex*) in connection with loftiness of spirit is suggestively close in language and sentiment to Cicero's depiction of *magnitudo animi* at *Off.* 1.63: 'Therefore we require men who are brave and of great spirit (*magnanimos*) also to be good and straightforward (*simplices*), friends of truth and not in the least deceitful (*minimeque fallaces*; cf. Barbaro at 2.6.17 *simplex* [*ingenium*] ... *et minime subdolum*): such are the central qualities for which justice is praised' (tr. Griffin and Atkins 1991: 26).

quam facillime, quia et simplex erit, ut diximus, et minime subdolum; et a pueritia maxime iuditium solemus ferre qualisquumque[168] futurus sit vir. Nam sive statim cuius ingenii puer sit deprehendamus,[169] sive, ut in plerisque[170] contingit, nulla sit via discernendi (latentes enim quidam ita sunt atque reconditi ut vix ante cognoscantur quam [52r] adoleverint et paterni imperii iugum excusserint), erit tamen facile iudicare sintne ii quales desiderabimus. **18** In iis enim qui sese quales futuri sint statim aperiunt,[171] nullus error intercidet; eos quoque qui iuditium . . .[172] nostrum aut fallent aut effugient, hoc ipso quod se non patiantur intelligi cognoscemus non esse ad caelibatum idoneos. Simplices nanque sint est necesse qui se ad vitam caelestem accingunt.

19 Desyderarem autem in hoc sanguinis minus quam in eo qui ad rempublicam aspirabit, cuius rei signum facile ex oris vultusque alacritate aut ex colore sumemus. Nam exhilarat sanguis, ut dicitur, plurimum, et coloris vigorem in membris omnibus, praecipue in genis et fronte, praescribit, ex corporis item robore et lacertorum firmitate indicium aliquod ducimus. **20** Nam et [52v] fortius pellunt et resistunt qui sanguinis multum habent et ad laborem aliquem vehementem tolerantius durant; sed animo nequaquam tantundem valent, nam et ab ira cito decidunt et sententias suas minus pertinaciter tuentur, quod signum iocundi et magni etiam cordis est; sed et temperatioris sunt complexionis, ideoque et quam longissime vivunt si modum cupiditatibus ponant. **21** Iccirco nos sanguineos quidem malumus, quam aut biliosos aut melancholicos aut humettos: non tamen multum, nam

---

[168] *quales*- MS.
[169] *deprae*- MS.
[170] *plaer*- MS.
[171] *aperunt* MS.
[172] A one-word space is left blank in the MS.

because it will be unaffected, as I said,[173] and not at all deceitful; and it's very much on the basis of boyhood that we usually form a judgment as to what sort of man he's going to be. For whether we recognize at once what temperament a boy has or (as happens in most cases) there's no way of telling (for certain boys are so retiring and reserved that we hardly get to know them before they've come of age and thrown off the yoke of their fathers' authority), it will nevertheless be easy to judge if they are the sort we'll want. **18** For in the case of those who immediately reveal themselves in terms of what they'll be like, no mistake will occur. As for those, too, who will either beguile or elude our judgment, we shall recognize that they are ill suited to celibacy from the very fact that they don't allow themselves to be understood; for those getting ready for the celestial[174] life must necessarily be straightforward.

19 In this person I'd want less blood than in one who'll aspire to public service, and we shall easily infer a token of this from the brisk vitality of mouth and face, or from one's colour.[175] For blood very much brightens the complexion, they say, and determines the force of coloration in all the body parts, especially the cheeks and brow; similarly, we draw a telling indication from the body's robustness and muscular tautness. **20** For those with a good supply of blood are stronger in exerting force or withstanding it, and they have greater powers of endurance for any strenuous work. But they aren't nearly as strong in mind; for they quickly subside after an angry outburst, and they guard their own opinions less firmly (which is a sign of an agreeable and even generous spirit).[176] But they are also of a rather balanced constitution, and for that reason they also live to the longest possible extent, if they limit their desires. **21** Hence I prefer full-blooded types over the bilious or melancholic or those wet with phlegm.[177] But I don't much prefer them: since

---

[173] 2.6.8, 16; cf. 2.6.18.

[174] Again the play on *caelebs/caelibatus* and *caelestis*; cf. 2.2.2-3 and nn. 9-11.

[175] Barbaro's portrayal of the body and mind requiring nourishment in 2.6.14 'Hence ... needs' eases his transition to the theme of blood in 2.6.19-21, at least from the perspective of ancient physiological theory. So, e.g., in Aristotle blood is theorized as 'the final nutrient (*trophē*) for the blooded animals' (*Part. an.* 2.3 650a34-5 [tr. Lennox 2001: 24]; cf. 2.3 650b11-13, 2.4 651a14-15), and as the raw material out of which the entire body is constructed (cf. 3.5 668a4-8; further, Boylan 2015: 55–61 with Lennox 199–200 on 2.3 650a32-5 and 650b2).

[176] Loose adaptation of the Aristotelian idea that thick, fibrous blood makes for strength and a hot, passionate temperament, whereas thin, watery blood is connected to intelligence and (if excessively watery) timorousness; see, e.g., *Part. an.* 2.4 650b18-51a5 with Boylan 2015: 60-1.

[177] In accordance with Hippocratic humoral theory (see, e.g., *Nat. hom.* 4 [6.38-40 Littré] with Jouanna 2012: 335–59), blood here constitutes one of the four humours along with yellow bile, black bile, and phlegm in Barbaro's *biliosos ... humettos* (see also 3.6.53 and n. 281).

quom esse continentissimum sit necesse eum, quem instituimus, nimius obstaret sanguis: quare, ut nos arbitramur, necesse est parum consistat ut ad id, quod optatur, sine molestia pervenire puer possit.

22 Sed nimium provehi in alieno opere videor; quo minus verendum est ne laudem aliquam mereri voluisse iudican[**53r**]dus sim.[178] scio enim esse aliquam culpam; sed consulendum fuit rei magnitudini quam tractamus. Quare ad reliqua transibimus, venia impetrata.

---

[178] *sim, scio* Br.

the boy we are training necessarily has to be very restrained, too much blood would be a disadvantage. Therefore, as I see it, it's essential that the blood isn't particularly thick in substance,[179] so that the boy can reach his desired goal without trouble.

22 But I seem to be carrying on unduly on a business that belongs to others. All the less reason to fear that I'm to be judged as having wanted to earn a modicum of praise! For I know that there's an element of blame; but there had to be regard for the sheer scale of the topic I'm treating. Hence, if forgiveness is granted, I shall move on to the matters that remain.

---

[179] See n. 176 above. For the connection between the humours and human temperament cf. 4.2.75 and n. 211.

Bibliography

Allen, James. 'The Stoics on the Origin of Language and the Foundations of Etymology,' in *Language and Learning: Philosophy of Language in the Hellenistic Age*, edited by Dorothea Frede and Brad Inwood, 14–35. Cambridge: Cambridge University Press, 2005.
Archibald, Elizabeth. 'Sex and Power in Thebes and Babylon: Oedipus and Semiramis in Classical and Medieval texts,' *The Journal of Medieval Latin* 11 (2001): 27–49.
Banfi, Luigi. 'Ermolao Barbaro, Venezia e il patriarcato di Aquileia,' *Nuova antologia* 111 (1950): 421–8.
Bausi, Francesco, ed. *Ermolao Barbaro-Giovanni Pico della Mirandola. Filosofia o eloquenza?* Naples: Liguori Editore, 1998.
Beagon, Mary. *The Elder Pliny on the Human Animal: Natural History, Book 7.* Oxford: Oxford University Press, 2005.
Bellavitis, Anna. 'Patrimoni e matrimoni a Venezia nel Cinquecento,' in *Le ricchezze delle donne: diritti patrimoniali e poteri familiari in Italia (XIII-XIX secc.)*, edited by Giulia Calvi and Isabelle Chabot, 149–60. Turin: Rosenberg and Sellier, 1998.
Bianchi, Luca. *Studi sull'aristotelismo del Rinascimento.* Padua: Il Poligrafo, 2003.
Bianchi, Luca. 'Continuity and Change in the Aristotelian Tradition,' in *The Cambridge Companion to Renaissance Philosophy*, edited by James Hankins, 49–71. Cambridge: Cambridge University Press, 2007.
Bigi, Emilio. 'Barbaro, Ermolao,' *Dizionario biografico degli Italiani* 6 (1964): 95–9.
Biow, Douglas. *Doctors, Ambassadors, Secretaries: Humanism and Professions in Renaissance Italy.* Chicago and London: The University of Chicago Press, 2002.
Bloomer, W. Martin. 'Quintilian on the Child as a Learning Subject,' *Classical World* 105, no. 1 (2011): 109–37.
Bonazza, Mirna. 'Ferrara, Biblioteca Comunale Ariostea, Classe II, Cl. II.9,' *Manus Online* 2008 (http://manus.iccu.sbn.it/; identifier: CNMD\\0000051337).
Bonazza, Mirna. 'Biblioteca Comunale Ariostea,' in *I manoscritti datati di Ferrara*, edited by Gilda P. Mantovani and Silvia Rizzi, 3–13. Florence: SISMEL (Società Internazionale per lo Studio del Medioevo Latino), Edizioni del Galluzzo, 2017.
Boylan, Michael. *The Origins of Ancient Greek Science: Blood–A Philosophical Study.* Abingdon and New York: Routledge, 2015.
Branca, Vittore, ed. *Ermolao Barbaro: Epistolae, orationes et carmina.* 2 vols. Florence: Bibliopolis, 1943.

Branca, Vittore. 'Un trattato inedito di Ermolao Barbaro: il *De coelibatu libri*,' in *Bibliothèque d'Humanisme et Renaissance* 14, no. 1 (1952): 83-98.
Branca, Vittore. 'Ermolao Barbaro e l'Umanesimo veneziano,' in *Umanesimo europeo e Umanesimo veneziano*, edited by Vittore Branca, 193-212. Florence: Sansoni, 1963.
Branca, Vittore, ed. *Ermolao Barbaro, De coelibatu, De officio legati*. Florence: Leo S. Olschki, 1969.
Branca, Vittore. 'Fermezza cristiana e impegno filologico del Patriarca Ermolao Barbaro,' in *Miscellanea Gilles Gérard Meersseman*, 2 vols: 2.687-94. Padua: Antenore, 1970.
Branca, Vittore. 'Ermolao Barbaro and late Quattrocento Venetian Humanism,' in *Renaissance Venice*, edited by John R. Hale, 218-43. London: Faber and Faber, 1973.
Branca, Vittore. 'L'Umanesimo veneziano alla fine del Quattrocento. Ermolao Barbaro e il suo circulo,' in *Storia della cultura veneta, 3.1: Dal primo Quattrocento al Concilio di Trento*, edited by Girolamo Arnaldi and Manlio Pastore Stocchi, 123-75. Vicenza: Pozza, 1980.
Branca, Vittore. 'Umanesimo veneziano fra Barbaro e Bembo,' in *Una famiglia veneziana nella storia: I Barbaro. Atti del Convegno di studi in occasione del quinto centenario della morte dell'umanista Ermolao, Venezia, 4-6 Novembre 1993*, edited by Michela Marangoni and Manlio Pastore Stocchi, 9-42. Venice: Istituto Veneto di Scienze, Lettere ed Arti, 1996.
Branca, Vittore. *La sapienza civile. Studi sull'Umanesimo a Venezia*. Florence: Leo S. Olschki, 1998.
Branca, Vittore, and Roberto Weiss. 'Carpaccio e l'iconografia del più grande umanista veneziano (Ermolao Barbaro),' *Arte veneta* 17 (1963): 35-40.
Breen, Quirinus. 'Giovanni Pico della Mirandola on the Conflict of Philosophy and Rhetoric,' *Journal of the History of Ideas* 13, no. 3 (1952): 384-412.
Brown, Patricia F. *Venetian Narrative Painting in the Age of Carpaccio*. New Haven and London: Yale University Press, 1988.
Brown, Patricia F. *Venice and Antiquity: The Venetian Sense of the Past*. New Haven and London: Yale University Press, 1996.
Brown, Peter. *The Body and Society: Men, Women and Sexual Renunciation in Early Christianity*. New York: Columbia University Press, 1988.
Bruez, Véronique, tr. *Le Pogge: Un vieux doit-il se marier?* Paris: Les Belles Lettres, 1998.
Butler, Shane, ed. and tr. *Angelo Poliziano, Letters. Volume I: Books I-IV*. The I Tatti Renaissance Library 21. Cambridge, MA, and London: Harvard University Press, 2006.
Carotti, Natale. 'Un politico umanista del Quattrocento: Francesco Barbaro,' *Rivista Storica Italiana* 54, no. 2 (1937): 18-37.
Céard, Jean. 'Ermolao Barbaro,' in *Centuriae Latinae: Cent une figures humanistes de la Renaissance aux Lumières offertes à Jacques Chomarat*, edited by Colette Nativel, 79-84. Travaux d'Humanisme et Renaissance 314. Geneva: Librairie Droz, 1997.

Chojnacki, Stanley. *Women and Men in Renaissance Venice: Twelve Essays on Patrician Society*. Baltimore and London: The Johns Hopkins University Press, 2000.

Claassen, Jo-Marie. 'Documents of a Crumbling Marriage: The Case of Cicero and Terentia,' *Phoenix* 50, nos 3–4 (1996): 208–32.

Clark, Albert C. 'The Reappearance of the Texts of the Classics,' *The Library* ser. 4–2, no. 1 (1921): 13–42.

Cooper, John M. 'Aristotle on the Goods of Fortune,' *Philosophical Review* 94, no. 2 (1985): 173–96.

Cox, Virginia. 'Rhetoric and Humanism in Quattrocento Venice,' *Renaissance Quarterly* 56, no. 3 (2003): 652–94.

Dasen, Véronique. *Dwarfs in Ancient Egypt and Greece*. Oxford: Oxford University Press, 1993.

Davison, Claire C., with the collaboration of Birte Lundgreen; edited by Geoffrey B. Waywell. *Pheidias: The Sculptures and Ancient Sources*. Bulletin of the Institute of Classical Studies Supplement 105. 3 vols. London: Institute of Classical Studies, School of Advanced Study, University of London, 2009.

Dean-Jones, Lesley. *Women's Bodies in Classical Greek Science*. Oxford: Oxford University Press, 1994.

D'Elia, Anthony F. *The Renaissance of Marriage in Fifteenth-Century Italy*. Cambridge, MA, and London: Harvard University Press, 2004.

Diller, Aubrey. 'The Library of Francesco and Ermolao Barbaro,' *Italia medioevale e umanistica* 6 (1963): 253–62.

Dorandi, Tiziano. 'Potamone di Alessandria,' *Zeitschrift für Papyrologie und Epigraphik* 199 (2016): 33–5.

Dubois, Edward C. 'Does Happiness Die with Us? An Aristotelian Examination of the Fortunes of the Deceased,' *Journal of Philosophy of Life* 4, no. 1 (2014): 28–37.

Dyck, Andrew R. *A Commentary on Cicero, De Officiis*. Ann Arbor: The University of Michigan Press, 1996.

Egerton, Frank N., ed. *Edward Lee Greene: Landmarks of Botanical History, Part II*. Stanford, CA: Stanford University Press, 1983.

Falco, Riccardo. '*Litterae* e *philosophia* nel rapporto tra Ermolao Barbaro, Antonio de Ferrariis e la cultura aragonese,' in *Letteratura fra centro e periferia: Studi in memoria di Pasquale Alberto De Lisio*, edited by Gioacchino Paparelli and Sebastiano Martelli, 261–84. Naples: Edizioni Scientifiche Italiane, 1987.

Fantazzi, Charles. 'Revival of Classical Texts,' in *Brill's Encyclopedia of the Neo-Latin World: Macropaedia*, edited by Philip Ford, Jan Bloemendal, and Charles Fantazzi, 101–11. Leiden and Boston: Brill, 2014a.

Fantazzi, Charles. 'Imitation, Emulation, Ciceronianism, Anti-Ciceronianism,' in *Brill's Encyclopedia of the Neo-Latin World: Macropaedia*, edited by Philip Ford, Jan Bloemendal, and Charles Fantazzi, 141–53. Leiden and Boston: Brill, 2014b.

Fava, Domenico. *La Biblioteca Estense nel suo sviluppo storico, con il catalogo della mostra permanente e 10 tavole*. Modena: G. T. Vincenzi e Nipoti, 1925.

Ferracin, Antonio. 'Trevisan, Zaccaria senior,' *Dizionario biografico degli Italiani* 96 (2019): 744–6.
Ferrero, Giuseppe G., ed. *Pauli Iovii Opera I: Lettere, volume primo (1514–1544)*. Rome: Istituto Poligrafico dello Stato, 1956.
Ferriguto, Arnaldo. *Almorò Barbaro: L'alta cultura del settentrione d'Italia nel 400, i 'sacri canones' di Roma e le 'sanctissime leze' di Venezia (con documenti inediti)*. Miscellanea di storia veneta, series 3, 15.2. Venice: A Spese della Società, 1922.
Figliuolo, Bruno. *Il diplomatico e il trattatista: Ermolao Barbaro ambasciatore della Serenissima e il* De officio legati. Naples: Guida, 1999.
Forlivesi, Marco. 'Vernia, Nicoletto,' *Dizionario biografico degli Italiani* 98 (2020): 811–16.
Fortenbaugh, William W. *Theophrastus of Eresus: Sources for His Life, Writings, Thought and Influence. Commentary Volume 6.1: Sources on Ethics*. Leiden: Brill, 2011.
Frank, Erich. 'The Fundamental Opposition of Plato and Aristotle,' *American Journal of Philology* 61, no. 1 (1940): 34–53.
Frank, Richard I. 'Augustus' Legislation on Marriage and Children,' *California Studies in Classical Antiquity* 8 (1975): 41–52.
Garin, Eugenio, ed. *Prosatori latini del Quattrocento*. Milan: Riccardo Ricciardi Editore, 1952.
Garrod, Raphaële. 'Aristotelianism and Scholasticism,' in *Brill's Encyclopedia of the Neo-Latin World: Macropaedia*, edited by Philip Ford, Jan Bloemendal, and Charles Fantazzi, 589–602. Leiden and Boston: Brill, 2014.
Geanakoplos, Deno J. *Greek Scholars in Venice: Studies in the Dissemination of Greek Learning from Byzantium to Western Europe*. Cambridge, MA: Harvard University Press, 1962.
Giannetto, Nella. *Bernardo Bembo, umanista e politico veneziano*. Florence: Leo S. Olschki, 1985.
Giglioni, Guido. 'Philosophy,' in *The Oxford Handbook of Neo-Latin*, edited by Sarah Knight and Stefan Tilg, 249–62. Oxford: Oxford University Press, 2015.
Giovio, Paolo. *Elogia virorum literis illustrium, quotquot vel nostra vel avorum memoria vixere*. Basel: Peter Perna, 1577.
Gnesotto, Attilio, ed. *Francesci Barbari* De re uxoria liber in partes duas, *Atti e Memorie della R. Accademia di Scienze, Lettere ed Arti in Padova* n.s. 32 (1915–16): 6–105.
Gothein, Percy. *Francesco Barbaro. Früh-Humanismus und Staatskunst in Venedig*. Berlin: Verlag Die Runde, 1932.
Gothein, Percy. *Zaccaria Trevisan il vecchio: la vita e l'ambiente*. Venice: La Reale Deputazione Editrice, 1942.
Grafton, Anthony. *Joseph Scaliger: A Study in the History of Classical Scholarship*. 2 vols. Oxford: Oxford University Press, 1983–93.
Graham, Daniel W., ed. and tr. *The Texts of Early Greek Philosophy*. 2 vols. Cambridge: Cambridge University Press, 2010.
Grendler, Paul F. *The Universities of the Italian Renaissance*. Baltimore and London: The Johns Hopkins University Press, 2002.

Griffin, Miriam T., and E. Margaret Atkins, eds. *Cicero, On Duties.* Cambridge Texts in the History of Political Thought. Cambridge: Cambridge University Press, 1991.
Griggio, Claudio, ed. *Francesco Barbaro, Epistolario, I: Le tradizione manoscritta e a stampa.* Florence: Leo S. Olschki, 1991.
Griggio, Claudio, ed. *Francesco Barbaro, Epistolario, II: La raccolta canonica delle 'Epistole'.* Florence: Leo S. Olschki, 1999.
Griggio, Claudio. 'Barbaro Francesco, umanista e uomo di stato,' in *Nuovo Liruti. Dizionario biografico dei friulani, II: L'età veneta*, edited by Cesare Scalon et al., 383–91. Udine: Forum, 2009.
Griggio, Claudio. 'Francesco Barbaro, *De re uxoria.* II: Nota sul testo, testo critico, traduzione, commento,' in *Francesco Barbaro*, De re uxoria, edited by Claudio Griggio and Chiara Kravina, 151–343. Florence: Leo S. Olschki, 2021.
Gualandi, Michelangelo. *Nuova raccolta di lettere sulla pittura, scultura ed architettura, scritte da' più celebri personaggi dei secoli XV. a XIX.* 3 vols. Bologna: A Spese dell'Editore ed Annotatore, 1844–56.
Gualdo, Germano. 'Barbaro, Francesco,' *Dizionario biografico degli Italiani* 6 (1964): 101–3.
Guthrie, William K. C. *A History of Greek Philosophy, V. The Later Plato and the Academy.* Cambridge: Cambridge University Press, 1978.
Guthrie, William K. C. *A History of Greek Philosophy, VI. Aristotle: An Encounter.* Cambridge: Cambridge University Press, 1981.
Hatzimichali, Myrto. *Potamo of Alexandria and the Emergence of Eclecticism in Late Hellenistic Philosophy.* Cambridge: Cambridge University Press, 2011.
Hett, Walter S., ed. and tr. *Aristotle*, On the Soul, Parva naturalia, On Breath. 2nd edn. Loeb Classical Library 288. Cambridge, MA, and London: Harvard University Press, 1957.
Hieatt, A. Kent, and Maristella Lorch, tr. *Lorenzo Valla*, On Pleasure: De voluptate. New York: Abaris Books, 1977.
Hrabar, Vladimir E., ed. *De legatis et legationibus tractatus varii. Bernardi de Rosergio* Ambaxiatorum brevilogus*; Hermolai Barbari* De officio legati*; Martini Garrati Laudensis* De legatis maxime principum*; ex aliis excerpta qui eadem de re usque ad annum MDCXXV scripserunt.* Tartu (Dorpat): C. Mattiesen, 1906.
Hufnagel, Glenda L. *A History of Women's Menstruation from Ancient Greece to the Twenty-First Century: Psychological, Social, Medical, Religious, and Educational Issues.* Lewiston, NY: Edwin Mellen Press, 2012.
Jouanna, Jacques. *Greek Medicine from Hippocrates to Galen: Selected Papers.* Leiden and Boston: Brill, 2012.
Kallendorf, Craig W. *Virgil and the Myth of Venice: Books and Readers in the Italian Renaissance.* Oxford: Oxford University Press, 1999.
Kallendorf, Craig W., ed. and tr. *Humanist Educational Treatises.* The I Tatti Renaissance Library 5. Cambridge, MA, and London: Harvard University Press, 2002.

Katz, Phyllis B. 'Educating Paula: A Proposed Curriculum for Raising a 4th-Century Christian Infant,' in *Constructions of Childhood in Ancient Greece and Italy*, edited by Ada Cohen and Jeremy B. Rutter, 115–27. *Hesperia* Supplement 41. Princeton, NJ: The American School of Classical Studies at Athens, 2007.

King, John E., ed. and tr. *Cicero: Tusculan Disputations*. 2nd edn. Loeb Classical Library 141. Cambridge, MA, and London: Harvard University Press, 1945.

King, Margaret L. 'Caldiera and the Barbaros on Marriage and the Family: Humanist Reflections of Venetian Realities,' *Journal of Medieval and Renaissance Studies* 6 (1976): 19–50.

King, Margaret L. *Venetian Humanism in an Age of Patrician Dominance*. Princeton, NJ: Princeton University Press, 1986.

King, Margaret L. 'Humanism in Venice,' in *Renaissance Humanism: Foundations, Forms, and Legacy*, edited by Albert Rabil, 3 vols: 1.209–34. Philadelphia: University of Pennsylvania Press, 1988.

King, Margaret L. *Humanism, Venice, and Women: Essays on the Italian Renaissance*. Aldershot: Ashgate, 2005.

King, Margaret L. 'Concepts of Childhood: What We Know and Where We Might Go,' *Renaissance Quarterly* 60, no. 2 (2007): 371–407.

King, Margaret L., ed. and tr. *Renaissance Humanism: An Anthology of Sources*. Indianapolis and Cambridge: Hackett Publishing Company, Inc., 2014.

King, Margaret L., ed. and tr. *Francesco Barbaro, The Wealth of Wives: A Fifteenth-Century Marriage Manual*. The Other Voice in Early Modern Europe: The Toronto Series, 42. Toronto: Iter Academic Press; Tempe, AZ: Arizona Centre for Medieval and Renaissance Studies, 2015.

Kohl, Benjamin G., and Ronald G. Witt, eds, with Elizabeth B. Welles. *The Earthly Republic: Italian Humanists on Government and Society*. Philadelphia: University of Pennsylvania Press, 1978.

Kravina, Chiara. 'Una fortunata triade pedagogica: il *De re uxoria* di Francesco Barbaro e i trattati educativi del primo Quattrocento,' in *Le carte e i discepoli: Studi in onore di Claudio Griggio*, edited by Fabiana di Brazzà et al., 161–74. Udine: Forum, 2016.

Kravina, Chiara. 'Tradizione e fortuna del *De re uxoria* di Francesco Barbaro: censimento dei manoscritti,' in *Acta Conventus Neo-Latini Vindobonensis: Proceedings of the Sixteenth International Congress of Neo-Latin Studies (Vienna 2015)*, edited by Astrid Steiner-Weber and Franz Römer, 412–22. Leiden and Boston: Brill, 2018.

Kravina, Chiara. 'Significato e ricezione del *De re uxoria*,' in *Francesco Barbaro, De re uxoria*, edited by Claudio Griggio and Chiara Kravina, 1–149. Florence: Leo S. Olschki, 2021.

Kraye, Jill. 'Philologists and Philosophers,' in *The Cambridge Companion to Renaissance Humanism*, edited by Jill Kraye, 142–60. Cambridge: Cambridge University Press, 1996.

Kraye, Jill. 'Pico on the Relationship of Rhetoric and Philosophy,' in *Pico della Mirandola: New Essays*, edited by Michael V. Dougherty, 13–36. Cambridge: Cambridge University Press, 2008.

Kristeller, Paul O. 'Un codice padovano di Aristotele postillato da Francesco e Ermolao Barbaro: il manoscritto Plimpton 17 della Columbia University Library a New York,' *La Bibliofilia* 50, no. 2 (1948): 162–78.

Kristeller, Paul O. *Eight Philosophers of the Italian Renaissance.* Stanford, CA: Stanford University Press, 1964.

Labalme, Patricia H. 'Secular and Sacred Heroes: Ermolao Barbaro on Worldly Honour,' in *Una famiglia veneziana nella storia: I Barbaro. Atti del Convegno di studi in occasione del quinto centenario della morte dell'umanista Ermolao, Venezia, 4–6 Novembre 1993*, edited by Michela Marangoni and Manlio Pastore Stocchi, 331–44. Venice: Istituto Veneto di Scienze, Lettere ed Arti, 1996.

Laks, André, and Glenn W. Most, eds and trs. *Early Greek Philosophy V: Western Greek Thinkers.* Part 2. Loeb Classical Library 528. Cambridge, MA, and London: Harvard University Press, 2016.

Lattimore, Richmond, tr. *The Odyssey of Homer.* New York: Harper & Row, 1967.

Lazzarini, Lino. 'Francesco Petrarca e il primo Umanesimo a Venezia,' in *Umanesimo europeo e Umanesimo veneziano*, edited by Vittore Branca, 63–92. Florence: Sansoni, 1963.

Leão, Delfim F. 'A Statesman of Many Resources: Plutarch on Solon's Use of Myth and Theatricality for Political Purposes,' in *A Man of Many Interests: Plutarch on Religion, Myth, and Magic. Essays in Honour of Aurelio Pérez Jiménez*, edited by Delfim F. Leão and Lautaro Roig Lanzillotta, 41–58. Brill's Plutarch Studies 2. Leiden: Brill, 2019.

Lefkowitz, Mary R., and Maureen B. Fant, eds. *Women's Life in Greece and Rome. A Source Book in Translation.* 3rd edn. Baltimore: The Johns Hopkins University Press, 2005.

Lennox, James G., tr. *Aristotle*, On the Parts of Animals *I-IV*. Oxford: Oxford University Press, 2001.

Lindsay, Wallace M., ed. *Sexti Pompei Festi de verborum significatione quae supersunt.* Leipzig: Teubner, 1913.

Lines, David A. 'Aristotle's *Ethics* in the Renaissance,' in *The Reception of Aristotle's Ethics*, edited by Jon Miller, 171–93. Cambridge: Cambridge University Press, 2013.

Lohr, Charles H. 'Medieval Latin Aristotle Commentaries: Authors G-I,' *Traditio* 24 (1968): 149–245.

Long, A. A., and David N. Sedley, eds. *The Hellenistic Philosophers.* 2 vols. Cambridge: Cambridge University Press, 1987.

López-Ríos, Santiago. 'A New Inventory of the Royal Aragonese Library of Naples,' *Journal of the Warburg and Courtauld Institutes* 65 (2002): 201–43.

Mahoney, Edward P. 'Aristotle and Some Late Medieval and Renaissance Philosophers,' in *The Impact of Aristotelianism on Modern Philosophy*, edited by Riccardo Pozzo, 1–34. Studies in Philosophy and the History of Philosophy 39. Washington, D.C.: The Catholic University of America Press, 2004.

Manetti, Aldo. 'Review of Vittore Branca, ed. *Ermolao Barbaro*, De coelibatu, De officio legati. (Florence: Leo S. Olschki, 1969),' *La Bibliofilia* 73, no. 3 (1971): 305–11.

Manuwald, Gesine, ed. and tr. *Fragmentary Republican Latin III: Oratory, Part I*. Loeb Classical Library 540. Cambridge, MA, and London: Harvard University Press, 2019.

Marcon, Susy, and Laura Moretti, eds. *Daniele Barbaro 1514–70: Letteratura, scienza e arti nella Venezia del Rinascimento*. Venice: Antiga Edizioni, 2015.

Margolin, Jean-Claude. 'Sur la conception humaniste du "barbare": À propos de la controverse épistolaire entre Pic de la Mirandole et Ermolao Barbaro,' in *Una famiglia veneziana nella storia: I Barbaro. Atti del Convegno di studi in occasione del quinto centenario della morte dell'umanista Ermolao, Venezia, 4–6 Novembre 1993*, edited by Michela Marangoni and Manlio Pastore Stocchi, 235–76. Venice: Istituto Veneto di Scienze, Lettere ed Arti, 1996.

Marshall, Tina, ed. and tr. *Coluccio Salutati:* On the World and Religious Life. The I Tatti Renaissance Library 62. Cambridge, MA, and London: Harvard University Press, 2014.

Matino, Gabriele, and Patricia F. Brown, eds. *Carpaccio in Venice: A Guide*. Venice: Marsilio, 2020.

Mazzatinti, Giuseppe. *La biblioteca dei re d'Aragona in Napoli*. Rocca S. Casciano: Licinio Cappelli Editore, 1897.

McDonnell, Myles. 'The Speech of Numidicus at Gellius, *N.A.* 1.6,' *American Journal of Philology* 108, no. 1 (1987): 81–94.

McLaughlin, Martin L. *Literary Imitation in the Italian Renaissance: The Theory and Practice of Literary Imitation in Italy from Dante to Bembo*. Oxford: Oxford University Press, 1995.

Meloni Trkulja, Silvia. 'Cristofano di Papi dell'Altissimo,' *Dizionario biografico degli Italiani* 31 (1985): 54–7.

Mensch, Pamela, tr., with James Miller, ed. *Diogenes Laertius:* Lives of the Eminent Philosophers. Oxford: Oxford University Press, 2018.

Mercer, R. G. G. *The Teaching of Gasparino Barzizza, with Special Reference to His Place in Paduan Humanism*. London: Modern Humanities Research Association, 1979.

Modrak, Deborah K. W. *Aristotle's Theory of Language and Meaning*. Cambridge: Cambridge University Press, 2001.

Moffitt, John F. 'Sluter's *Pleurants* and Timanthes' *Tristitia Velata*: Evolution of, and Sources for, a Humanist Topos of Mourning,' *Artibus et Historiae* 26, no. 51 (2005): 73–84.

Mohr, Richard D. 'The Number Theory in Plato's *Republic* VII and *Philebus*,' *Isis* 72, no. 4 (1981): 620–7.

Mosshammer, Alden A. 'Thales' Eclipse,' *Transactions of the American Philological Association* 111 (1981): 145–55.

Müntz, Eugène. 'Le musée de portraits de Paul Jove,' *Mémoires de l'institut national de France, Académie des inscriptions et belles lettres* 36, no. 2 (1901): 249–343.

Nauert, Charles G. 'Caius Plinius Secundus,' in *Catalogus Translationum et Commentariorum* IV, edited by F. Edward Cranz, 297-422. Washington, D.C.: The Catholic University of America Press, 1980.
Nauert, Charles G. *Humanism and the Culture of Renaissance Europe*. 2nd edn. Cambridge: Cambridge University Press, 2006.
Nisbet, Robin G. M., and Niall Rudd. *A Commentary on Horace*, Odes, *Book III*. Oxford: Oxford University Press, 2004.
Notopoulos, James A. 'The Name of Plato,' *Classical Philology* 34, no. 2 (1939): 135-45.
O'Sullivan, Patrick. 'Aeschylus, Euripides, and Tragic Painting: Two Scenes from *Agamemnon* and *Hecuba*,' *American Journal of Philology* 129, no. 2 (2008): 173-98.
Ogilvie, Brian W. *The Science of Describing: Natural History in Renaissance Europe*. Chicago and London: The University of Chicago Press, 2006.
Ostwald, Martin. 'The Reform of the Athenian State by Cleisthenes,' *Cambridge Ancient History*[2] 4 (1988): 303-46.
Panizza, Letizia. 'Ermolao Barbaro e Pico della Mirandola tra retorica e dialettica: Il *De genere dicendi philosophorum* del 1485,' in *Una famiglia veneziana nella storia: I Barbaro. Atti del Convegno di studi in occasione del quinto centenario della morte dell'umanista Ermolao, Venezia, 4-6 Novembre 1993*, edited by Michela Marangoni and Manlio Pastore Stocchi, 277-330. Venice: Istituto Veneto di Scienze, Lettere ed Arti, 1996.
Panizza, Letizia. 'Pico della Mirandola e il *De genere dicendi philosophorum* del 1485: L'encomio paradossale dei "barbari" e la loro parodia,' *I Tatti Studies in the Italian Renaissance* 8 (1999): 69-103.
Panizza, Letizia. 'Pico della Mirandola's 1485 Parody of Scholastic "Barbarians",' in *Italy in Crisis: 1494*, edited by Jane Everson and Diego Zancani, 152-74. Oxford: Legenda, 2000.
Parish, Helen. *Clerical Celibacy in the West: c. 1100-1700*. Farnham: Ashgate, 2010.
Paschini, Pio. *Tre illustri prelati del Rinascimento: Ermolao Barbaro, Adriano Castellesi, Giovanni Grimani*. Rome: Facultas Theologica Pontificii Athenaei Lateranensis, 1957.
Pease, Arthur S., ed. *M. Tulli Ciceronis* De natura deorum *libri tres*. 2 vols. Cambridge, MA: Harvard University Press, 1955-8.
Pesic, Peter. 'Shapes of Proteus in Renaissance Art,' *Huntington Library Quarterly* 73, no. 1 (2010): 57-82.
Petrucci, Armando. 'Bracciolini, Poggio,' *Dizionario biografico degli Italiani* 13 (1971): 640-6.
Pincus, Debra. 'Venice and the Two Romes: Byzantium and Rome as a Double Heritage in Venetian Cultural Politics,' *Artibus et Historiae* 13, no. 26 (1992): 101-14.
Pistilli, Gino. 'Guarini, Guarino,' *Dizionario biografico degli Italiani* 60 (2003): 357-69.
Powell, Jonathan G. F., ed. *Cicero*, Cato Maior de Senectute. Cambridge Classical Texts and Commentaries 28. Cambridge: Cambridge University Press, 1988.

Pozzi, Giovanni, ed. *Hermolai Barbari Castigationes Plinianae et in Pomponium Melam*. 4 vols. Thesaurus Mundi 11, 14, 18, 19. Padua: Antenore, 1973–9.
Pozzi, Giovanni. 'Appunti sul *Corollarium* del Barbaro,' in *Tra latino e volgare per Carlo Dionisotti*, edited by Gabriella Bernardoni-Trezzini et al., 2 vols: 2.619–40. Padua: Antenore, 1974.
Price Zimmermann, T. C. *Paolo Giovio: The Historian and the Crisis of Sixteenth-Century Italy*. Princeton, NJ: Princeton University Press, 1995.
Queller, Donald E. 'The Civic Irresponsibility of the Venetian Nobility,' in *Economy, Society, and Government in Medieval Italy: Essays in Memory of Robert L. Reynolds*, edited by David Herlihy et al., 223–35. Kent, OH: The Kent State University Press, 1969.
Queller, Donald E. *The Venetian Patriciate: Reality versus Myth*. Urbana and Chicago: University of Illinois Press, 1986.
Rackham, Harris, ed. and tr. *Pliny, Natural History, Volume IX: Books 33–35*. Loeb Classical Library 394. Cambridge, MA, and London: Harvard University Press, 1952.
Raines, Dorit. 'La biblioteca manoscritta di Daniele Barbaro: raccolta, uso e dispersione di una collezione veneziana,' in *Daniele Barbaro 1514–70: Letteratura, scienza e arti nella Venezia del Rinascimento*, edited by Susy Marcon and Laura Moretti, 101–13. Venice: Antiga Edizioni, 2015.
Ramminger, Johann. 'A Commentary? Ermolao Barbaro's Supplement to Dioscorides,' in *On Renaissance Commentaries*, edited by Marianne Pade, 65–85. Noctes Neolatinae: Neo-Latin Texts and Studies 4. Hildesheim: Olms, 2005.
Reeds, Karen M. 'Renaissance Humanism and Botany,' *Annals of Science* 33, no. 6 (1976): 519–42.
Regnicoli, Laura. 'Sinibaldi, Antonio,' *Dizionario biografico degli Italiani* 92 (2018): 246–50.
Reynolds, Leighton D., and Nigel G. Wilson. *Scribes and Scholars: A Guide to the Transmission of Greek and Latin Literature*. 2nd edn. Oxford: Oxford University Press, 1974.
Riddle, John M. 'Dioscorides,' in *Catalogus Translationum et Commentariorum* IV, edited by F. Edward Cranz, 1–143. Washington, D.C.: The Catholic University of America Press, 1980.
Rinaldi, Michele. 'La lettera di dedica a Federico da Montefeltro del primo libro delle *Commentationes in centum sententiis Ptolemaei* di Giovanni Gioviano Pontano,' *Cahiers de Recherches Médiévales et Humanistes* 25 (2013): 341–55.
Rinaldi, Michele, tr. 'Appendice: Ermolao Barbaro, *De officio legati*,' in Luigi Robuschi, 'Il *De officio legati* di Ermolao Barbaro ed il pensiero politico nella Venezia di fine '400,' *Atti dell'Istituto Veneto di scienze, lettere ed arti. Classe di scienze morali, lettere ed arti* 172 (2013–14): 289–300.
Rist, John M. *The Mind of Aristotle: A Study in Philosophical Growth*. Toronto: University of Toronto Press, 1989.

Robuschi, Luigi. 'Il *De officio legati* di Ermolao Barbaro ed il pensiero politico nella Venezia di fine '400,' *Atti dell'Istituto Veneto di scienze, lettere ed arti. Classe di scienze morali, lettere ed arti* 172 (2013-14): 257-301.
Rodini, Elizabeth. 'The Politics of Marriage in Carpaccio's St. Ursula Cycle,' *Early Modern Women* 8 (2013): 85-117.
Roick, Matthias. 'From Lost Laughter to Latin Philosophy: On the Beginnings of Neapolitan Humanism,' *California Italian Studies* 3.1 (2012): http://escholarship.org/uc/item/91x000m2.
Roller, Matthew. 'The Dialogue in Seneca's *Dialogues* (and Other Moral Essays),' in *The Cambridge Companion to Seneca*, edited by Shadi Bartsch and Alessandro Schiesaro, 54-67. Cambridge: Cambridge University Press, 2015.
Ross, W. David, ed. *Aristotelis fragmenta selecta*. Oxford: Oxford University Press, 1955.
Ross, W. David, tr. *Aristotle: The Nicomachean Ethics*. The World's Classics. Oxford and New York: Oxford University Press, 1980. Revised by John L. Akrill and James O. Urmson.
Sabbadini, Remigio. *Vita di Guarino Veronese*. Genoa: Istituto Sordo-Mutti, 1891.
Sabbadini, Remigio. 'La gita di Francesco Barbaro a Firenze nel 1415,' *Miscellanea di studi in onore di Attilio Hortis*, 2 vols: 2.615-27. Trieste: Caprin, 1910.
Sabbadini, Remigio, ed. *Epistolario di Guarino Veronese*. 3 vols. Venice: A Spese della Società, 1915-19.
Saxonhouse, Arlene. 'Xanthippe: Shrew or Muse,' *Hypatia* 33, no. 4 (2018): 610-25.
Scaglione, Aldo. 'Review of Vittore Branca, ed. *Ermolao Barbaro*, De coelibatu, De officio legati (Florence: Leo S. Olschki, 1969),' *Modern Philology* 69, no. 4 (1972): 338-9.
Schenkeveld, Dirk M., and Jonathan Barnes. 'Language,' in *The Cambridge History of Hellenistic Philosophy*, edited by Keimpe Algra et al., 177-225. Cambridge: Cambridge University Press, 1999.
Sedley, David N. *Plato's Cratylus*. Cambridge: Cambridge University Press, 2003.
Sharples, Robert W. 'Peripatetics on Happiness,' in *Greek and Roman Philosophy 100 BC-200 AD*, edited by Richard Sorabji and Robert W. Sharples, 627-37. Bulletin of the Institute of Classical Studies Supplement 94. London: Institute of Classical Studies, University of London, 2007.
Shepherd, William. *Poggii Bracciolini Florentini Dialogus an seni sit uxor ducenda*. Liverpool: Geo. F. Harris Publisher, 1807.
Smith, Stephen C. 'Brutus as an Earthborn Founder of Rome (Livy 1.56),' *Mnemosyne* 60, no. 2 (2007): 285-93.
Sorabji, Richard. *Animal Minds and Human Morals: The Origins of the Western Debate*. Cornell Studies in Classical Philology 54. Ithaca, NY: Cornell University Press, 1993.
Soubiran, Jean, ed. and tr. *Vitruve*, De l'architecture: *Livre IX*. Paris: Les Belles Lettres, 1969.
Stacey, Peter. '*Hispania* and Royal Humanism in Alfonsine Naples,' *Mediterranean Historical Review* 26, no. 1 (2011): 51-65.

Stickney, Trumbull. *De Hermolai Barbari vita atque ingenio*. Paris: Société Nouvelle de Librairie et d'Édition, 1903.

Taylor, Christopher C. W. 'The Role of Women in Plato's *Republic*,' in *Virtue and Happiness: Essays in Honour of Julia Annas*, edited by Rachana Kamtekar, 75–87. Oxford Studies in Ancient Philosophy Supplementary Volume. Oxford: Oxford University Press, 2012.

Todd, Robert B. 'Themistius,' in *Catalogus Translationum et Commentariorum* VIII, edited by Virginia Brown, 57–102. Washington, D.C.: The Catholic University of America Press, 2003.

Touwaide, Alain. 'Printing Greek Medicine in the Renaissance. Scholars, Collections, Opportunities, and Challenges: Introduction,' *Early Science and Medicine* 17, no. 6 (2012): 371–7.

Tredennick, Hugh, ed. and tr. *Aristotle*, Metaphysics, *Books I-IX*. Loeb Classical Library 271. Cambridge, MA, and London: Harvard University Press, 1933.

Treggiari, Susan. *Terentia, Tullia and Publilia: The Women of Cicero's Family*. London and New York: Routledge, 2007.

Trithemius, Johannes (Tritheim, Johann). *Liber de scriptoribus ecclesiasticis*. Basel: Johann Amerbach, 1494.

Ulery, Robert W., ed. and tr. *Pietro Bembo: History of Venice. Volume I: Books I-IV*. The I Tatti Renaissance Library 28. Cambridge, MA, and London: Harvard University Press, 2007.

Ullman, Berthold L. *The Origin and Development of Humanistic Script*. Rome: Edizioni di storia e letteratura, 1960.

Vecchio, Silvana. '*De uxore non ducenda*: La polemica antimatrimoniale fra XIII e XIV secolo,' in *Gli Zibaldoni di Boccaccio: memoria, scrittura, riscrittura. Atti del Seminario internazionale di Firenze-Certaldo (26–28 aprile 1996)*, edited by Michelangelo Picone and Claude Cazalé Bérard, 53–64. Florence: Franco Cesati Editore, 1998.

Vendruscolo, Fabio. 'Ateneo e Dioscoride: le ultime fatiche dell'umanista Ermolao Barbaro e il codice Par. gr. 3056,' *Maia* 69, no. 3 (2017): 583–95.

Vendruscolo, Fabio. 'Per la biblioteca di Francesco ed Ermolao Barbaro: cinquant'anni dopo,' in *Griechisch-byzantinische Handschriftenforschung: Traditionen, Entwicklungen, neue Wege*, edited by Christian Brockmann et al., 101–28. Berlin and New York: Walter de Gruyter, 2020.

Vickers, Brian. *In Defence of Rhetoric*. Oxford: Oxford University Press, 1988.

Vottero, Dionigi, ed. *Lucio Anneo Seneca: I Frammenti*. Bologna: Pàtron Editore, 1998.

Walsh, P. G., ed. and tr. *Augustine*, De bono coniugali, De sancta virginitate. Oxford Early Christian Texts. Oxford: Oxford University Press, 2001.

Wardle, David. *Cicero*: On Divination, *Book 1*. Oxford: Oxford University Press, 2006.

Waters, Matt. *Ancient Persia. A Concise History of the Achaemenid Empire, 550–330 BCE*. Cambridge: Cambridge University Press, 2014.

Weiss, Roberto. *The Renaissance Discovery of Classical Antiquity*. 2nd edn. Oxford: Basil Blackwell, 1988.

Whidden, Christopher. 'The Account of Persia and Cyrus's Persian Education in Xenophon's *Cyropaedia*,' *Review of Politics* 69, no. 4 (2007): 539–67.
Williams, Gareth D. 'Style and Form in Seneca's Writing,' in *The Cambridge Companion to Seneca*, edited by Shadi Bartsch and Alessandro Schiesaro, 135–49. Cambridge: Cambridge University Press, 2015.
Wilson, Katharina M. '*De Conjuge non Ducenda*: Heavenly Persuasion to Wifelessness,' *Classica et Mediaevalia* 36 (1985): 213–23.
Wilson, Nigel G. *From Byzantium to Italy: Greek Studies in the Italian Renaissance*. 2nd edn. London and New York: Bloomsbury Academic, 2017.
Woodbury, Leonard. 'Socrates and the Daughter of Aristides,' *Phoenix* 27, no. 1 (1973): 7–25.
Zorzi, Marino. 'I Barbaro e i libri,' in *Una famiglia veneziana nella storia: I Barbaro. Atti del Convegno di studi in occasione del quinto centenario della morte dell'umanista Ermolao, Venezia, 4-6 Novembre 1993*, edited by Michela Marangoni and Manlio Pastore Stocchi, 363–96. Venice: Istituto Veneto di Scienze, Lettere ed Arti, 1996.

Index of Passages

Apuleius
Apologia
10.8-9 105 n.22

De dogmate Platonis
1.1.1 145 n.123

Aratus
Phaenomena
322 55 n.18
342-52 55 n.16

Aristotle
De anima
2.4 415a22-b2 137 n.100
3.4 429a29-b5 143 n.116

De interpretatione
1 105 n.17

De nobilitate
fr. 3 113 n.42

De partibus animalium
2.3 650a34-5 161 n.175
2.3 650b11-13 161 n.175
2.4 650b18-51a5 161 n.176
2.4.651a14-15 161 n.175
3.5 668a4-8 161 n.175

Ethica Nicomachea
1.7 1097a28-34, 1097b14-16 127 n.77
1.8 1099a31-3 127 n.77
1.10-11 1100a10-1101b9 133 n.91
1.13 1102b13-1103a10 83 n.91
4.1 1120b7-11 129 n.83
6.12 1143b34 67 n.44
6.13 1145a6-11 67 n.44
8.1 1155a16-21 137 n.99
10.7 1177a12-78a8 69 n.50
10.7 1177a.28-9, 1177b1 67 n.44
10.7 1177a32-5 69 n.51
10.7 1177b26-78a8 81 n.87
10.8 1178a22-79a32 69 n.50
10.9 1179b31-81b22 67 n.44

Historia animalium
7[8] 588b22-589a3 137 n.100

Metaphysica
1.3 983b20-1 105 n.18
4.5 1009b17-19 145 n.122

Politica
1.2 1252a26-31 109 n.31
7.16 1334b29-36a2 109 n.31
7.16 1335a29 111 n.36

[Aristotle]
Athēnaiōn politeia
14.1-2 155 n.154

Augustine
De bono coniugali
3 107 n.28

Aulus Gellius
1.6.1-6 111 n.35
1.6.3 40 n.102

Barbaro, Ermolao
Epistolae (as in Branca 1943)
VIII (to Pope Sixtus IV) 23 and
    43 n.157, 30–1 and 45 n.198
XI (to Francesco Tron) 23 and
    43 n.154
XII (to Girolamo Donato) 31 and
    45 n.203

XXXI (to Nicoletto Vernia) 31 and
  45 n.200
LXVIII (to Giovanni Pico della
  Mirandola) 29 and 45 nn.185–
  6
LXXII (to Arnold of Bost) 5 and
  36 n.21
LXXVI (to Arnold of Bost) 4 and
  36 n.20
LXXX (to Giovanni Pico della
  Mirandola) 30 and 45 nn.185,
  194
LXXXI (to Giovanni Pico della
  Mirandola) 30 and 45 nn.185,
  195
CXXXI (to Marco Dandalo) 38 n.63
CXLVI (to Jacopo Antiquario) 2 and
  36 n.12
CXLVII (to Ugolino Verino) 3 and
  36 n.13
CLII (to Antonio Calvo) 3 and
  36 n.14
CLIV (to Jacopo Antiquario) 2 and
  36 nn.7–11
CLVI (to Pope Alexander VI) 24 and
  44 n.167

Orationes (as in Branca 1943)
III 31 and 45 n.205

Barbaro, Francesco
De re uxoria (as in Griggio 2021)
I.1 15 and 40 n.100
I.3 15-16 and 40 n.101
II.1-8 107 n.28
II.1 85 n.95
II.2 87 n.100
II.3 111 n.36
II.9-10 111 n.35, 113 n.43
III.1 16 and 40 nn.105, 107, 85 n.96
III.8 16 and 40 n.107
IV.4 111 n.36
VI.1 16 and 40 n.110
VI.6 16 and 40 n.109
VII.1 16 and 40 n.108

X.2 85 n.97
XII-XVI 20
XII.1 41 n.128, 85 n.98
XV.1 20 and 41 n.127
XVIII 17, 39 n.78
XVIII.17 38 nn.75, 77

Cicero
Academica
1.17 61 n.31

Brutus
145, 150 45 n.193

De divinatione
1.92 67 n.45
1.112 105 n.21

De finibus
1.49 147 n.138
2.45 53 n.11
2.68 95 n.122
3.60-1 147 n.138
3.64 63 n.34
5.11 69 n.50
5.34, 5.38 53 n.11
5.48-54 79 n.83
5.48-60 57 n.20
5.57 77 n.74
5.66 69 n.52
5.82 91 n.113
5.92 95 n.123
5.94 145 n.129

De legibus
1.22 53 n.11

De natura deorum
1.2, 1.63, 1.117 121 n.58
2.140-6, 2.150-1 65 n.39

De officiis
1.11 53 n.11, 87 n.100, 137 n.99
1.12 69 n.52
1.15 19

1.18 19, 67 n.47, 71 n.55
1.19 19, 67 n.47, 69 n.52, 71 n.57,
　79 n.83
1.20-41 19
1.22 63 n.34, 69 n.52
1.28 69 n.52
1.31 63 n.34
1.42-60 19
1.50 69 n.52
1.52 63 n.34
1.52-3 141 n.110
1.54 137 n.99
1.61-92 19
1.63 159 n.167
1.66 95 n.121
1.71 18, 69 n.52, 71 n.57, 79 n.83,
　83 n.92
1.72 157 n.159
1.93-151 19
1.101-2 81 n.88
1.107-9 151 n.147, 155 n.156
1.108 153 n.153
1.110, 1.114, 1.120 155 n.157
1.112 153 n.151
1.114 159 n.166
1.129 125 n.70
1.132, 1.141 81 n.88
1.153 73 n.60
1.155 18
1.155-6 71 n.57, 79 n.83, 83 n.92
1.157 73 n.60
1.158 73 nn.61–2
2.12 65 n.39
3.16 153 n.149
3.28, 3.30 63 n.34

De oratore
1.209-13 61 n.31
2.224 125 n.70

De republica
1.38.1-2 61 n.31
1.43.2 67 n.46
2.12 113 n.41

De senectute
16 139 n.106

Orator
74 135 n.95

Paradoxa Stoicorum
8-9 131 n.87

Tusculanae disputationes
1.38 77 n.75
1.83 97 n.128
1.85 91 n.113, 97 nn.128, 134
2.60 145 n.129, 147 nn.136, 138
2.61 147 nn.136, 138
2.66-7 147 n.138
3.70 97 n.134
5.9 79 n.83

Cornelius Nepos
Aristides
1.2, 1.4 153 n.149

Dante Alighieri
Inferno
5.52-60 61 n.28

Diodorus Siculus
2.6 61 n.28

Diogenes Laertius
1.21 95 n.122
1.23 105 n.21
1.26 105 n.19, 107 n.25
1.46-7 153 n.153
1.87 89 n.109
1.106-8 107 n.26
2.14 145 n.126
2.16 113 n.44
2.26 113 n.42
2.36-7 113 n.43
2.66 119 n.56
2.68 79 n.80
2.86, 2.97, 2.100 121 n.58

2.115 131 n.87
3.4 145 n.123
3.29, 3.31 105 nn.20, 22
4.1 121 n.62
4.3 147 n.141
4.6 145 n.124
4.40-1 121 n.62
4.44 145 n.125
4.46 121 n.60
4.48, 52, 54 121 n.59
4.53-4 121 n.61
5.3-4 121 n.62
5.67 145 n.124
7.37, 166 145 n.129
7.119 71 n.54

Herodotus
1.59 155 n.154
1.74.2 105 n.21
3.39-43, 3.120-5 95 n.123
3.134 59 n.27

Hippocrates/Hippocratic Corpus
De natura hominis
4 161 n.177

Homer
Iliad
3.2-6 65 n.38
6.243-6 97 n.132
24.496 97 n.133

Odyssey
4.363-570 153 n.152
11.492-3 135 n.92
11.538-40 135 n.93

Horace
Carmina
3.3.3 153 n.151
3.3.7-8 139 n.107

Sermones
1.6.121, 2.7.44 153 n.151

Jerome
Adversus Iovinianum
1.16, 1.47 59 n.24
1.48 59 n.26, 113 n.42
2.13 59 n.24

Epistulae
107 123 n.66, 125 n.72

Livy
1.56.7-8, 59.2, 59.8 155 n.155
45.40.7 97 n.134

Manilius
Astronomica
4.150-1 55 n.18
5.32-56 55 n.16
5.140-51 55 n.18

Ovid
Fasti
2.717-18 155 n.155
4.717-18 55 n.18

Pausanias
1.40.3 131 n.86

Plato
Apologia
24b 121 n.58

Cratylus 103 n.11

Leges
773b-e 107 n.28

Phaedo
62b, 67d, 82e 141 n.113

Phaedrus
237b-d 61 n.31

Protagoras
343a 107 n.26

Respublica
457c-461e 107 n.28

Pliny the elder
Naturalis historia
2.53 105 n.21
7.26 65 n.38
7.172 145 n.128
34.49 131 n.86

Plutarch
Moralia
227f 111 n.36
654c 105 n.19

Vitae
  Aemilius Paulus
  5.5 97, 35.1-3 97 n.134

  Aristides
  6.1, 7.6 153 n.149

  Cato maior/Cato the elder
  20.5 125 n.70

  Lycurgus
  15.1-2 111 n.36

  Solon
  7.1 105 n.19
  7.2 107 n.25
  8.1-3 153 n.153
  30.1-3, 30.5, 31.1 155 n.154

[Plutarch]
De liberis educandis 123 n.66
7 125 nn.69, 73
8 131 n.87

Quintilian
Institutio oratoria
Bks 1–2 123 n.66
1.1.9 125 n.72
1.2 125 n.69
1.6.36 103 nn.9–10
2.2.3-8 125 n.69
2.13.13 135 n.95

Sallust
Iugurtha
1.1-4 77 n.74

Seneca the younger
De matrimonio
fr. 30 59 n.26

Dialogi
1.1.5 71 n.54
1.6.1 95 n.121
2.5.6 131 n.87
2.8.2 71 n.54
8.3.5 69 n.51
8.5.3-8 57 and n.20
8.5.6-8 77 n.74
8.6.4-5 69 n.51
12.10.1-3, 12.1 133 n.89

Epistulae
9.1, 8, 15, 17-18, etc. 69 n.51
15.1-3 141 n.111
58.30 145 n.123
58.36 147 n.138
59.14 71 n.54
65.15-16 77 n.74
65.16-17, 21 141 n.113
65.22 141 n.111
66.35, 74.6 95 n.121
79.12 141 n.113
80.6 133 n.89
82.5 95 n.121
82.10-11 133 n.89
85.38 69 n.51
88.34 141 n.113
92.10 141 n.111
98.16 147 n.138
123.16 133 n.89

Quaestiones naturales
1 pref. 4-6, 9-11 77 n.74
3 pref. 11, 18 77 n.74

Sophocles
Electra
945 119 n.52

Terence
Andria
829 40 n.102

Hautontimorumenos
719 139 n.107

Theocritus
Idylls
15.139 97 n.133

Valerius Maximus
1.1.1 67 n.45
5.10.2 97 n.134
6.9 ext. 5 95 n.123
7.1.1 91 n.113
7.2 ext. 3 131 n.87
7.3.2 155 n.155
8.11 ext. 6 135 n.95

Valla, Lorenzo
De voluptate
1.45.1-11 65 n.37

Velleius Paterculus
1.10.3-5 97 n.134

Virgil
Aeneid
2.503 97 n.132
8.671-713 59 n.27

Vitruvius
De architectura
9.3.1 55 n.18

Xenophon
Cyropaedia
1.2.3, 1.2.6-9 67 n.46

General Index

Academics 104–5 and n.16
Accademia Pontaniana 42 n.146
Achilles' pride in Neoptolemus, his son 134–5 and n.94
active man
    always serves the community 66–7
    regulates contemplative study within the state 66–7, 78–9
    sometimes engages in contemplation 82–3
Aemilius Paulus Macedonicus, Lucius 97 n.131, 99 n.136
Alexander the Great 142–3 and nn.117–18
Amasis, Egyptian pharaoh 94–5 and n.123
Anaxagoras 144–5 and n.126
animals
    humankind a social animal 68–9 and n.52, 72–3 and n.61, 75 n.67
    natural affection for their young 136–7 and n.99
    no capacity for human reason 52–3 and n.11, 70–1 and n.56, 80–1
Antigonus II Gonatas 120–1 and n.60
Antipater of Tarsus 140–1 and n.110
Antipater of Tyre 141 n.110
Antiquario, Jacopo 1, 2
Antony and Cleopatra 58–9 and n.27
Aquileia, Patriarchate of ix, 1, 2, 27
Arcesilaus 120–1 and n.62, 144–5 and n.125
Archeanassa, Plato's alleged mistress 105 n.20
Archelaus, Socrates' teacher 112–13 and n.44

Argo Navis 54–5 and n.16
Aristides the Just 113 n.42, 150–3 and nn.148–50
Aristippus of Cyrene 78–9 and n.80, 118–19
Aristotle 5 and 36 n.21, 22–3, 31, 43 n.153, 61 n.30, 66–7 and n.44, 78–9, 82–3
    Barbaro's translations of 5, 22 and 42–3 n.150
    citing Empedocles 144–5 and n.122
    good health in relation to happiness 140–1 and n.111
    happiness in the contemplative life 68–9 and n.50
    happiness of the dead affected by descendants' fortunes 132–3 and n.91
    ideas/forms immanent in particulars 80–1 and n.87, 86–7 and n.101
    on marriage and reproduction 106–9 and n.31
    the mean 8, 33, 42 n.144
    on the nature of blood 161 nn.175–6
    obedience of impulse to reason 82–3 and n.91
    position on the derivation of names/naming 105 n.17
    scala naturae in 137 n.100
    senses impaired by overload 142–3 and n.116
    shameful conduct alleged 120–1 and n.62
    thirty-seven as male marital age most conducive to procreation 111 n.36

and Venetian ideology 22
Arnold of Bost 4, 5, 24
Athena Parthenos 131 nn.85–6
Atossa 58–9 and n.27
Augustine on marriage 14–15,
   107 n.28
Augustus' moral reforms 110–11 and
   n.37
Averroes 22

Barbaro, Daniele 42–3 n.150
Barbaro, Ermolao
  ambassador to Milan 3
  ambassador to Papal Curia 1
  and Aristotle 5 and 36 n.21, 22–3
    and 42 n.150
  as *barbarus* 23, 43 n.158
  Castigationes Plinianae primae 24,
    29, 32
  Compendium ethicorum librorum
    22 and 42 n.150
  Compendium scientiae naturalis
    ex Aristotele 42 n.150
  Corollarium in Dioscoridem 23
    and 43 n.160, 24
  De officio legati ix, x, xi, 29, 32
  devotion to his humanistic studies
    2–3, 4
  and Dioscorides ix, 5 and 36 n.21,
    23–4, 32
  dispute with Giovanni Pico della
    Mirandola 23, 29–31
  letters of 1–2, 3, 4–5, 23, 24, 29–30,
    31
  library of 36 n.18
  and manuscript collation 11
  in Naples (1471–3) 3, 21, 42
    n.146
  nomination to Patriarchate of
    Aquileia 1–2, 27
  in Padua (1474–9) 22
  'philosophy' of translation 22–3,
    29–31
  and Themistius 5 and 36 n.21, 22,
    23, 30–1
  as 'Venetian humanism's most
    genuine rebel' 21
  view of the relationship between
    verbum and *res* 31–2
Barbaro, Francesco 5, 12–17
  education 13
  in Florence (1415) 13
  De re uxoria 12–21
    Ciceronian style and diction in
      13 and 38 n.73, 32
    criteria for choosing wife
      85 n.96
    date of composition 14
    definition of marriage in
      85 n.95
    influence of Cicero's *De officiis*
      on 17–18
    meaning of title 16
    originality of 12–17
    translations and editions
      of 14
    two movements of 14 and
      39 n.83
  marriage to Maria Loredan
    39 n.84
Barbaro, Zaccaria 2, 6, 7, 12, 39 n.84,
   89 n.110
  ambassador to Naples 3
Barbo, Marco 1
Barzizza, Gasparino 13
Bassus, Gavius 103 n.9
Bembo, Pietro 27 and 44 n.179
Bias of Priene 88–9 and n.109, 130–1
   and n.87
Biblioteca Comunale Ariostea,
   Ferrara 5, 6
Bion of Borysthenes 120–1 and
   nn.59–61
birthsigns, influence of 54–5 and
   nn.16–18
blood, nature of 160–1 and nn.175–7
Boccaccio, Giovanni 40 n.93
Bracciolini, Poggio 17 and 40–1
   n.115
Branca, Vittore ix, x, 5, 31, 32, 33

Caecilius Metellus Macedonicus,
    Quintus 90-1 and n.113,
    96-7 and n.128, 99 n.136,
    111 n.35
Caecilius Metellus Numidicus,
    Quintus 111-12 and n.35
Calistus/Cybisthus, Thales' alleged
    son 106-7 and n.25
Calvo, Antonio 3
Carbone, Ludovico 39 n.86
Carpaccio, Vittore 26-9
Cavalcanti, Ginevra 13
celibate/celibacy
    blood, desirable constitution of
        160-3 and nn.175-7
    commerce, no engagement in
        128-9
    and contemplation 7
    as counterpart to noble wife in
        De re uxoria 20
    definition of 102-3
    education of 7, 8, 19, 124-5
    female 8-9
    god-like 7, 8, 70-1 and n.54,
        102-3 and n.9, 116-17,
        140-1 and n.112
    good health needed 7, 138-49
    home-schooled by tutor of
        impeccable integrity 124-5
    ill-suited to tasks beneath his
        contemplative capacities
        156-9
    like Stoic sage 71 n.54
    natural disposition sought in
        150-63
    natural manner of speech 33
    no recluse 68-9 and n.51
    parental duty of care 116-27
    practical resources needed for
        celibate-to-be 126-37
    qualities sought in 114-27
    relation between inner purity and
        external deportment 31-2
    religious formation 7, 122-3
    self-control 8
    two classes of 84-5
    utility to others 70-1 and n.57
    vivacious and cheerful 8, 21, 33
Chaeremon of Alexandria 59 n.24
childhood, concept of in
    Renaissance 9
Chojnacki, Stanley 12, 20
Cicero 17, 18-20, 29, 32 and 46 n.213,
    33, 72-3, 75 n.64, 76-7,
    78-9, 82-3, 96-7
    marriages 58-9 and n.26
    obedience of impulse to reason
        80-1 and n.88
    shifting stance in *De officiis* 1 on
        vita activa vs. *contemplativa*
        18-19, 71 n.57, 78-9 and
        n.83, 83 n.92
    virtue lies entirely in action 66-7,
        79 n.81
Claudius Caecus, Appius 138-9 and
    n.106
Cornelius Scipio Africanus, Publius
    142-3 and n.117
Cyrenaic school of hedonism 79 n.80,
    145 n.129
Cyrus the Great 67 n.46

Damian, Peter 101 n.4
Darius I of Persia 58-9 and n.27
Darius III of Persia 142-3 and n.117
De coelibatu
    archaisms in 34
    Barbaro's textual personality in
        21-2
    celibacy and contemplation,
        relationship of 7
    Ciceronian diction/style x, 21, 29,
        32 and 46 n.213, 33,
        117 n.49, 155 n.156
    composition and textual history
        4-6
    contemplative life as 'active' 7,
        18-19, 21, 24, 56-7 and
        n.20, 77 n.74, 148-9
        and n.143

content of the four books 7–9
in context of Venetian humanism 9–12
date of composition ix, 3
echoes of Francesco Barbaro's *De re uxoria* 20, 84–5 and nn.95–8
engagement with Cicero's *De officiis* x, 8, 18–19, 32, 53 n.11, 141 n.110, 151 n.147, 155 nn.156–7, 159 n.167
etymology of *caelebs/caelibatus* 102–3 nn.9–10
exempla in 10, 22, 33, 98–9 and n.136
gladiatorial arena, allusions to 10, 92–3 and n.118
grammatical and syntactical oddities in 34
marriage, definition of 84–5 and n.95
meaning of celibacy in 7
natural diversity of aptitudes/life-trajectories 54–7, 76–7
'naturalist' and 'conventionalist' approaches to naming 42 n.144, 102–3 and n.11, 104–5 and n.17
pleasures of marriage 92–3
in relation to Francesco Barbaro's *De re uxoria* 17–21
stylistic tendencies of 29–35
'surfeit of prosperity' argument 92–9 and n.119
title *De coelibatu* 100–1 and n.4
'two books of'? 5 and 36 n.21
variant spellings in 33–4
wordplay and verbal effect 34–5
De officio legati 48
Ciceronian Latinity 29, 32
date of composition ix, 3
manuscript tradition ix
'modern' diplomatic ethos in xi

non-Ciceronian diction 45–6 n.209
stylistic consistency and orthodoxy 34, 35
definition, philosophical stress on 60–1 and n.31, 102–3 and n.8
D'Elia, Anthony 15
de' Medici, Cosimo I 26
de' Medici, Lorenzo 13–14
dell'Altissimo, Cristofano 26, 27
Diogenes of Babylon 141 n.110
Diogenes of Sinope 146–7 and n.139
Dionysius of Heraclea 144–7 and nn.129, 136
Dionysius II of Syracuse 119 n.56
Dioscorides ix, 5, 23–4, 32
Donato, Girolamo 1, 26
Donato, Nicolò 2

Egnazio, Giovanni Battista 23, 24
Empedocles 144–5 and n.122
Epicurus/Epicureanism 117 n.49
epigraphy 10
Etruscan augury 66–7
Euripides 92–3 and n.117

Ferdinand I, King of Naples 6, 38 n.72
Florence
civic humanism in 15, 40 n.97
dowry inflation in 15

Gallerie dell'Accademia, Venice 27, 28
Gerson, Jean 101 n.4
Giovio, Paolo 25–6, 27
Giustiniani, Bernardo 38 n.63
Giustiniani, Leonardo 12
the golden mean 8
Grafton, Anthony 11
Griggio, Claudio 17–18
Guarini, Guarino 13, 14, 17
pioneer of Renaissance wedding oration 14
Gymnosophists 58–9 and n.25

hands, senses, etc., granted by divine beneficence 64–5 and n.39
Hannibal 142–3 and n.117
Hecuba 92–3 and n.117
Heniochus/Auriga 54–5 and n.17
Hippocratic humoral theory 161 n.177
Homer 74–5, 96–7, 132–5, 152–3
    Achilles conversing with Odysseus in underworld 134–5 and nn.92–3
    as philosopher 134–5
humanistic curriculum 8, 32–3

'If the sky falls in' 138–9 and n.107
Iphigenia 134–5 and n.95
Iunius Brutus, Lucius 152–5 and nn.154–5

Jerome on marriage 14–15, 59 n.24
Jovinian 59 n.24

Kallendorf, Craig 10
King, Margaret 10, 21
Kraye, Jill 30

Legenda Aurea of Jacopo da Varagine 26
Licinius Crassus, Lucius 45 n.193
Loredan, Maria 39 n.84
Lyco of Troas 144–5 and n.124

marriage
    anxious distractions arising in marriage 114–15
    definition of 84–5 and n.95
    ensures reproduction and generational succession 64–5 and n.37, 86–9 and n.100, 106–7
    joy and pride in offspring 88–91, 92–3
    shifting medieval and Renaissance attitudes to 14–15
McLaughlin, Martin 29

menstruation 61 n.29
misogyny 9, 14, 17
Mucius Scaevola Pontifex, Quintus 45 n.193
Myron of Eleutherae 74–5 and n.68
Myrto, allegedly married to Socrates 113 n.42
Myson of Chen 106–7 and n.26

numismatics 10

Oroetes, Persian satrap 95 n.123

Panaetius of Rhodes 19, 41 nn.117 and 122, 67 n.47
Peripatetics 60–1 and n.30, 68–9, 82–3, 104–5 and n.17
    position on 'externals' 94–5 and n.122, 126–7 and n.77, 128–9 and n.82
Persian education 66–7 and n.46
Persian kingly succession 118–19 and n.53
Petrarch 9, 13, 15 and 40 n.93
Pherecydes of Syros 144–5 and n.128
Phidias 128–31 and nn.85–6
Pico della Mirandola, Giovanni 23, 29–30
Pinacoteca Civica di Palazzo Volpi, Como 25
Pisistratus 152–3 and 155 n.154
Plato
    alleged lovers 104–5
    'conventionalist' vs. 'naturalist' naming in *Cratylus* 102–3 and n.11
    demiurge in *Timaeus* 98–9 and n.137
    etymology in *Cratylus* 103 n.11
    male-female unions of Guardians in *Republic* 106–7 and n.28
    mistress? 105 n.20
    never married 104–5
    numbers in relation to Forms 86–7 and n.101

originally named Aristocles
145 n.123
soul's bodily incarceration 140–1
and n.113
his soundness of body reflected in
his name 144–5 and n.123
theory of Forms 53 and n.13,
80–1 and n.87
Pliny the elder ix, 24, 32
[Plutarch] *De liberis educandis*
41 n.130
Poliziano, Angelo 11, 26
Polycrates of Samos 94–5 and
n.123
Pompey the Great 147 n.136
Pontano, Giovanni 42 n.146
Popes
    Alexander VI 2, 24, 29
    Benedict XIV 1
    Cyriacus 26–7, 28
    Innocent VIII 1
    Nicholas II 101 n.4
    Sixtus IV 23, 29, 30
Posidonius of Apamea 146–7 and
n.136
Potamo of Alexandria 42 n.144, 94–5
and n.122
Pozzi, Giovanni 23
Praxiteles 74–5 and n.68, 128–31 and
n.86
Priam of Troy 96–7 and n.128,
99 n.136
Proteus 152–3 and n.152
Publilia, Cicero's second wife 58–9
and n.26
pygmies vs. cranes 64–5 and n.38
Pyrrhus of Epirus 138–9 and n.106

Quinctius Cincinnatus, Lucius
55 n.18

rhetoric and philosophy,
compatibility of 23, 29–31
Riddle, John 23, 24
Rodini, Elizabeth 28

'royal humanism' in Neapolitan court
21 and 42 n.132

Sabine women, abduction of 110–13
and n.41
Saignet, Guillaume 101 n.4
Salutati, Coluccio 15, 65 n.37
scholastic Aristotelianism 22–3,
29–30
Scuola di Sant'Orsola, Venice 27
Semiramis 58–61 and n.28
Sinibaldi, Antonio 5–6, 38 n.72
Sluter, Claus (sculptor) 135 n.95
Socrates 103 n.11, 118–21 and n.58
    turns from natural philosophy to
ethics 112–13 and n.44
    two wives at same time 112–13
and nn.42–3
Solon 152–3 and n.153, 155 n.154
Sophocles 92–3 and n.117, 118–19
and n.52
Speusippus 120–1 and n.62, 146–7
and n.141
St. Ursula, legend of 26–8
Stilpo 130–1 and n.87
Stimmer, Tobias 26
Stoicism
    doctrine of 'affiliation' (*oikeiōsis*)
137 n.99
    position on 'externals' 93 n.119,
94–5 and nn.121–2, 126–7
and n.76, 133 n.89
    poverty as an indifferent/no evil
133 n.89
    soul's bodily incarceration 140–1
and n.113
    suicide 147 n.138
    virtue alone sufficient for
happiness 95 n.122, 126–7
and n.76, 141 n.111
    zeal for etymology 102–3 and n.10
Strato of Lampsacus 145 n.124

Tarquinius Superbus, Lucius
155 n.155

Taurus 55 and n.18
Thales of Miletus 104–7 and
    nn.18–19, 21, 25
Themistius 5, 22, 23, 24, 30–1
Themistocles 142–3 and n.117, 150–3
    and nn.147–50
Theodorus of Cyrene 118–19 and
    121 nn.58–9, 144–5 and
    n.127
Theophrastus 56–7 and 59 n.24
Timanthes of Cynthus 134–5 and
    n.95
Tiraqueau, André 39 n.83
Trevisan, Zaccaria 13, 14
Trithemius, Johannes 5

Uffizi Gallery 26

Valeriano, Pierio 26
Valla, Lorenzo 65 n.37
'veiled face,' humanist aesthetic of
    135 n.95
Venice
    bachelorhood in 12–13
    civic irresponsibility in patriciate
        11

diffusion of Greek in 10
dowry inflation in 12–13, 15–16,
    20, 27, 133 n.90
evolution of humanism in 9–12
legislation on inheritance 132–3
    and n.90
as 'new Rome' 10
patrician civic ideology in 3–4,
    12–13
printing, rise of 11, 43 n.153
prostitution in 13
three humanist generations in
    10–11
unanimitas, myth of 10, 11
Vergerio, Pier Paolo 22, 41–2 n.130
Verino, Ugolino 3
Vernia, Nicoletto 31, 32
Vestal Virgins 65 n.37

Xanthippe, wife of Socrates 49 on
    2.2.19, 112–13 and nn.42–4
Xenocrates of Chalcedon 144–5 and
    n.124
Xerxes I of Persia 142–3 and n.117

Zeno of Citium 145 n.129, 146–7

Index of Latin Words

animantes 137 n.99
appetitus vs. *ratio* 80–1 and n.88

caelebs/*caelestis* 7, 102–3 and
    nn.9–10, 160–1 and n.174

dulciolus 35

honestum 67 n.47
humanitas 31

minutulus 35
motiuncula 35
munire viam 48 on 1.4.12

nisi forte 35, 59 n.27
non null-/*nonnull-* 49 on 2.2.7

omnia referre ad voluptatem 117 n.49

quamvis/*quanvis* 66 n.42

res uxoria 16 and 40 n.103

simplex 159 n.167

unanimitas 10, 11
utilis/*utilitas* 24, 63 n.34

verbum and *res*, 'word' and 'essence'
    31
veri cognitio 67 n.47, 71 n.55
voluptatum fuga 31, 32
vultus 153 n.151
vultus velatus 135 n.95

Index of Greek Words

ἄθεος/θεός 118 n.51, 121 n.58
ἀνάμνησις 81 n.87

ἠίθεος 103 n.9

μισανθρωπεῖν 107 n.26

οἰκείωσις 137 n.99
ὁρμή 81 n.88

πάθημα 105 n.17
περίπατος 61 n.30
πλατύς 145 n.123

www.ingramcontent.com/pod-product-compliance
Lightning Source LLC
Chambersburg PA
CBHW052115300426
44116CB00010B/1677